"*No Shortcut to Success* tells it like it is. Rhodes is correct that there are too many 'shortcut hopefuls' with simplistic formulas that promise less time and effort with guaranteed results. His view from the field is of a journeyman in the trenches, crying out for would-be disciple makers and church planters (particularly among Muslims) to get real, count the cost, and be ready to pay it!"

Greg Livingstone, Founder, Frontiers

"I love this book! Some people will find it disturbing, but Rhodes does not provoke for provocation's sake. His key ideas challenge many core presuppositions that underlie modern missions. He reminds us that the Protestant missionary enterprise was born when William Carey wrote of our obligation to use 'means' to bring people to Christ, and warns, 'Today, as in Carey's day, the "means" are in danger of being despised.' While critical of popular contemporary shortcuts to ministry, Rhodes's proposal is careful and constructive. His practical suggestions deserve serious consideration. Even if one disagrees with Rhodes, this book will sharpen our thinking about missions practice. The church desperately needs to read this book."

Jackson Wu, Professor of Theology, International Chinese Theological Seminary; Editor, *Themelios*

"I am extremely grateful for this honest, commonsense, reasonable, and respectful response to current trends at play among us who labor tirelessly in the unreached regions. This book is not for the faint of heart or the 'weekend warrior missionary,' but for the bold and courageous. I recommend this book to anyone who wants to follow our Savior deeply into the lives and societies of the unreached. Maybe, like me, some who are a bit weary from the 'long approach' will find refreshment herein to quicken their pace and catch a second wind. Please, I beckon you, whoever you are, to consider deeply the contents of this book. Let us wrestle deeply with each one of the issues Rhodes has addressed. Why? Unreached people's very salvation is at stake!"

Matt Arnold, church planter; Missionary Trainer, Ethnos360

"Never have I read such a timely book on the imperative of global outreach. Currently there are countless moving parts in mission strategies and Rhodes has examined many of these through a biblical lens that ultimately brings the reader back to the wonderful basics. He illustrates that the foundation of missions has historically been commitment to gaining fluency in both culture and language. Rather than proposing a 'silver-bullet' approach, he calls us back to the hard work of being professional ambassadors of the gospel. I hope this book will be read by all those contemplating missionary service and those in leadership, in sending churches and mission organizations alike."

Mark Dalton, Director of Missions, Shadow Mountain Community Church

"For years I've been asked, 'What can I read to get a balanced view of the radical changes happening in missions today?' *No Shortcut to Success* is an indispensable tool, not only addressing destructive trends in today's missiology, but also making a persuasive, scriptural case for historic methods and values that have been set aside. For those wanting solid, well-researched data and biblically sound principles that allow us to evaluate today's methods, this book is a vital resource."

Brad Buser, church planter, Southeast Asia; Founder, Radius International

"New missions (like Narcissus of old) has become so enamored with its own image that it struggles to see beyond itself. To any who believe that modern missions has had the last word, *No Shortcut to Success* is a merciful wake-up call, taking us back to the first words of Scripture and the sound wisdom of generations of missionary endeavors. With thoroughness and thoughtfulness, each chapter explores and critiques current trends in missions, but rather than promoting yet another new strategy, it instead urges a return to the solid foundation of biblical and historical mission. This is one of those books you must read slowly, with pen in hand, as each page proves to be both provoking and refreshing, sobering and heartening, challenging and encouraging."

Jacob Edwards, church planting team leader, North Africa

"In a day when there are so many voices advocating for new methods and what can appear to be formulaic approaches to ministry among the unreached, I find Rhodes's book to be full of helpful corrections. I especially appreciate his clarification on our role as ambassadors for the King. I believe he is spot-on in calling us to clarity, credibility, and boldness in our communication. I hope that all those aspiring to be a part of what God is doing cross-culturally in our day will read and heed the encouragement to approach the task of proclaiming Jesus seriously and with great care and preparation."

Dave Myers, global pastor, Chicago, Illinois

"Matt Rhodes has stated very clearly that there truly is 'no shortcut to success.' It takes time and involvement for an extended period to learn another culture, including another language. We don't all learn at the same pace, but it is necessary for missionary church planters to go through the learning process in order to communicate the message of the gospel with clarity and understanding. The Holy Spirit, in creating understanding, does not bypass the process. I commend *No Shortcut to Success* to you as a critical component in the process of evangelizing and planting churches among unreached peoples."

Gary Coombs, Missions Pastor, Shadow Mountain Community Church; President, Southern California Seminary

"Biblical, wise, encouraging, and practical. This combination of adjectives is rarely apropos to a contemporary book on missions. From the deft hand of a current practitioner in the field, we have been given a gift of clear biblical thinking regarding Christ's mission for his church and the way sacred Scripture prescribes for fulfilling it. I look forward to getting this book into the hands of pastors, missions committees, and missions candidates."

Chad Vegas, Senior Pastor, Sovereign Grace Church; Founding Board Chairman, Radius International

"Rarely does a person agree with every point in a book, and this book is no different. What is different about this book is the call back to the Scriptures and away from the fad and allure of new things in missions. Rhodes pushes us to consider the mundane, ordinary, and hard work of missionary efforts. We can no longer trust in shiny, new, quick fixes if the 3.1 billion unreached people are going to be truly reached by the powerful gospel of Jesus. We need people with grit and perseverance who will see his kingdom come and his will be done. *No Shortcut to Success* is that herald in the wilderness of missions strategy, calling people to not despise the small beginnings. To do the long, hard work of seeing the church planted among the unreached. If you are in the vicinity of missions, you should read this book."

Justin Raby, Campus Pastor, South Overland Park Campus; Director of Mobilization, Campus Support

"I deeply enjoyed reading this short but very informative book from a current frontline practitioner. Missions, and its ever-changing terminology, can feel inaccessible to the average lay person, but this is a great resource to help them understand what is being said in the current missions discussion. Filled with history and wisdom from the likes of Paton, Judson, Taylor, and Carey, this book is a must-read not only for lay people but also for pastors, missions pastors, and anyone involved in the Great Commission."

Brooks Buser, President, Radius International

No Shortcut to Success

Other 9Marks Books

Edited by Mark Dever and Jonathan Leeman

One Assembly: Rethinking the Multisite and Multiservice Church Models, Jonathan Leeman (2020)

The Rule of Love: How the Local Church Should Reflect God's Love and Authority, Jonathan Leeman (2018)

Church in Hard Places: How the Local Church Brings Life to the Poor and Needy, Mez McConnell and Mike McKinley (2016)

Why Trust the Bible?, Greg Gilbert (2015)

The Compelling Community: Where God's Power Makes a Church Attractive, Mark Dever and Jamie Dunlop (2015)

The Pastor and Counseling: The Basics of Shepherding Members in Need, Jeremy Pierre and Deepak Reju (2015)

Who Is Jesus?, Greg Gilbert (2015)

Nine Marks of a Healthy Church, 3rd edition, Mark Dever (2013)

Finding Faithful Elders and Deacons, Thabiti M. Anyabwile (2012)

Am I Really a Christian?, Mike McKinley (2011)

What Is the Gospel?, Greg Gilbert (2010)

Biblical Theology in the Life of the Church: A Guide for Ministry, Michael Lawrence (2010)

Church Planting Is for Wimps: How God Uses Messed-Up People to Plant Ordinary Churches That Do Extraordinary Things, Mike McKinley (2010)

It Is Well: Expositions on Substitutionary Atonement, Mark Dever and Michael Lawrence (2010)

What Does God Want of Us Anyway? A Quick Overview of the Whole Bible, Mark Dever (2010)

The Church and the Surprising Offense of God's Love: Reintroducing the Doctrines of Church Membership and Discipline, Jonathan Leeman (2010)

What Is a Healthy Church Member?, Thabiti M. Anyabwile (2008)

12 Challenges Churches Face, Mark Dever (2008)

The Gospel and Personal Evangelism, Mark Dever (2007)

What Is a Healthy Church?, Mark Dever (2007)

No Shortcut to Success

A Manifesto for Modern Missions

Matt Rhodes

Foreword by Mark Dever

:: CROSSWAY®

WHEATON, ILLINOIS

Cover design: Lindy Martin, Faceout Studios
First printing 2022
Printed in the United States of America

Trade paperback ISBN: 978-1-4335-7775-8
ePub ISBN: 978-1-4335-7778-9
PDF ISBN: 978-1-4335-7776-5
Mobipocket ISBN: 978-1-4335-7777-2

Library of Congress Cataloging-in-Publication Data
Names: Rhodes, Matt, 1979– author.
Title: No shortcut to success : a manifesto for modern missions / Matt Rhodes ; foreword by Mark Dever.
Description: Wheaton, Illinois : Crossway, 2022. | Series: 9Marks | Includes bibliographical references and index.
Identifiers: LCCN 2021014534 (print) | LCCN 2021014535 (ebook) | ISBN 9781433577758 (hardcover) | ISBN 9781433577765 (pdf) | ISBN 9781433577772 (mobipocket) | ISBN 9781433577789 (epub)
Subjects: LCSH: Missions.
Classification: LCC BV2061.3 .R475 2022 (print) | LCC BV2061.3 (ebook) | DDC 266—dc23
LC record available at https://lccn.loc.gov/2021014534
LC ebook record available at https://lccn.loc.gov/2021014535

Crossway is a publishing ministry of Good News Publishers.

BP		32	31	30	29	28	27	26	25	24	23	22
15	14	13	12	11	10	9	8	7	6	5	4	3

Contents

Small Beginnings (Zechariah's Hymn)

MATT RHODES

Do not despise the day of small beginnings,
when mountains do not move, when we must wait
upon a silent world, still slowly brimming
up, but not yet full. Do not forsake
these small tasks. God seeds humble, human labor
with hidden strength, and every seed, when sown,
seems weak beneath the mountains' weight, but later,
tiny shoots spring up and split the stones.
Our waiting—like all waiting—serves a purpose:
faith is forged through heat and long exposure.
One day it will emerge, mature and perfect.
Today, the mountains still loom, cold and sober,
and we are formed beneath the frozen surface
in rooms where magma seethes and boils over.

Foreword

THE AUTHOR OF THIS BOOK is no friend of mine. I don't mean to suggest I dislike him. Rather, I simply don't know him. As far as I can remember, we have never met or directly communicated. He hasn't asked me to write this foreword. And, what's more, I don't think he knows I'm doing it. He may not even use it!

Then why am I writing this?

Because some mutual friends sent me the manuscript of this book. I read it, and concluded that I not only liked this book, but thought that it would be important for it to be published and read widely.

What I know of the author is good. He has experience professionally working with statistics. And he has, for some years, been a full-time Christian worker in a fairly closed country. It's out of that experience that he raises questions about much current missions thinking.

Those of us who are pastors know that much missions literature these days reads like "get rich quick" testimonials. "I did this and that and then thousands and thousands of churches were started and millions came to Christ!" Did you know that there were Christian fads that lure young Christians and even pastors to think that the best missions work can be done cheaply and quickly?

I should be careful with the word "lure." That sounds ominous. One of the things this author does is to assume and even show the good motives of so many of those who are presenting missions in new, exciting, and yet ultimately unbiblical ways.

This book tries to help us recover what so many generations of heroic Christians before us knew—this work of taking the gospel where it has never been is normally work that is hard and long. But in our generation, a number of writers have risen up (and the author names them and quotes them) who would deny this, or at least would reshape what the effort is. Language learning and in-country residence are contrasted with prayer and remote, nonresidential missionaries. And, what's more, in many circles this new thinking has prevailed.

Like those whose methods he's questioning, our author wants to see churches planted among people who previously didn't know the gospel. Unlike those he's questioning, our author doesn't see years of careful preparation as being opposed to such church planting, but as the normal means of it. We prepare like ambassadors, because we represent the King.

One thing this book is clear on is the importance of teaching to the missionary task. Whether it is verbal preaching or writing, knowledge of the local language is essential to what missionaries are called to do. Missionaries should work to be able to proclaim their message clearly, credibly, and boldly.

Particularly important are chapters 2, 3, 6, and 9. In chapters 2 and 3, the author lays out specific criticisms of contemporary "church planting" and "disciple making" movements. In chapter 6 he lays out a careful argument for great energy and time being given to language learning. And in chapter 9, he gives wise counsel for finding, sending, and sustaining missionaries.

I could say more, but I'm keeping you from reading the book. Head on into the book. It's well done. And it's important if we're going to use the means that God has given us to reach the nations with the gospel.

Mark Dever
April 2020

Series Preface

THE 9MARKS SERIES of books is premised on two basic ideas. First, the local church is far more important to the Christian life than many Christians today perhaps realize.

Second, local churches grow in life and vitality as they organize their lives around God's Word. God speaks. Churches should listen and follow. It's that simple. When a church listens and follows, it begins to look like the One it is following. It reflects his love and holiness. It displays his glory. A church will look like him as it listens to him.

So our basic message to churches is, don't look to the best business practices or the latest styles; look to God. Start by listening to God's Word again.

Out of this overall project comes the 9Marks series of books. Some target pastors. Some target church members. Hopefully all will combine careful biblical examination, theological reflection, cultural consideration, corporate application, and even a bit of individual exhortation. The best Christian books are always both theological and practical.

It is our prayer that God will use this volume and the others to help prepare his bride, the church, with radiance and splendor for the day of his coming.

With hope,
Jonathan Leeman
Series Editor

Introduction

The "New Missions"

MY BROTHER PATRICK is a high-school teacher. A few years ago, his administration introduced new methods for teaching mathematics to children: the "new math," they called it. The phrase struck me because I remember, back when we were children, teachers were *also* introducing a "new math." Presumably, in the years since then, more than a few "new maths" have come and gone. Today's is newer than yesterday's, and tomorrow's will be newer still. There has *always* been a new, cutting-edge way of teaching mathematics to children.

This push toward newness, of course, shows up in many disciplines—parenting, psychology, technology, the list goes on. Fads come and go, and each arrives with the thunderous certainty of absolute truth.

As we talked about this, Patrick said something that caught my attention. He said, "After ten years of teaching, I finally feel like I'm starting to become a good math teacher." Ten years! It took that much time for him to excel in his profession. Why? Because teaching math is complicated. It requires imparting complex information. But it also requires holding students' attention. And a good teacher must know how to motivate and how to discipline, when and how to involve parents, how to help when children have issues at home that keep them from focusing in school, how to deal with self-esteem and relationship issues, and how to value the awkward but precious teenage souls that are given into his care.

I'm a missionary, and I've been one long enough to realize that fads come and go in missions too. Insider movements, business as mission, the Camel Method, CPM, DMM, T4T: I've seen them all roll over us. I've read the stories and statistics. I've heard the proponents of each new methodology claim that it's *the solution we've been looking for!* I've seen these methodologies presented as the only true way back to the New Testament pattern.

But there's a difference between the "new math" and the "new missions." People don't uproot their families in order to teach the "new math" to the uneducated. Teachers don't die on the mathematics field. Fads in missions—if they are just fads—are more dangerous than fads in math teaching because what missionaries teach is more important than math.

We can learn from these fads, of course. Each has unique strengths. But I'm becoming more and more certain that it may be impossible to become a "good missionary"—just as it is impossible to become a "good math teacher"—without the slow acquisition of professional skills. After all, like good math teachers, we're trying to impart information. We also do so in a complex world of relationships, self-esteem issues, and family problems. And because we work cross-culturally, we struggle to understand the complexities of that world. Perhaps it will take more than ten years to become a good missionary?

It may bother people to suggest that we need professional skills to be good missionaries. We don't mind saying that someone is a good math teacher based on whether he or she *knows how to teach well.* But we struggle with the idea that missionaries—after all they have given up—might still be fundamentally ineffective if they don't master the ropes of their job. We think to ourselves, *Even if missionaries don't learn languages well, even if they're unfamiliar with the cultures they work in, even if they have no more theological insight than most believers, surely they'll be okay. After all, teaching the message of Jesus must be different than teaching math! Won't Jesus's message be obvious in missionaries' joyful, loving lives, even if they can't communicate that message in ordinary language to the people they're ministering to?*

I suppose this can happen. God works in mysterious ways, and we should never set limits on him. All the same, depending on God to work in unlikely ways just because he *can* do so is unwise. My mother met my father at a Bible study when they were in high school. She remembers thinking that he was handsome, and after he said something that she thought was wise, she went home and scrawled in her journal that she was going to marry him. They eventually started dating and were married a few years later. Today, they have a vibrant and happy marriage and are living proof that God *can* use love at first sight to point us in the direction of a good marriage partner. But the fact that this *can* happen doesn't mean we should expect it! In the same way, simply being a loving Christian *can* win people to Christ, but that doesn't mean it's enough to make someone a capable missionary.

This is hard for us to grasp because we think of missions as fundamentally different than secular vocations. But it's not. We all work "unto the Lord." Christian doctors, Christian firefighters, and Christian math teachers all have to master a set of professional skills before they can expect God to bless others through their work. It is no different for missionaries. The Spirit works in unique ways in each vocation, but—and this is critically important—he does not bypass our humanity when he works through us. Jesus said, "As the Father has sent me, even so I am sending you" (John 20:21). And just as God worked through Jesus's ordinary human presence, Jesus's ordinary human touch, Jesus's ordinary human words, so God works through our humanity. When the Spirit works in New Testament missionaries, he does not bypass ordinary patterns of human communication, relationships, or reasoning. Instead, he works *through* them.

Christian doctors, Christian firefighters, and Christian math teachers all have to master a set of professional skills before they can expect God to bless others through their work. It is no different for missionaries. The Spirit works in unique ways in each vocation, but . . . he does not bypass our humanity when he works through us.

Take Paul, for example. People are convinced of Christ as Paul and other missionaries engage in ordinary, human processes of discussion and debate (Acts 17:2–3; 18:4, 28; 26:28). Discipleship occurs in the trusting, human relationships (2 Cor. 11:29; 12:14; 1 Thess. 2:11–12) that Paul builds over time. Discipleship depends on human processes of learning and teaching (Acts 20:20). In the following chapters, we'll examine the Scriptures in detail to see how these processes work in the ministries of Paul and other New Testament missionaries.

For now, I simply want to suggest that missionaries, like math teachers, have a set of very human skills they need to learn. The most difficult of these skills have to do with communication, since most missionaries work in foreign cultures and languages. While basic linguistic and cultural competency can be achieved within a year or two, it takes considerably longer to reach the fluency we need to navigate or even partake in spiritual conversations marked by high emotions, nuanced concepts, and fast, colloquial speech. Simply put, missionaries need to master the languages and cultures we are working in to a level that few missionaries today even imagine is possible. Fortunately—as missionaries of past generations knew well—this level of mastery is entirely possible. But amid all our other tasks, we're going to reach it only if we believe it's an indispensable part of being a "good missionary."

This work, of course, is difficult. Perhaps we tell ourselves that bypassing these efforts saves time. This is particularly tempting today when missions agencies sprint around the globe, touting newfangled methods that dangle the carrot of easy, explosive movements of thousands or even millions of new believers. Such stories tend to be hyperanecdotal and impossible to verify. They're rarely, if ever, what they seem; in fact, as I will explain, these methods tend to make long-term success *less* likely.

So we need to rethink our easy acceptance of these new, silver-bullet methods. We've too quickly abandoned the painstaking, time-honored path to professionalism that William Carey, Adoniram Judson, Hudson Taylor, and others pursued. They spent years studying Scripture, acquiring a new language, and understanding the culture of those to whom they ministered. They discipled people slowly and patiently. The Spirit multiplied their efforts and gave their work success.

I can't promise results—those are still in God's hands. I can't offer shortcuts or magical formulas—there are none. But while there's no one-size-fits-all road map to success, there are key guideposts along the way. In this book, I will describe a scriptural path for missionaries to follow. I will show how it wove through the ministries of great missionaries of the past, and I will describe what it means for missionaries today.

It can be painful for missionaries who have invested so much to question their approach to their work. But it will be worthwhile if it sharpens them in their efforts to reach the lost. After all, I'm writing this book for the lost, for those we hope to reach using every means within our grasp. But I'm also writing for the missionaries who have given up so much for the cause of Christ. I want their efforts to succeed. In my career overseas, I've been consistently humbled by the quality of the men, women, and even children I've had the privilege to work alongside, many of whose shoes I am not worthy to untie. If these insights contain some grain of truth—if they're not simply my own personal missions fad, of which I too will repent in another ten years—then I hope to bless these great men and women.

PART ONE

WHERE SHORTCUTS HAVE LED US: SURVEYING THE PROBLEM

1

Professionalism and the
Use of "Means"

WE NO LONGER HAVE a highly professional missionary force. Many in the missions community are untroubled by this. In fact, professionalism is widely panned. Consider these quotes from influential modern-day missions thinkers:

- Ying Kai, architect of the widely practiced Training for Trainers (T4T) church-planting methodology, blames his sense of professionalism for his decision not to share the gospel with a dying man: "I had a chance, but my professional mind thought, 'This is not good timing.'"[1]
- David Garrison, author of *Church Planting Movements: How God Is Redeeming a Lost World*, writes that "Church planting is not rocket science (so don't leave it for the professionals; everyone should be planting churches)."[2]
- David Watson, principal designer of the Disciple Making Movements (DMM) methodology, writes that "Professional leadership in the church has resulted in a reduction of those who feel qualified

---

1 Steve Smith, *T4T: A Discipleship Re-Revolution* (Bangalore, India: WIGTake resources, 2011), ch. 12.
2 David Garrison, *Church Planting Movements: How God Is Redeeming a Lost World* (Bangalore, India: WIGTake Resources, 2007), 308.

to minister. The net result is a weaker church, one that does not have the infrastructure to multiply, expand, or grow."[3]

We could go on, but for now these quotes will suffice. Professionalism, of course, is a stale-sounding word. It evokes images of old textbooks quietly molding away on library shelves. To some of us, applying such a word to missions work may seem classist and Pharisaical. Even worse, it can come across as an attempt to wrench the work of ministry out of the Spirit's lively control and put it in the cold hands of an elite, seminary-trained few. To others, the word "professional" might sound clinical, distant, and impersonal. We want missionaries to be loving, relational, and dynamic—not *professional*.[4]

3   David Watson and Paul Watson, *Contagious Disciple Making: Leading Others on a Journey of Discovery* (Nashville: Thomas Nelson, 2014), 52.

4   In John Piper, *Brothers, We Are Not Professionals: A Plea to Pastors for Radical Ministry* (Nashville: B&H, 2013), Piper never precisely defines professionalism, but perhaps comes the closest to it when he says, "professionalization carries the connotation of an education, a set of skills, and a set of guild-defined standards which are possible without faith in Jesus. Professionalism is not supernatural. The heart of ministry is" (x). Piper's objection here is not to investing in adequate theological education, acquiring mastery of the language and culture we minister in, avoiding shortcuts of time and resources in our tasks, and evaluating practical circumstances as we make decisions, which are the four basic criteria I will offer several pages from now in applying professionalism to missions. Indeed, Piper was instrumental in founding a seminary (Bethlehem College and Seminary), and his church began a missions organization (Training Leaders International) that trains pastors overseas in many of the things I will advocate. Rather, Piper's objection is to the extrabiblical cultural expectations we can place on pastors, expectations that often mimic the marketplace, with the implied encouragement for pastors to put their trust in those things, as if they are the special key that will unlock ministerial success. When writing the first edition of his book, he had managerial and therapeutic expectations in mind: the professionalism of "the three-piece suit and the stuffy upper floors" and things "learned in pursuing an MBA" (xi). By the second edition of his book, his concern had switched to a younger generation with its emphasis on "communication and contextualization." It's the "understated professionalism of torn blue jeans and the savvy inner ring." It's about "being in the know about the ever-changing entertainment and media world. This is the professionalization of ambience, and tone, and idiom, and timing, and banter. It is more intuitive and less taught. More style and less technique. More feel and less force" (xi). To be utterly clear, I'm not advocating what Piper is opposing. I would oppose what he opposes, too. In fact, I would say his exacting and studious approach to the pastorate models precisely what I will be using this book to call for among missionaries.

But perhaps these ways of understanding professionalism are a bit uncharitable. And I wonder, would we really prefer amateurism?

In every other area of life, we clearly wouldn't. It would sound absurd to apply statements like those that we read above with regard to other vocations:

- Imagine a police officer blaming her "professional mind" for her decision not to rescue a child in danger. Would she not blame her *lack* of professionalism?
- Imagine a medical professor telling students that "Surgery is not rocket science (so don't leave it for the professionals; everyone should be doing surgery)."
- Imagine a dentist lamenting the fact that professional practice in dental work had resulted in a reduction of those who felt qualified to pull teeth.

When we do business with people of other vocations, we know that we are at their mercy. We depend on their diligence and expertise. If they take shortcuts or don't have the skills they need, then we're going to get hurt. We may suffer financial loss, injury, or even death.

Perhaps ministry is not so different. Perhaps missionaries, like practitioners of other vocations, can be guilty of malpractice, and for the same reason: people under our care can be *hurt* by our negligence and lack of professionalism just as they could be hurt by the amateurism of untrained medical professionals, marriage counselors, or mechanics. A burning heart and a Bible are not enough.

Perhaps missionaries, like practitioners of other vocations, can be guilty of malpractice, and for the same reason: people under our care can be hurt by our negligence and lack of professionalism just as they could be hurt by the amateurism of untrained medical professionals, marriage counselors, or mechanics.

Sadly, I've seen this play out. I've seen inexperienced pastors give glib marital advice. I've watched untrained preachers badly misinterpret Scripture. I've seen missionaries miscommunicate important truths in languages they don't know. All of these individuals can do real damage in people's lives. "Whoever is slack in his work is a brother to him who destroys" (Prov. 18:9). If we believe in the importance of the missionary calling, then we need to realize that unprofessional, slipshod missions work may do far more damage than unprofessional, slipshod medical work.

The Case against Professionalism

Where does our distaste for professionalism come from? Political and social analyst Yuval Levin suggests that within society at large, "confidence in our institutions has been falling and falling."[5] This has resulted in "widespread doubt of many forms of professional authority—of the physician, the scholar, the scientist, the journalist, the expert of any kind."[6] If Levin is right, our distaste for professionalism in missions circles may be a result of broader trends in secular thinking. But even from a secular perspective, these trends are unfortunate. Levin reminds us that professionalism helps us by providing "broadly accepted general standards, means of training new professionals . . . and a strong ethic and straightforward set of common commitments."[7] Couldn't missionaries benefit from having clearer standards to guide them?

Of course, Christian teachers who minimize the importance of professionalism in ministry do so with the best of intentions. They believe their ideas are grounded in solid theology, not taken from streams of secular thought. Let's see if their reasons for dismissing professionalism hold up.

First, they rightly emphasize that missionaries and other ministers are not a superior caste of Christians. David and Paul Watson write,

---

5   Yuval Levin, *A Time to Build: From Family and Community to Congress and Campus, How Recommitting to Our Institutions Can Revive the American Dream* (New York: Hachette), 29.
6   Levin, *Time to Build*, 38.
7   Levin, *Time to Build*, 81.

In place of the doctrine of the priesthood of all believers, we now see
a strengthening of the priesthood of the pastor only. . . . By promoting and insisting on a professional clergy, the church has limited its
ability and capacity to reach the world for Christ.[8]

The Watsons are correct to insist on the priesthood of both laypeople
and clergy. But if laypeople and clergy share the same priesthood,
why should we imagine that the clergy can work effectively without
professional qualifications when laypeople cannot? After all, the Watsons acknowledge elsewhere that discipling people through emotional
problems "may mean a professional counselor."[9] If God uses the training
of professional counselors to disciple people through emotional problems, why wouldn't he use the training and expertise of missionaries to
disciple them in other parts of their spiritual lives? Indeed, missionaries aren't so different from other believers. Diligent, excellent work is
commended throughout Scripture (see Prov. 14:4; 20:4; 24:30; Eccles.
10:10; Col. 3:23), and like other believers, we need to offer the best we
can to God in our work. Tim Keller writes,

There may be no better way to love your neighbor . . . than to simply
do your work. But only skillful, competent work will do.[10]

Second, those who argue against the need for professionalism in
missions rightly want to guard us against depending on our own
efforts rather than the grace of God and the power of the Spirit.
But it doesn't need to be an either/or. As Dallas Willard has written, "Grace is not opposed to effort but is opposed to earning."[11] We
certainly cannot earn the salvation of the unsaved, but in missions,

---

8 Watson and Watson, *Contagious Disciple Making*, 51–52.

9 Watson and Watson, *Contagious Disciple Making*, 226.

10 Timothy Keller, *Every Good Endeavor: Connecting Your Work to God's Work* (New York:
Penguin, 2012), 67.

11 Dallas Willard, *The Great Omission: Rediscovering Jesus' Essential Teachings on Discipleship* (New York: HarperCollins, 2006), 166. Willard's concern here is to point out that,
though no effort we make can earn our salvation—or that of others—God still chooses

as in other vocations, the Holy Spirit works through our efforts. For example, Paul writes,

> I planted, Apollos watered, but God gave the growth. So neither he who plants nor he who waters is anything, but only God who gives the growth. . . . each will receive his wages according to his labor. For we are God's fellow workers. . . .
>
> According to the grace of God given to me, like a skilled master builder I laid a foundation, and someone else is building upon it. *Let each one take care how he builds upon it.* (1 Cor. 3:6–10)

God gives the growth, but he gives it through our planting and watering, so we should do good work. The Spirit's work isn't disconnected from our human efforts just because they're human. Rather, he inhabits our efforts, as human as they are.

Jesus says, "As the Father has sent me, even so I am sending you" (John 20:21). The Father sent Jesus into the world "in human form" (Phil. 2:8), and God worked in Jesus's human words, human presence, and human touch. God will also work through our humanity and through the human qualities we bring to ministry. To forget this is to take a subtle step toward *gnosticism*,[12] imagining that the human

---

to work through our efforts. Willard has missionaries' efforts—among others—in mind, as he continues:

> . . . the evangelical tradition is filled with effort—for example, the great missionaries (Judson and Carey and others) who went out. Some said to them, "Don't you believe God is going to save who He is going to save?" And they would reply, in effect, "Yes, that's exactly why I am going. I want to be there when it happens." Grace is a tremendous motivator and energizer when you understand and receive it rightly.

12 Gnosticism was a set of first- and second-century Christian heresies that saw a sharp distinction between the material and spiritual worlds; the observable, material world was seen as corrupt while the spiritual world was seen as pure and untainted. Many gnostics did not think it was possible for God to become human and believed salvation was acquired by transcending one's humanity through "secret knowledge from above" (*gnōsis*) that opened up the mysteries of the spiritual world (Bart D. Ehrman, "Christianity Turned on Its Head: The Alternative Vision of the Gospel of Judas," in *The Gospel of Judas from Codex Tchacos*, ed. Rudolf Kasser, Marvin Meyer, and Gregor Wurst [Washington DC: National Geographic, 2006], 77–120). The Christian doctrine

aspects of our work and ministry are contemptible and incompatible with the pure, untainted work of the Spirit. But God is pleased to reveal his divine power through ordinary, material things.[13] He works through things as human and as seemingly "unspiritual" as study, intelligence, relational instincts, and the professional wisdom that can be acquired only through years of experience.[14] In fact, the first person mentioned in Scripture as being filled with the Spirit is Bezalel, who builds the tabernacle. Moses states,

> [The LORD] has filled him with the Spirit of God, with skill, with intelligence, with knowledge, and with all craftsmanship, . . . to work in gold and silver and bronze, in cutting stones for setting, and in carving wood, . . . with skill to do every sort of work done by an engraver or by a designer . . . by any sort of workman or skilled designer . . . in whom the LORD has put skill and intelligence to know how to do any work in the construction of the sanctuary. (Ex. 35:31–36:1)

Can the Spirit really work through such "human" things as the intelligence and skill of engravers, workmen, and designers? Might he be at work in the "human" skills and abilities of missionaries too? I believe he is. Paul echoes this passage[15] when he writes of his own skill as a builder of God's sanctuary:

---

of the incarnation, in contrast, held that God was at work in both the spiritual and the material, and that a harsh distinction should not be drawn between the two, as Christ was both God and man.

13 Theologians describe this by saying that God's saving grace (theologians call it *special grace*) is dispensed through natural means (theologians call this *common grace*, God's goodness in creation that is available to saved and unsaved alike). For example, I believe and am saved (special grace) when God's Word falls on my natural human ears in ordinary human language (common grace). And I shouldn't expect someone to believe the truths of the Scriptures (special grace) if I can't explain those truths to them in their own language (common grace).

14 Indeed, God is at work not only in us but all around us in seemingly mundane things: flowers don't bloom, seasons don't change, and stars don't shine except through his constant, sustaining power.

15 Paul likely has the description of Bezalel's work in mind, since he also discusses the building of a sanctuary by skilled men whom God has gifted, and since his description

According to the grace of God given to me, like a skilled master builder I laid a foundation. . . . Let each one take care how he builds upon it . . . with gold, silver, precious stones, wood. . . . each one's work will become manifest. . . . Do you not know that you are God's temple? (1 Cor. 3:10–16)

Human work—and the human ways in which we do the work—have always been part of God's plan. In the beginning, he ordained humans to work, to "fill the earth and subdue it, and have dominion over" it (Gen. 1:28). In the end, we will still "reign forever and ever" (Rev. 22:5; see also 2 Tim. 2:12). As surprising as it may be, we still find human work at the center of God's plan for the world.

To illustrate how starkly we forget this, I'd like to share an email that recently went around a major mission board's discussion forum. The situation it describes—and the writer's evaluation of it—is not at all unusual. Rather, it's indicative of a widespread approach to missions in which the Holy Spirit is seen as working in ways that entirely bypass ordinary human relationships, communication patterns, and realities. Here's what the email said:

Subject: To all the saints who have thought . . . do I have what it takes . . .

We invited 6 university students to come spend two weeks with us. They didn't know the language; the[y] didn't know the culture. All they knew was that they loved Jesus, and they prayed, and they did what they felt God was leading them to do.

So, one day as they were leaving their hotel to go to our institute, one of the young ladies, "D", felt led to put a 10-rupee note in her pocket. After getting dropped off at the end of our street, they noticed in the early morning light that the street was empty, except for one woman sweeping the street. As the group was filing past her, a girl

---

of building "with gold, silver, precious stones, wood . . ." (1 Cor. 3:12) closely echoes the description of Bezalel's work done "in gold and silver and bronze, in cutting stones for setting, and in carving wood . . ." (Ex. 35:32–33).

in the front of the group smiled to her. The woman smiled back. "D", at the back of the group, felt that the 10 rupees she had put in her pocket was for this woman, so she gave the woman the 10-rupee note.

The two women locked eyes. Not knowing the language or what to say, "D" just said, "Jesus, Jesus, Jesus, Jesus, Jesus." The street sweeper's eyes filled with tears and she fell into "D's" arms, embracing her for some time. When she stepped back, the woman looked upward, put her hands together as if in prayer, pointed toward Heaven, and said, "Thank you. Thank you."

As a cross-cultural worker for 6–7 years, when I heard about this encounter, it struck me (once again) that effectiveness in ministry comes from Jesus, his presence, his power, his sovereignly ordaining events—and perhaps our childlike trust & dependence upon his leading. May it always be so in our work here. Amen.

There's much to commend in the story above. The six university students took a bold step in coming to a country where they didn't know the language or culture. They clearly desired to obey the Holy Spirit. They showed compassion and generosity to the impoverished street-sweeper. Their kindness touched her and may have helped her find hope. In all these things, I believe God was honored.

Nevertheless, let us return to the subject line of the email: "To all the saints who have thought . . . do I have what it takes . . ." This story is about a group of people who—though bold and charitable—clearly didn't possess many vital parts of what it takes to do missionary work well. They didn't speak this woman's language and couldn't share the gospel with her—all they could do was pronounce Jesus's name. The woman seemed to understand the one word the student said to her, "Jesus," so she might assume that Jesus is generous. On the other hand, in the absence of any other teaching or guidance, receiving free money in Jesus's name could also lead her to understand a very different gospel than the one Jesus preached.

Note that the writer of the email—himself a long-term missionary—sees the situation as not only healthy, but emblematic. In his view, the enormous obstacles posed by these students' lack of training are irrelevant because "effectiveness in ministry comes from Jesus, his presence, his power." He's half-right. Effectiveness in ministry *does* come from Jesus. But the success Jesus gives in ministry is usually mediated through practical abilities, including the ability to speak the language of the people with whom we hope to share his message.

Going Back to the Start

I am hoping, then, to reintroduce a question that is as old as the Protestant missionary enterprise itself: Every missionary acknowledges the vital role of the Spirit, but what role do *we* play? When William Carey first proposed sending missionaries to unreached nations, he was famously rebuked by an older pastor who told him, "Young man, sit down! When God pleases to convert the heathen, he'll do it without your help or mine either."[16] Carey responded by writing a pamphlet titled *An Enquiry into the Obligations of Christians to Use Means for the Conversion of the Heathens.* This groundbreaking pamphlet became the "charter for Protestant missions."[17] In it, Carey explained that appeals to God's sovereignty don't take away our obligation to responsibly steward the "means" he has given us for the spread of the gospel. Rather, God sovereignly plans for his Spirit to work through the skills and choices of ordinary men and women. Carey's observation is a timely reminder for us. Today, as in Carey's day, the "means" are in danger of being despised.

Today, as in Carey's day, the "means"
are in danger of being despised.

---

16 Joseph Belcher, *William Carey: A Biography* (Philadelphia: American Baptist Society, 1853), 19.

17 *The New Encyclopaedia Britannica* (Chicago: Encyclopaedia Britannica, Inc., 1998), 356 (accessed August 1, 2018, https://www.britannica.com/biography/William -Carey).

What Would a Professional Approach to Missions Look Like?

Can I take a short detour to provide a working definition of professionalism here? When I speak of professionalism, I'm not necessarily thinking of a seminary education, which may help some missionary candidates but will be prohibitively expensive for others. Rather, when I speak of professionalism in missions work, I'm suggesting that we approach ministry with responsibility and devotion to excellence. This includes:

- investing in adequate theological education;
- acquiring technical skills—including mastery of the language and culture we minister in—to clearly proclaim the gospel of Jesus among peoples who have never heard;
- avoiding shortcuts by allocating adequate time, energy, and resources to the task;
- and evaluating practical circumstances as we make decisions.

What human *means* are necessary as we proclaim the gospel? Might pragmatic wisdom really be a part of how we seek God's will? And is it really possible that God might work through something as bland and everyday as the acquisition of "technical skills"?

It is very possible indeed. When William Carey wrote his pamphlet, he addressed the need not only to *send* missionaries but also to equip them to deal with the practical problems of reaching the unreached, including "their distance from us . . . the difficulty of procuring the necessaries of life, or the unintelligibleness of their languages."[18]

Carey knew missionaries needed to navigate the distance and the harsh living conditions. They needed to prepare for cross-cultural communication. They needed to know the Scriptures. They needed to acquire a high degree of fluency in foreign languages and cultures. One of his biographers put it this way: "[Carey and his colleagues] regarded

---

18 William Carey, *An Inquiry into the Obligation of Christians to Use Means for the Conversion of the Heathen* (Leicester, UK: Ann Ireland, 1792), 67.

it as the duty of a missionary to obtain as complete a knowledge as possible of the language and religious institutions, the literature, and the philosophy of the people among whom [they] labored."[19]

Early missionary statesmen like Carey, John Eliot, Adoniram Judson, Hudson Taylor, and John Paton first acquired these skills. And only then—after long, patient years honing their abilities—did they begin to teach.[20] But why does it matter what missionaries did centuries ago? Perhaps times have changed, or perhaps we've come to know better or learn more quickly than the Adoniram Judsons and Hudson Taylors of history? To be sure, we understand *some* things better than earlier missionaries. But they may have also understood some things better than we do. Yuval Levin reminds us that in any profession, those who have gone before us can both provide expertise and show us how to put that expertise to use.[21] So before we turn from the path they so carefully carved for us, we had better make sure we know what we're doing. We may need to focus more on rebuilding the traditions they left us than on tearing them down, more on renewal than on revolution.

Sequentialism, and How We Turned from It

Sadly, many modern missions efforts not only leave historic missions practices behind—they disdain them as primitive and dangerous. It's impossible to overstate how David Garrison's book, *Church Planting Movements: How God Is Redeeming a Lost World*, has influenced the missions community. Garrison writes,

> Missionaries naturally think in sequential steps. First, you learn the language, then you develop relationships with people, then you share a witness, then you win and disciple converts, then you draw them into a congregation.[22]

19 J. C. Marshman, *The Life and Times of Carey, Marshman, and Ward*, vol. 1 (London: Longman, Brown, Green, Longmans, & Roberts, 1859), 465–66.
20 We will discuss the extensive training they pursued in chapter 6.
21 Levin, *Time to Build*, 41.
22 Garrison, *Church Planting Movements*, 243.

Garrison calls this type of thinking "sequentialism" and labels it "the third deadly sin" of church-planting work.[23] Mike Shipman—the architect of Any-3, a widely used approach to missions—agrees that such an approach is dangerous, explaining that learning a people's culture and beliefs before sharing the gospel with them is actually *detrimental* to missions work. Shipman explains, "We find being a bit 'dumb' [is] better than being too smart, as expertise in the local culture can provoke defensiveness."[24]

Garrison's and Shipman's ideas are widely popular on the field. But do you notice how different their approaches are from those of previous generations? What Judson and Taylor and Carey considered necessary is now considered "deadly."

I've seen firsthand how influential these modern ideas have become. Veteran team leaders discouraged me from seeking out formal training in the Scriptures before going to the field, and throughout the first years of my ministry I was encouraged to invest less in language learning in order to become more involved in "ministry." I've lived in three North African cities. Surprisingly, in every city, the vast majority of long-term missionaries had little theological understanding of either Christianity or Islam, the area's predominant religion. Most missionaries also had a poor grasp of the local languages and cultures. None of this disturbed them as they went about trying to share the gospel. Missionaries tended to focus on seeking out "divine appointments," praying for the sick, and telling the simple stories about Jesus their limited language abilities allowed. They operated on the assumption that if they "lived out the gospel" and prayed hard enough for a "breakthrough," their ministries would bear fruit. Again, this approach is colored with a kind of gnosticism or hyper-spiritualism that overlooks God's pattern of working through ordinary, human means. Does it make sense to pray for "divine appointments" to share the gospel with people

---

23 Garrison, *Church Planting Movements*, 243.

24 Mike Shipman, "Any-3: Lead Muslims to Christ Now!" *Mission Frontiers* (July/August 2013): 22.

while neglecting to learn their language well enough for them to understand the gospel when I explain it?

Of course, there are exceptions, but this kind of amateur approach to missions is happening around the world. But why? What instincts and assumptions have contributed to this trend away from and even against professionalism? I can think of a few.

An Overemphasis on Speed

As early as 1900, missionaries were developing plans for "the evangelization of the world in this generation!"[25] Since then, no less than nineteen such campaigns have been devised.[26] Let me be clear: The need around the world *is* urgent—indescribably so!—as people live and die without the saving knowledge of Christ. But none of these plans appears to have reached its goal. Is it possible that working too quickly makes us ineffective? In the intense pressure they feel to complete the Great Commission, missionaries often bypass the slow, unflashy work of acquiring professional skills like theological education and language fluency.

An Overdependence on "Silver-Bullet" Strategies

Missions has been inundated by a stream of "silver-bullet" strategies. Many of these make lavish promises, ensuring well-meaning participants that after reading a book or completing a short training they are now ready to lead huge movements of unreached people to Christ.

For example, Mike Shipman describes his widely practiced method, Any-3, this way: "A person can learn Any-3 in an hour, practice it with a friend that afternoon, and have fruitful interaction with Muslims that evening!"[27] According to these strategies, explosive replication of churches is a healthy norm: "If a church didn't reproduce itself after

25 John K. Mott, *The Evangelization of the World in This Generation* (New York: Student Volunteer Movement for Foreign Missions, 1900).

26 David Hesselgrave, *Paradigms in Conflict: 10 Key Questions in Christian Mission* (Grand Rapids, MI: Kregel, 2005), ch. 9.

27 Shipman, *Any-3: Lead Muslims to Christ Now!*, 18.

six months it was considered an unhealthy church."[28] Such methods aim to bring hundreds of thousands—even millions—of unbelievers to Christ through rapid, exponential growth. But this emphasis on speed rarely leaves time for the careful discipling of new church leaders. After all, Jesus spent three years, rather than six months, with his apostles. The insistence on both speed and silver-bullet reproducibility works against a more careful, professional approach. At the time of this writing, the most dominant of these new strategies include *Church Planting Movements* (CPM)[29] and other closely related approaches like *Disciple Making Movements* (DMM),[30] *Training for Trainers* (T4T),[31] and *Any-3*.[32]

An Oversized Role Given to Short-Term Mission Trips

Up until 1945, largely due to the difficulty of international travel, short-term mission trips were essentially nonexistent.[33,34] In the 1960s, short-term missionaries made up approximately 2 percent of the Protestant missionary force; twenty years later, this rate had increased to more than 50 percent—and it is presumably higher today. This increase has blurred the lines between senders and traditional, long-term missionaries. In fact, short-term missionaries are increasingly seen as vital to the completion of the Great Commission. I don't mean to demean the good work that often happens on short-term trips. But short-term missionaries, by definition, won't have the professional commitment of long-term workers, nor will they have time to develop the professional skills (e.g., fluency

28 Garrison, *Church Planting Movements*, 195.

29 See Garrison, *Church Planting Movements*.

30 See Watson and Watson, *Contagious Disciple Making*.

31 See Smith, *T4T*.

32 Mike Shipman, *Any 3: Anyone, Anywhere, Anytime* (Monument, CO: WIGTake Resources, 2013).

33 C. Philip Slate, "A History of Short-Term Missions Associated with Churches of Christ in North America," *Missio Dei* 3/1 (February 2012).

34 Meredith Long, "The Increasing Role of Short-Term Service in Today's Mission," in *Mission Handbook: North American Protestant Ministries Overseas*, 10th ed., ed. Edward R. Dayton (Monrovia, CA: MARC, 1973), 17.

in the language) that long-term missionaries historically have felt were indispensable.

An Overweening Skepticism of Intellectual Preparedness

Many evangelical churches in the United States feel an unfortunate distrust of intellectualism, which has led them to discount the importance of training in ministry.[35] This trend shows up in missions circles, too. For example, David Garrison encourages us that enormous movements of people may turn to Christ through "simple actions that anyone can take."[36] Jerry Trousdale explains that discipleship is so simple that no teaching is needed: "Do not teach or preach; instead . . . when people are simply exposed to the scriptures, God will reveal the truth to them." He goes on to quote a missions leader explaining that this is because of "the simplicity of the Bible."[37] If the task and message are simple, then are training and a professional skill-set really necessary? Shouldn't it be enough simply to love people and "be Jesus" to them?

Indeed, there is a beautiful simplicity to many core truths of the gospel. But while the most profound truths of Scripture ("God loves you") are simple, most people still need to work through complicated and deeply personal questions before they come to believe in these simple truths.[38]

---

35 See, for example, Henry Blamires, *The Christian Mind: How Should a Christian Think?* (Vancouver, BC: Regent, 1963), 16: "Christianity is emasculated of its intellectual relevance. It remains a vehicle of spirituality and moral guidance at the individual level perhaps; at the community level it is little more than an expression of sentimentalized togetherness . . . we meet only as worshipping beings and as moral beings, not as thinking beings." See also Mark A. Noll, *The Scandal of the Evangelical Mind* (Grand Rapids, MI: Eerdmans, 1994).

36 Garrison, *Church Planting Movements*, 307.

37 Jerry Trousdale, *Miraculous Movements: How Hundreds of Thousands of Muslims Are Falling in Love with Jesus* (Nashville: Thomas Nelson, 2012), 108.

38 In Western culture, for example, some of the complex questions that stand in the way of many unbelievers coming to know Christ include: Does science disprove the Bible? Why does God forbid some types of sexual expression? Why would a good God allow suffering? How could a good God send people to hell? People of other cultures have similarly complex questions. Answers—at least in part—may exist, but if we assume that the answers will be *simple* or glib, we are not going to be very helpful.

There's an undeniable trend toward doing things more quickly and with less preparation. Countless good-hearted men and women have been trained to think this way and have been sent out under these assumptions. They've sacrificed greatly to go and live overseas. And so, questions that strike at the heart of their method will be painful. But we must ask them all the same: Is it wise to downplay a methodical, professional approach to missions? Or have we lost irreplaceable tools for communicating the gospel by encouraging lower levels of preparation?[39]

In this book, I'm going to argue for a different approach to missions. I'm going to argue that there is in fact a set of knowledge and skills that missionaries need to acquire in order to do their work well. I'm going to describe what a professional approach to the missionary calling might look like.

Furthermore, I'm going to argue that despite the proliferation of success stories that fill bookstores and various organizations' fundraising letters, our increasing acceptance of amateurism has significantly reduced our effectiveness in the missionary task. Simply put, we've pursued a task without the necessary skills and without committing the necessary time and resources. In many cases, we might not even be aware there is a set of necessary skills or resources we are missing.

I want to be clear: acquiring these skills doesn't guarantee we'll succeed in raising up healthy churches. A doctor who has finished medical school cannot guarantee that she'll be able to treat your cancer. In ministry, as in medicine, outcomes rest in God's hands. But without these skills, we will find ourselves lost and unprepared, in the same way a tribal healer might be if he tried to treat that same cancer with a cocktail of mud, roots, and leaves. Despite his good intentions and insistence that his method has worked in the past, this tribal healer will leave a lot of people uncured and unhelped.

In the same way, amateur missions work can leave behind immature converts, unformed churches, and untaught disciples. Even worse,

---

39 I'm not arguing here that God can't use hastily executed, slipshod missionary efforts. God can do whatever he wants! But these efforts may succeed *despite* the overemphasis on quickness and efficiency and multiplication, not *because of* it.

it can leave behind unconverted converts, false churches, and disciples who don't know whom they're supposed to be following. We may mistakenly assume that people have believed or rejected the gospel when in fact they've never understood it.

A few clarifications will be helpful at this point.

First, I realize the word "professional" carries some baggage in ministry circles. Could people interpret it in ways I don't intend? Yes, that is a risk. Sadly, professionalism can exist in distorted, unscriptural forms. It can be pursued in isolation from other virtues, or apart from the Spirit's life-giving power. But all virtues can be twisted in these ways. So let's try to embrace the best and most scriptural of what professionalism can be, rather than dismissing it outright simply because distorted forms of it exist. After all, we have a shortage of words to describe work done thoroughly and well, and "professional" may serve as a timely reminder for today's missions community. It conveys a set of biblical ideas we have largely forgotten, such as the importance of hard, excellent work in ministry, and particularly in the parts of ministry that seem most human and pragmatic. Our era is rife with trends and assumptions that are effectively "anti-professional" in a way that I believe is harmful to the cause of the Great Commission, as I will argue. The term "professional" captures much of what is needed to correct these trends and return us to a more biblical path. So if you have mixed feelings about the word "professional," or if it has negative connotations for you that are not what I'm intending, please hear me graciously. I'm not asking you to like the word yet. I'm simply asking you to let yourself imagine as you read: if we put the negative connotations aside, might there be ways professionalism could be a positive, healthy, and even necessary part of successful missions work?

Second, I'm looking at missions in a narrow sense. That is, I'm specifically concerned with the type of missions that sees its goal as establishing Christ-centered churches that are sufficiently mature to multiply and endure among peoples who have had little or no access to Jesus's message.

In any professional undertaking, we need to be clear about our goals,[40] and I restrict my definition of the missionary vocation because the word *missions* has acquired an impossibly broad range of meanings. Nearly twenty-five years ago, Ralph Winter noted that the word *missions* now encompasses "any Christian volunteering to be sent anywhere in the world at any expense to do anything for any time period."[41] We do not only use it, as I will, to describe the planting of churches among peoples that previously had little or no exposure to the gospel. We also use it to describe humanitarian projects overseas with Christian organizations such as World Vision or Samaritan's Purse. We use it to describe community outreaches. We use it to describe parachurch ministries like InterVarsity or Cru. I'm glad Christians are engaged in all of these ministries, but I can't possibly discuss them all. I will limit my discussion of *missions* to the planting of churches among unreached peoples because this is my area of expertise and experience, and because it's the most direct expression of Christ's Great Commission:

> All authority in heaven and on earth has been given to me. Go therefore and make disciples of all nations, baptizing them in the name of the Father and of the Son and of the Holy Spirit, teaching them to observe all that I have commanded you. And behold, I am with you always, to the end of the age. (Matt. 28:18–20)

In recent years, I've heard an increasing chorus of voices argue that it's unwise and even immoral to divorce the proclamation of the gospel in new cultures from humanitarian ministries, especially those that provide aid to people in poverty. I'm not attempting to "divorce" the two—they're not mutually exclusive. But because the relationship between them can be complex, we'll discuss how they interact in chapter 4.

---

40 Indeed, the statement above will need to be unpacked further. What constitutes a mature church? How are such churches established? We will address these questions in chapter 8. For now, however, a brief definition of our goal should be adequate.

41 Ralph Winter, "The Greatest Danger . . . The Re-Amateurization of Missions," *Mission Frontiers Bulletin* 5 (March/April 1996).

Third, it's important to note that a missionary who is highly trained in one field—perhaps as a medical specialist—may still lack the ability to effectively proclaim the gospel. There are many highly qualified doctors, dentists, and other medical professionals in missions. There is, however, a shortage of people who are highly qualified in the missionary calling.

Fourth, it is important to remember that most missionaries work in teams and that most teams have a variety of members who play different roles. In missionary work, as in ministry at home, "There are varieties of gifts, . . . and there are varieties of service" (1 Cor. 12:4–5), which the Spirit "apportions to each one individually as he wills" (v. 11). While it would behoove members of missions teams to acquire as many professional skills as possible, it's possible for an individual to be a useful and even critically important member of a missionary effort without acquiring all of the skills that a wider team should aim to master.

Lastly, while I'm deeply concerned about the lack of professionalism I see in the missionary community, I don't assume there's any laziness or sinful agenda behind it. It is driven by misunderstanding, not malice.

I'll begin in chapters 2 and 3 by addressing some of these misunderstandings and where they've led us. Today's missions community believes it is ministering more effectively than ever before, so these chapters may offer a sobering reassessment of modern missions. We'll see how severely today's frenzied, speed-at-all-costs missions efforts undermine their own success by failing to invest adequate time, energy, and resources in their endeavors. I'll spend the remainder of this book describing a healthier approach to the missionary task.

I don't begin with critique to camp on where people have gone wrong but because we need to understand both the problem and its fallout before we can understand why a solution is necessary. I have no desire to condemn missionaries who are doing the best they know how. Indeed, most missionaries I've met are wonderful, hard-working, and humble people. I'm not trying to add to their burden. Instead, I write out of love and concern for them. I want them to succeed. I've seen too many wonderful people come back feeling defeated and confused after spending long years on the field without seeing the "fruit" they had prayed for and had been taught to expect. I think of friends who have faithfully given of themselves, prayed for the sick, and spoken of Jesus. Yet these friends also failed to acquire professional skills, including even a low-level mastery of the local language. My intent is not to berate these friends for their lack of professionalism. It is to say that there's a still more excellent way, a "means" that will help us succeed in carrying God's good news to the nations.

2

Movements and Rumors
of Movements

NO ONE WANTS to rain on a good parade.

How, then, do we call for self-reflection in today's missions world? Today's missions leaders believe they have discovered "the most effective means in the world" to bring the world's lost millions to a saving knowledge of Jesus Christ.[1] Success stories are everywhere. In recent years, unprecedented waves of people in the Muslim world have reportedly turned to Christ.[2,3,4] In Northern India, a leading missions thinker reports more than 80,000 churches born and 2 million Hindus baptized in a few short years among the people group he worked with.[5] Later, this number reportedly

1   David Garrison, *Church Planting Movements: How God Is Redeeming a Lost World* (Bangalore, India: WIGTake Resources, 2007), 28.

2   Jerry Trousdale, *Miraculous Movements: How Hundreds of Thousands of Muslims Are Falling in Love with Jesus* (Nashville: Thomas Nelson, 2012).

3   David Garrison, *A Wind in the House of Islam: How God Is Drawing Muslims around the World to Faith in Jesus Christ* (Monument, CO: WIGtake Resources, 2014).

4   Tom Doyle, *Dreams and Visions: Is Jesus Awakening the Muslim World?* (Nashville: Thomas Nelson, 2012).

5   David Watson and Paul Watson, *Contagious Disciple Making: Leading Others on a Journey of Discovery* (Nashville: Thomas Nelson, 2014), xiii.

grew to 4 million,[6] then to 5.4 million,[7] and then finally to 10 million baptized believers.[8]

These amazing successes have supposedly resulted from new methods that depart markedly from the slow, thorough path I'll be advocating. And I must admit: the numbers are enticing. What missionary doesn't dream of such success? And who but the most hard-hearted could doubt that these stories are true? After years on the field with little tangible success, many missionaries are ready to try something new; many missions organizations, after long years in the doldrums, eagerly embrace new methods. And so they send their missionaries to be trained.

I repeat: no one wants to rain on a good parade. But if we care about the lost, we must do our due diligence. As much as we may want the above stories to be true—as much as we may hope that a silver bullet has been found that will crack open the most difficult mission fields all at once—we simply can't jump on board without substantiating these reports. In any other profession, this would be seen as obvious: *of course* we should seek verification when we hear of easy, rapid success on unprecedented levels. But we feel shy doing so. Andy Johnson describes the difficulty many of us feel questioning success stories from the mission field:

> This will almost seem rude. . . . To debate whether a method works is offensive enough, but to question the fundamental approach to Scripture that informs the method is intolerable. But we need to get over that reaction. We need to ask the deeper, more uncomfortable questions politely, lovingly, and directly.[9]

6   David Watson, "David Watson: My Journey with Disciple Making Movements," *Movements with Steve Addison*, podcast audio, August 29, 2016, accessed January 3, 2019, http://www .movements.net/blog/2016/08/29/121-david-watson-my-journey-with-disciple-making -movements.html.

7   "David Watson's Testimony," narrated by David Watson, *Accelerate Training*, accessed January 3, 2019, https://www.acceleratetraining.org/index.php/resources/61-david-watson -s-testimony-90-min-mp3/file.

8   Victor John, "How the Bhojpuri Movement Has Fostered Other Movements," *Mission Frontiers* (January/February 2018): 33.

9   Andy Johnson, "Pragmatism, Pragmatism Everywhere!" *9Marks Journal* (February 2010).

Unfortunately, the allure of the numbers makes it difficult to consider these things. Edward Ayub, a Muslim-background believer ministering in Bangladesh, complains that in the West "numbers are held to be the most important evidence of God's blessing."[10]

The Numbers Game

Sadly, what Ayub says is almost undeniable. In the foreword for Ying and Grace Kai's *Training for Trainers*, David Garrison asks a startling question: "If you knew there was someone God had used to bring two million souls to salvation in Jesus Christ, who were baptized into 150,000 new churches in 10 years' time, wouldn't you want to know more? I know I did."[11]

In fact, I *would* want to know more. Numbers should influence our thinking to some extent. But the problem today is that *numbers influence our thinking in ways that nothing else does.* Popular books on missions methods now invariably open with stories of thousands or millions coming to Christ. Books that aren't written in this way, it seems, simply don't sell. This is concerning. After all, Jesus declined to start movements of thousands (e.g., John 6:10–15), and ended his earthly ministry with a group of disciples "in all about 120" (Acts 1:15). One wonders whether a book written today about a ministry like Jesus's could even sell. Consider the following popular missions books:

- David Garrison begins his book on *Church Planting Movements* (CPM) by discussing the work of David Watson, who "made an incredible claim. . . . Their report listed nearly a hundred cities, towns, and villages with new churches and thousands of new

---

10 Edward Ayub, "Observations and Reactions to Christians Involved in a New Approach to Mission," in *Chrislam: How Missionaries Are Promoting an Islamicized Gospel,* ed. Joshua Lingel, Jeff Morton, and Bill Nikides (Garden Grove, CA: i2 Ministries, 2012), ch. 5.3.

11 David Garrison, foreword to Ying Kai and Grace Kai, *Ying and Grace Kai's Training for Trainers: The Movement That Changed the World* (Monument, CO: WIGTake Resources, 2011).

believers."[12] He goes on to tell stories of other reports of CPM success:

"Last year my wife and I started 15 new house churches."[13]

"We've started 65 new churches in the last nine months."[14]

"A missionary strategist began working with three small house churches of 85 members. . . . Seven years later membership had swelled to more than 90,000 believers."[15]

- David Watson begins his book promoting his enormously popular method—*Disciple Making Movements* (DMM)—by telling the story of his own work which, in its first nine years, had reportedly resulted in 26,911 churches and more than 930,000 baptized believers.[16] Later in the book, Watson describes his amazement at learning that this number had grown to over a million baptized believers: "I couldn't stop the tears. . . . I never dreamed [God] would make me a millionaire."[17]
- Steve Smith opens his book *Training for Trainers* (T4T) by describing the multiplication of churches under the ministry of Ying Kai, the architect of the method. "Within a few months of the beginning of the movement, over 12,000 people had been baptized and 908 small churches formed."[18] After five years, more than 15,000 churches and over 150,000 new believers were reported; by the time Smith wrote his book, he reported over 150,000 churches and 1.7 million believers.[19]

12 Garrison, *Church Planting Movements*, 15.
13 Garrison, *Church Planting Movements*, 16.
14 Garrison, *Church Planting Movements*, 17.
15 Garrison, *Church Planting Movements*, 17.
16 Watson and Watson, *Contagious Disciple Making*, Introduction.
17 Garrison, *Church Planting Movements*, 233.
18 Steve Smith, *T4T: A Discipleship Re-Revolution* (Bangalore, India: WIGTake resources, 2011), ch. 1.
19 Smith, *T4T*, ch. 1.

- Ying Kai's own book on T4T similarly opens with "Our Story," in which he describes thirty farmers from his ministry "leading more than 10,000 people to believe in Jesus [in] only 13 months."[20] His book is billed as "the remarkable inside story of the global Training for Trainers (T4T) movement that produced 150,000 new church starts and saw 2 million baptisms in a decade."[21]
- Mike Shipman, the architect of the *Any-3* method, begins his book by reporting that after seven years using his method, "more than 5,000 Muslims from the people group with whom we have served have professed faith in Jesus Christ. . . . We are seeing believers and churches reproduce. . . . Of the more than 450 groups that have formed . . . one third of them are fourth generation and beyond."[22]
- Kevin Greeson begins his book *Camel Method* by telling of a movement which "had its origins in the late 1980s" and by 2003 had "more than 100,000 baptized Muslim-background believers."[23]

These authors have good intentions in speaking about the number of people who came to Christ through them. Ying Kai, for example, is described by one of his reviewers as having "humbly modeled the sacrificial spirit of faith."[24] We should all assume that this is the case. Likely, Kai and the other authors mentioned above firmly believe in their methods and only tell such incredible success stories to help us embrace their methods, too.

But we shouldn't overlook the skewed emphasis demonstrated by such a strong and consistent focus on numbers. Nor can we afford to overlook the influence that such reported numbers have on

20 Ying Kai and Grace Kai, *Ying and Grace Kai's Training for Trainers: The Movement That Changed the World* (Monument, CO: WIGTake Resources, 2018).

21 "The T4T Book," T4T Global, accessed May 31, 2019, http://www.t4tglobal.org/book.

22 Mike Shipman, *Any 3: Anyone, Anywhere, Anytime* (Monument, CO: WIGTake Resources, 2013), ch. 1.

23 Kevin Greeson, *The CAMEL: How Muslims Are Coming to Faith in Christ* (Monument, CO: WIGTake Resources, 2010), ch. 1.

24 Steve Smith, "What Others Are Saying," in Ying Kai and Grace Kai, *Ying and Grace Kai's Training for Trainers: The Movement That Changed the World* (Monument, CO: WIGTake Resources, 2018).

missionaries. A new team leader working in an organization where DMM was heavily promoted writes about his struggle to consider DMM from a biblical perspective:

> **It has been a significant struggle to get to a place where I can say to myself "it's OK to not follow DMM 100%"—and I wonder why this is?**
> I realized this when as a team we were engaging with Scripture over a particular aspect of DMM, and a team member presented a strong argument from Scripture which stood at odds with DMM methodology. It was compelling, and I agreed with his reasoning and with his conclusion—I had no counter-argument to offer—and yet I remained unwilling to accept it . . . I had unwittingly subordinated Scripture to my own convictions about pursuing a particular methodology, and I was blind to consider alternatives . . .
> I have realized that my unwillingness to critique DMM was not born out of theological convictions . . . but rather out of more personal motivations: **it has to do with promises I have taken up that I am not willing to lay down again.** And this pertains to the strong statements that DMM uses. Several times during my Level 1 training, examples were cited where a certain team followed all but one of DMM's critical elements, and once this final ingredient was added . . . the movement began. DMM's branding makes extensive use of these before and after stories, and the repetition of these stories creates a narrative with an implicit promise . . . failure to follow any one of the DMM principles will mean failure to catalyze a movement properly. This is an "all or nothing" condition, with a lot at stake. All of us want to see God's kingdom come in our midst, hundreds of thousands of Muslims coming to Christ, a transformation of our people groups and our cities and our countries through the powerful message of Jesus. I yearn for a movement to Christ. **Whether implicitly or explicitly, DMM promises to deliver this, and not following DMM means failure.**
> I wish I could claim that what attracted me most to DMM was the rational conviction that this was the best Biblical approach. But

instead it is the emotional desire to see Kingdom impact, and the fervor and zeal to take hold of a method that promises this. The DMM training is full of examples of thousands and tens of thousands of churches planted, millions of Muslims coming to Christ. It is awesome and awe-inspiring. The sheer weight of these statistics means that (emotionally) it is hard to have a clear head for Biblical critique; the reason I am "buying in" is because I want results. I want DMM to be Biblical because I want its promises to be true. . . . But the truth is—and I think most will agree—that DMM cannot make promises about Kingdom fruit—only God can, and only promises found in Scripture are promises worthy of us putting hope in . . .[25]

This team leader is not unique in being swayed by the promises of DMM. Sadly, what is unique is that he was insightful enough to realize how the "implicit promise" of numbers—rather than Scripture—had begun to drive him. He knows how easily numbers can dominate our thinking. Every missionary dreams of success. But the problem is that DMM ties such success exclusively to the method or others like it. Rather than presenting these methods as one option to consider, many DMM proponents paint these methods as "what God is doing . . . today."[26]

As one put it, "Over the last 50 years and especially since the turn of the 21st century, the Spirit of God has been birthing a new concept in the earth. Instead of addition, the Spirit of God is calling forth multiplication."[27] This "new concept" of "multiplication" is thought to be so significant that some "believe that another 'Reformation' is underway."[28]

25 Personal correspondence. Name withheld for security reasons. June 18, 2015, emphasis original.

26 Trousdale, *Miraculous Movements*, 17.

27 Jerry Trousdale and Glenn Sunshine, *The Kingdom Unleashed* (Murfreesboro, TN: DMM Library, 2015), ch. 1.

28 Harry Brown, foreword to Jerry Trousdale and Glenn Sunshine, *The Kingdom Unleashed* (Murfreesboro, TN: DMM Library, 2015). Similarly, Robby Butler states that, "A revolution is unfolding in the Church—perhaps even a second Reformation" (Robby Butler, "Are Movements the Seeds of a Second Reformation," *Mission Frontiers* [March/April 2016]: 4–5).

In a way, the exaggeration doesn't worry me. I'm sure most mission-aries won't be too convinced by comparisons that put the innovations of the past thirty years on a par with the Reformation. Nonetheless, the importance that's placed on these newer missions methods is prob-lematic when it leads their proponents to accuse Christians who reject their methods of having poor motives:

> God is doing something extraordinary *in our day*. As he draws a lost world to himself, Church Planting Movements appear to be the *way* he is doing it. . . . when we act out of our own reasoning rather than aligning ourselves with God's ways, we are like an obstinate goat that puts itself at cross purposes with its master's will. . . . Without exaggeration we can say that Church Planting Movements are *the most effective means in the world today for drawing lost millions into saving, disciple-building relationships with Jesus Christ*.[29]

Many portray alternate methods as slow and unbiblical. They com-pare straw-man caricatures of old methods to new methods—and then dismiss them out of hand. For example, we're told we must choose between new methods and their rapidly multiplying "rabbit churches," and the slow, cumbersome "elephant churches" of other methods.[30,31] We're told we must choose between new methods that result in the conversion of entire communities, and old methods that set their goal as reaching only "one person at a time."[32] David and Paul Watson even argue that the traditional approaches result in "good odds for Satan—he will encourage us to win one and lose ten or more as a result of these methodologies."[33] The Watsons repeat this claim, stating that new churches planted through traditional methods will "find it very

---

29 Garrison, *Church Planting Movements*, 28, emphasis original.

30 Garrison, *Church Planting Movements*, 194.

31 Trousdale and Sunshine, *Kingdom Unleashed*, ch. 6.

32 Watson and Watson, *Contagious Disciple Making*, 108.

33 Watson and Watson, *Contagious Disciple Making*, 108.

difficult to reproduce. . . . [In] our opinion, Satan is at work in these extraction methodologies."[34]

These comments add up, and their message is clear: *Only our methods really work. Other methods are foolish, or even dishonoring to God.* As we continue, we'll explore whether these newer methods are aligned with Scripture. For now, it's enough to note that this narrative places enormous pressure on young missionaries who find aspects of these newer methods unwise or unscriptural. I've seen couples in more than one missions organization pushed off teams because they held scriptural concerns. In some cases, these missionaries didn't know what they were getting into. Many large missions agencies no longer feel that training in other methods is worth promoting. I mention this to explain why I find it necessary to examine newer methods in light of Scripture; I'm not simply going out of my way to pick at details and find fault. I'm trying to buy room for young missionaries to breathe and for other strategies to be considered. If we want to do our work professionally, then we must have room to consider other options. And we must look more at the health and long-term stability of our work than at apparent, immediate growth.

How, then, can we respond biblically to reports of enormous movements? Consider the following:

1. Scriptural Principles Are More Important Than Numbers

Simply put, big numbers don't define success in ministry—whether locally or globally. Andy Johnson writes, "Far too many of our books, articles, trainings, and conversations seem to operate at the level of 'what works' rather than 'what is most faithful to Scripture.'"[35]

Johnson's comment is insightful. What might lead us to focus on what works at the expense of focusing on what's biblical? I wonder if we have a subconscious assumption that scriptural principles do *not*

---

34 Watson and Watson, *Contagious Disciple Making*, 108. The Watsons use the phrase "extraction methodologies" to refer to the way they believe traditional church planting methods "extract" new believers from their communities of origin.

35 Andy Johnson, "Pragmatism, Pragmatism Everywhere!"

work very well in the real world, or at least not in today's world. I wonder if slower, less flashy growth may not always be the type of growth we want. The Mormon church grew rapidly in the late 1800s and throughout the 1900s. The preaching of prosperity gospels has grown explosively throughout the United States, Africa, and Latin America. This growth has been entirely regrettable. The Mormon church spread heresies incompatible with Christian doctrine. Prosperity-gospel churches contain dangerous deceptions. I don't mean to imply that DMM proponents make errors of this magnitude. I simply want to say that we shouldn't assume numerical growth means the growth of healthy churches that will stand the test of time. It's encouraging to hear reports of churches growing rapidly, but numbers alone don't make a method worth using.

Johnson proposes an alternative: "We need to be thinking about ways to evaluate our workers' performance more on their biblical faithfulness and much less on reported numbers of immediate, visible responses."[36] Ultimately, "success" in ministry isn't a matter of numbers but of ministering in a way that honors the Lord. Of course, this doesn't mean that numbers don't matter. But numbers can be gained in many ways, and in the end, "the fire will test what sort of work each one has done. If the work that anyone has built on the foundation survives, he will receive a reward" (1 Cor. 3:13–14).

Numerically large ministries are apparently successful. But if they are not built on a solid foundation of scriptural wisdom, they will not survive. At times, Jesus turned away from crowds of thousands to focus on teaching his disciples (Matt. 5:1; 8:18–23; John 6:15–22). Ever the long-term thinker, Jesus prioritized *healthy* over *huge*.

Ever the long-term thinker, Jesus prioritized healthy over huge.

----

36 Andy Johnson, "Pragmatism, Pragmatism Everywhere!"

2. Numbers May Be Incorrect or Misinterpreted

In the late 1980s, the *insider movement* (IM) methodology[37] reportedly led to enormous movements, including one in which between 300,000 and 1 million people turned to Christ in Bangladesh.[38] Yet subsequent reports leave reason to doubt these figures. Edward Ayub reports that,

> Someone abroad asked me whether 10,000 mosques have been converted to churches in Dhaka. I had to answer correctly that I knew of none. Did he hear that number correctly? If he heard the number correctly, that would indicate that almost all the mosques in Dhaka had been converted into churches. Even if he heard 1,000, that number could not possib[ly] be true. I do not know of even one . . . We do not want hyperbolic reports published. There is no spiritual benefit for the Church from these false reports.[39]

Another Muslim-background believer, Anwar Hossein, states that,

> Personally, I went to some places where the movement took place. And I did not find the reality. If it had been true then definitely there would be newspaper reports everywhere, television and charges, but nobody knows. Because this is a very hot issue. If it were to happen somewhere, [it would] immediately come to the church or radio or

---

37 "Insider movements can be described as movements to obedient faith in Christ that remain integrated with or inside their natural community. . . . Believers *retain their identity* as members of their socio-religious community while living under the Lordship of Jesus Christ and the authority of the Bible" (Rebecca Lewis, "Insider Movements: Honoring God-Given Identity and Community," *International Journal of Frontier Missiology* 26/1 (Spring 2009): 19). Insider movement approaches have been controversial because they encourage believers in Christ to maintain their previous religious identity. For example, a Muslim-background believer would still identify himself as a Muslim, rather than a Christian, and would still participate in the religious life of the Muslim community, including worship at the mosque, etc.

38 Joshua B. Lingel and Bill Nikides, "Chrislam: Insider Movements Moving in the Wrong Direction," *Christian Research Journal* 35/2 (2012).

39 Ayub, "Observations and Reactions to Christians Involved in a New Approach to Mission."

television. I think some of our brothers are giving false reports to impress supporters.[40]

Missiologists share these concerns:

> The missionaries talk about the hundreds of thousands who have come to Christ, but one insider who left the IM and became a visible Christian reports that the number of insiders couldn't be more than ten thousand. Other former insiders have reported publicly that many insiders are really Muslims who will do whatever it takes for the jobs and money they are offered by pro-IM ministries to feed their families. Likewise, a significant percentage of insider leaders in Bangladesh were already baptized Christians who were convinced by missionaries to revert to their former Muslim identities.[41]

> When asked where these people are, the answer is often, "We cannot tell you because of security concerns." . . . Although each method claims a large following, some leaders have admitted that the numbers are much less than originally thought.[42]

None of these quotes *prove* that insider movement leaders exaggerated their claims, but they certainly suggest we should be careful about accepting such claims without examination.

Might similar, well-intended optimism be inflating reported results from today's popular methodologies? Sadly, as Aubrey Sequeira reports, movement numbers can even be intentionally inflated to impress missionaries:

> What my Western brothers and sisters often don't understand is that most Indian "ministries" have learned what excites people in the

---

40 Anwar Hossein, quoted in Lingel and Nikides, "Chrislam: Insider Movements Moving in the Wrong Direction."

41 Lingel and Nikides, "Chrislam: Insider Movements Moving in the Wrong Direction."

42 Georges Houssney, "Position Paper on the Insider Movement" (Boulder, CO: Biblical Missiology, 2010), 3.

West. . . . massive numbers . . . dazzle the Western church . . . and when supporting partners in the West are impressed, that typically means the dollars will rush in. Unfortunately, Western churches seldom—if ever—learn that in many cases, the numbers are inflated, testimonies fabricated, and the "gospel work" that they've been investing in is a mirage.[43,44]

Today, David Watson's ministry among the Bhojpuri in India is said to have resulted in more than 10 million baptized believers.[45] Above, we examined Watson's description of the moment when he first heard that over a million people had been baptized as a result of his ministry: "I never dreamed God would make me a millionaire," he said. Then he continued: "We pray, with all our hearts, that you become millionaires as well."[46]

Here, again, is the implicit promise: *Follow this method and perhaps millions will come to Christ through you too.* But is the promise true? Should we listen to it more keenly because of Watson's claims? In any other profession, we would carefully verify such astounding results before assuming they were true. Imagine, for example, that a foreign branch of a business reported massive growth from an unorthodox strategy. Would we instantly implement this branch's business approach elsewhere, or would we first do our due diligence to make sure the growth was real and not a pyramid scheme? For some reason, in

---

43 Aubrey Sequeira, "A Plea for Gospel Sanity in Missions," *9Marks Journal* (December 2015).

44 Indian pastor Harshit Singh agrees:

> If we were able to compile all the reports of conversions reported by various agencies in India, we would find that India has been reached and converted many times over already. There have been movements reported that unfortunately [are] often inflated, grossly exaggerated, and sometimes outrightly false. And again, what is the motivation behind that? Rapid growth (Harshit Singh, "How Western Methods Have Affected Missions in India," 9Marks' First Five Years Conference, Columbus, OH, August 4, 2017. Accessed May 3, 2019, https://www.9marks.org/message/how-western-methods-have-affected-missions-in-india).

45 John, "How the Bhojpuri Movement Has Fostered Other Movements," 33.

46 David Watson, in Watson and Watson, *Contagious Disciple Making*, 233.

missions, simply making such claims is enough to profoundly impact strategies across the world.

In fact, God does seem to have brought many Bhojpuri people to himself since the early 1990s. For this, we should be profoundly grateful.[47] But while the salvation of new brothers and sisters is cause for rejoicing, we must remember that Watson argues for the validity of DMM, in part, by claiming that *millions* of Bhojpuri came to Christ, and that this happened through *his* ministry. How credible are these claims?

In fact, it isn't clear at all that DMM is responsible for what happened among the Bhojpuri. Other missionaries were working among the Bhojpuri. Before Watson's arrival, there were at least thirty churches that were actively evangelizing and planting new churches.[48] Might their ministries have been as important as Watson's? Indeed, Watson himself may be in a poor position to evaluate which factors proved critical in bringing people to Christ. He had little direct involvement in the Bhojpuri ministry. He was a "nonresidential missionary"[49,50,51] for the duration of his ministry to the Bhojpuri. He was stationed in Delhi—far from the Bhojpuri homeland—during his brief stay in India[52] and had little time to attain fluency in Hindi or in the Bhojpuri language while there.[53] Indian missionaries who worked with the Bhojpuri report

---

47 See Victor John and David Coles, *Bhojpuri Breakthrough: A Movement That Keeps Multiplying* (Monument, CO: WIGTake, 2019). I see no reason to doubt the individual stories of changed lives published or to doubt that many Bhojpuri people came to Christ.

48 Jim Slack, Scott Holste, and J. O. Terry, *An Analysis of Church Growth among the Bhojpuri of Northern India: Executive Summary of Full Report* (Richmond, VA: IMB Global Research Department, 2000), 1.

49 Watson and Watson, *Contagious Disciple Making*, 11.

50 "David Watson: My Journey with Disciple Making Movements."

51 "David Watson's Testimony."

52 John and Coles, *Bhojpuri Breakthrough*, 8.

53 Watson reports living in India for only eighteen months ("David Watson: My Journey with Disciple Making Movements"). As we will see in chapter 6, this is not enough time for a native English speaker to master even one Indian language under the best of conditions. And Watson was stationed in Delhi during this time—far from the Bhojpuri homeland and not an ideal environment for learning Bhojpuri—and he reports having attempted to study *three* languages at once ("David Watson's Testimony"), enrolling in a doctoral program studying Sanskrit ("David Watson: My Journey with Disciple Making Movements") as well as, presumably, studying Hindi and Bhojpuri.

that he came and "met a couple of times a year" with them during this time.[54] By 1994, before the Bhojpuri movement began, Watson had already left India, and from this time onward he lived with his family in Singapore, "twenty-five hundred miles and an ocean" away.[55,56,57] So how can Watson confidently state that *millions* came to Christ through his ministry, or at all? Indeed, Watson's assessment of his ministry's success seems wildly optimistic. He reports,

> We got audio Bibles and just said "Hey, just hand out audio Bibles." We handed out a thousand audio Bibles and saw 627 churches started . . . Think about that. No evangelist, just an audio Bible. And a guy went by every two weeks and . . . replaced the batteries in the player.[58]

How does Watson know that 627 "churches" were formed when his contact with them was limited to sending "a guy" to visit every two weeks—not to evangelize or to verify what was happening but to simply provide batteries? What kind of "church" can be formed around a single audio Bible? Watson also speaks with excitement of "eight-year-olds starting churches! Fourteen-year-old girls who can't read or write any language starting churches."[59]

Unfortunately, no reliable evidence has been presented to verify claims of millions of Bhojpuri coming to Christ. How, as Anwar Hossein asks above, would such an amazing movement occur in a country known to respond to conversion with hostility, all without any mention in "newspaper . . . or radio or television"?[60] Indeed, publicists of the Bhojpuri movement acknowledge that "sometimes people travel through an area where a movement has been reported and they don't

54 John and Coles, *Bhojpuri Breakthrough*, 8.
55 Watson and Watson, *Contagious Disciple Making*, xi.
56 "David Watson: My Journey with Disciple Making Movements."
57 Garrison, *Church Planting Movements*, 15.
58 "David Watson's Testimony."
59 "David Watson: My Journey with Disciple Making Movements."
60 Anwar Hossein, interview with Bill Nikides, "Interview of a Former Insider, Anwar Hossein," in *Chrislam: How Missionaries Are Promoting an Islamized Gospel*, ch. 5.1.

see evidence of it" but assure us that "you can walk in a jungle and never
see any animals. That doesn't mean there are no animals in the jungle."[61]
This may be true, but it becomes less plausible when the type of jungle
animal in question is purported to have a population of 10 million
and when all of the other jungle animals object noisily to its presence!
Furthermore, how were such great numbers of Bhojpuri believers
collected and verified? Demographics is a complex science—the US
census would have needed 20,000 census takers to count a population
of 10 million people.[62] Counting 10 million Bhojpuri Christians would
be more difficult because of India's demographic instability and Indian
Christians' fear of persecution, which might make Christian converts
hard to identify. In fact, Indian census data from 1991 to 2011 show a
net *decrease* in the number of Christians in Bihar and Uttar Pradesh,[63,64]
where the movement was centered[65] and where the Bhojpuri people
primarily live.

So where do Watson's numbers come from? Watson assures us that
"external audits" are taken to confirm the size of the movement every
five years,[66,67,68] but the only details published from these audits are
reports written by foreigners who were unfamiliar with the local lan-

61 David Coles, "A Still Thriving Middle-Aged Movement: An Interview with Victor John
    by Dave Coles," *Mission Frontiers* (May/June 2019): 16–19.

62 Based on 2010 numbers from "2010 Fast Facts," U.S. Census Bureau, accessed January 3,
    2019, https://www.census.gov/history/www/through_the_decades/fast_facts/2010_fast
    _facts.html. The 2010 US Census employed approximately one census taker for every 485
    Americans, and would have needed more than 20,000 census takers to count 10,000,000
    people.

63 A. P. Joshi, M. D. Srinivas, and J. K. Bajaj, *Religious Demography of India* (Chennai, India:
    Centre for Policy Studies, 2003), 36–39.

64 "Christian Religion Census 2011," Census 2011, accessed January 22, 2019, https://www
    .census2011.co.in/data/religion/3-christianity.html.

65 Slack, Holste, and Terry, *Analysis of Church Growth among the Bhojpuri*.

66 "David Watson: My Journey with Disciple Making Movements."

67 "David Watson's Testimony."

68 Initially, the IMB—the mission board of the Southern Baptist Convention, which sent
    Watson—participated in these audits, so they weren't actually "external," independent
    audits. After participating in the 2008 audit, the IMB confirms it was no longer comfort-
    able—for reasons not disclosed—putting its name on the audits, and these audits are not
    publicly available (personal communication).

guage and culture.[69] Even worse, the audits themselves admit that they "project growth based on various assumptions."[70] Strangely, they never explain what these assumptions are.[71,72]

Well, what's wrong with that? I worked in population-based statistics for eight years before going to the mission field, so I'll try to explain:

The Bhojpuri movement began in 1994, so it's more than twenty-five years old at the time of this writing.[73] Projecting compound growth over such time periods can produce wildly inaccurate results if your estimates are off by even a tiny margin. For example, US stocks increased in value by roughly 13 percent during the first three months of 2019 (when I first wrote this chapter).[74] If we projected that stocks were going to keep growing at that rate, we'd expect five dollars invested today to grow to over a million dollars twenty-five years from now. Sadly, it's not quite that easy to invest. This would be a terrible way to plan for retirement! My point here is simple: when you're projecting growth, you have to be really careful. If growth rates are even slightly inflated, your estimates will be wildly unstable. And the growth rates reported by audits of the Bhojpuri movement are certainly inflated— perhaps massively so. I say this because these audits examine growth rates in a small sample of *surviving* churches, but never attempt to correct for attrition rates in churches that didn't survive.[75] This is a basic statistical error that's old enough to have its own name: we call it *selection bias*.

Here's how selection bias influences estimates. Suppose a "movement" started with 100 churches. Suppose at the end of the year, the first 75 churches had collapsed and the remaining 25 had survived and

69 Slack, Holste, and Terry, *Analysis of Church Growth among the Bhojpuri*.

70 Slack, Holste, and Terry, *Analysis of Church Growth among the Bhojpuri*.

71 Jim Slack, "Church Planting Movements: Rationale, Research, and Realities of Their Existence," *Journal of Evangelism and Missions* 6 (2007): 29–44.

72 Slack, Holste, and Terry, *Analysis of Church Growth among the Bhojpuri*.

73 Garrison, *Church Planting Movements*, 15.

74 Here, I report statistics on stocks from the S&P 500 index of companies.

75 Slack, "Church Planting Movements," 39. Slack reports that in creating his reports, "churches to be interviewed [were] randomly selected from the total number" of churches in a movement and asked to give a history of their growth.

had each planted a new church. You're left with only 50 churches, right? The "movement" is only half as large as when it began. It is collapsing!

Now suppose that when you audit the movement, you select a sample from those 50 surviving churches and interview them about their rates of church growth. These churches are from the small segment of your movement that doubled in size in the past year, so you'll assume—based on their stories—that your movement has doubled in size.[76] Selection bias has tricked you into thinking your collapsing movement is multiplying rapidly.

All this is typical of reports of large movements in missions literature. Reported numbers of churches and believers are based on slapdash statistics that are never clearly explained or justified.

Staggering numbers—simply by virtue of being reported—are expected to be believed. I'm not suggesting that Watson and his coworkers are being deliberately dishonest. I'm simply pointing out that it's entirely impossible for the men who write of such enormous movements to know whether the numbers they report are real or fanciful.[77] Might well-meaning optimism have inflated their estimates? I believe so—partly because of something Watson claimed that came a little closer to home.

Let me explain. In 2013, David Watson wrote, "The following was received from our church leader that will be overseeing the Disciple Making Movements in North Sudan. . . . 'We have seen 100's of churches planted and thousands of disciples raised.'"[78]

---

76   Indeed, the only published audit of the Bhojpuri movement suffers from additional biases; the sample of churches interviewed was not taken "randomly" but was selected from attendees of a large conference—but pastors of healthy, growing churches are much more likely to attend Christian conferences, and this sample cannot have been representative of a larger movement.

77   I am not suggesting that no one came to Christ or that no lives were changed! Instead, I am examining the *numbers* of reported believers, since reported numbers are clearly presented in ways that exert enormous persuasive power as people choose whether or not to use DMM and other CPM-style methods.

78   David Watson, "Loving Our Neighbors in North Sudan," *David L. Watson*, accessed May 29, 2018, https://web.archive.org/web/20150928121505/https://www.davidlwatson.org /2013/08/30/loving-our-neighbors-in-north-sudan/.

MOVEMENTS AND RUMORS OF MOVEMENTS   65

There's one problem with this: I served in Sudan during the time period discussed. Sudan's missionary community was tightly woven, and we had strong relationships with the national church. We were all aware of what was happening. And to be sure, I saw encouraging signs in certain parts of the country. I saw people come to Christ. But I have little reason to believe Watson's group and methodology had much to do with this, nor do I have reason to believe there were hundreds of churches planted. Similarly, a colleague in Ethiopia writes that reports of "thousands of house churches" planted there using DMM are "highly exaggerated."[79] Sadly, I've seen this more than I would care to remember, often in sincere prayer letters sent out by sincere missionary coworkers.[80] The simple fact is that statistics can lie, and numbers shouldn't be trusted without verification.[81]

3. What Worked through God's Grace in One Place May Not Work Everywhere

In 1995, Rick Warren published *The Purpose Driven Church*.[82] Warren had pastored Saddleback Church from a forty-person congregation

---

79 Personal correspondence. Name withheld for security reasons. May 23, 2015.

80 For example, in the Muslim world, where I work, missionaries can easily be confused. If a few friends agree to pray to God to forgive their sins (a very sensible thing for any practicing Muslim to do, according to most Muslim theology!), after I share about Jesus (an accepted Muslim prophet), this does not necessarily mean that they have put their faith in him, *even if the prayer makes some reference to Jesus*. In situations like this, well-meaning missionaries—seeing what seems to be a small group of new believers in front of them—may report that a church has been planted.

81 Here is a dissertation idea for a young student who might be interested in a PhD in missiology: study those cities or regions where a CPM movement is said to have taken hold ten to twenty years after the fact. Don't rely on the hearsay and slapdash statistics that have often characterized reports about such movements. Scratch beneath the surface and look for real evidence: How many "churches" remain? How strong is their public witness? Have they transformed the cities they grew up in? Is Christianity thriving? What do they in fact leave behind after the initial rush of statistics? To be sure, I would love to discover that the answer is hundreds, even thousands, of thriving and healthy churches, and cities that have been impacted by such growth. I fear that that's not the case, but may I at least suggest that we ask the question?

82 Rick Warren, *The Purpose Driven Church: Growth without Compromising Your Message and Mission* (Grand Rapids, MI: Zondervan, 1995).

in 1980 to a megachurch which, by 2017, reported 22,000 members. Even in 1995, Saddleback was already enormous, and the book became an instant best-seller. What followed was predictable: other churches and other pastors began following his model in the hopes that becoming "purpose-driven churches" would help them become larger and healthier. They met with varying degrees of success, but those I'm aware of experienced only modest attendance growth, if any.

Our innate desire for success leads us to try to mimic what worked before: perhaps if we set up our churches like Rick Warren's, they will grow as his did; perhaps if we minister like the eighteenth-century revivalists, we will unlock the keys of revival. But God doesn't always work in the same ways. Rick Warren—or the eighteenth-century revivalists—may be gifted in ways you and I are not. And when God does bring about revivals or incredible church growth, we should not necessarily attribute what he's done to the ministry methods of the leaders through whom great movements happened. God may have worked through their methods at times, and he may have worked *despite* their methods at other times.

Conclusion

So let's not get caught up in the numbers game. It's not that we don't *care* about numbers—numbers count people, and people are important. But numbers give us a one-dimensional picture of what God is doing in people's lives. We can't put our trust in numbers. They're no replacement for the multifaceted, long-term wisdom of Scripture. They can be wildly inaccurate. And even when they are accurate, there's no guarantee that what worked for someone else will work for us. Let's make sure our decisions and strategies are driven by Scripture, not by numbers.

With that in mind, let's turn to the Scriptures and examine some of today's most popular movement methodologies and how they came to be.

3

In the Scales of the Scriptures

BEFORE WE EXAMINE today's methods in light of the Scriptures, we'll need some background on what those methods are. By far the most influential techniques today are *Church Planting Movements* (CPM) and other related methodologies.[1] Throughout this chapter, I'll refer to the Church Planting Movements methodology as *CPM*. I'll refer to the cluster of related techniques as *CPM-style methods*. All of the CPM-style methods I will discuss were developed by missionaries from the International Mission Board (IMB), the missionary arm of the Southern Baptist Convention. The IMB is the largest missions organization in the world. Because of its size, methods which gain traction in the IMB often reverberate throughout the larger missions community. Most of these methods also gained widespread popularity through books published by WIGTake Resources, a publishing house founded by IMB missionary David Garrison and his wife, who played a key role in developing CPM-style methods. While these methods differ in some respects, it shouldn't be surprising that they also share common overriding features.

---

1 The most influential CPM style methods at the time of this writing are:
   • Church Planting Movements (CPM) (Garrison, *Church Planting Movements*).
   • Disciple Making Movements (DMM) (Trousdale, *Miraculous Movements*).
   • Training for Trainers (T4T) (Smith, *T4T*).
   • Any-3 (Shipman, *Any-3: Lead Muslims to Christ Now!*).

In the early 1980s, the IMB by and large did not work in restricted-access countries. Because of this, they recognized that many of the world's largest unreached people groups were simply out of their reach. In an effort to evangelize the entire world by 2000,[2] the IMB began exploring ways to accelerate their efforts. They looked at "ways . . . a Non-Resident Missionary (NRM) [could] get the gospel to [an] unreached people group in a restricted access country."[3] By 1988, the IMB appointed David Garrison as "the first director of the NRM program."[4,5] Two years later, Garrison wrote *The Nonresidential Missionary*,[6] in which he argued that missionaries could live far from the people they hoped to reach and still act as catalysts for movements to Christ among those peoples. A single conviction underlay these ideas: "all the ESSENTIAL ingredients to see a people group reached reside within that people group."[7] Therefore, direct missionary involvement was unnecessary. Rather than ministering themselves, nonresident missionaries "merely check that someone does" the ministry.[8]

You might be wondering: but how would this distant missionary even communicate with locals? According to nonresident missionary theorists, only "market fluency" in the language was required, since nonresident missionaries needed to spend at least 70 percent of their time *away* from the people with whom they worked. Nonresident missionaries would work to coordinate "overall strategy" and to catalyze

---

2   R. Bruce Carlton, *Strategy Coordinator: Changing the Course of Southern Baptist Missions* (Eugene, OR: Wipf & Stock, 2011) 86, 229.

3   Richard Bruce Carlton, "An Analysis of the Impact of the Non-Residential/Strategy Coordinator's Role in Southern Baptist Missiology" (DTh diss., University of South Africa, 2006), 52–53.

4   Carlton, "Non-Residential/Strategy Coordinator's Role," 11.

5   Carlton, "Non-Residential/Strategy Coordinator's Role," 55.

6   V. David Garrison, *The Nonresidential Missionary*, vol. 1 of Innovations in Mission (Monrovia, CA: MARC, 1990).

7   William Smith, "Additional Document," emailed to Bruce Carlton November 16, 2004, cited by Richard Bruce Carlton, "An Analysis of the Non-Residential/Strategy Coordinator's Role in Southern Baptist Missiology" (DTh diss., University of South Africa, 2006), 210.

8   David B. Barrett and James W. Reapsome, *Seven Hundred Plans to Evangelize the World: The Rise of a Global Evangelization Movement* (Birmingham, AL: New Hope, 1988), 36.

"new work and approaches" via "phone, modem, electronic mail."[9,10] Eventually, nonresident missionaries became "strategy coordinators."[11] Their job involved little more than presiding over movements from a distance, and with little direct involvement. Such missionaries were seen as "a super-apostle of sorts, delegating various aspects of ministry to volunteers from the United States and from the field."[12] These emphases had a profound effect on CPM-style methodologies.

By the mid-1990s, a handful of strategy coordinators began reporting remarkable success stories that seemed to validate Garrison's approach. As these stories were analyzed, a new set of methods emerged. CPM came first; it was born in part by examining the work of David and Jan Watson. I've mentioned the Watsons already. They lived in Singapore as nonresidential missionaries / strategy coordinators for the Bhojpuri people in India.[13]

CPM was first publicized by Garrison in a pamphlet,[14] and eventually finalized in a book, *Church Planting Movements: How God Is Redeeming a Lost World*.[15] These publications caught the attention of the wider missions community, and CPM quickly gained far-reaching traction. Watson later branched off on his own. In partnership with Patrick Robertson, Jerry Trousdale, and others, he developed another CPM-style method, which they called *Disciple Making Movements* (DMM).[16]

---

9 *Market fluency* is not a technical term, but we can assume it refers to the ability to buy and sell items in a local market. This is far below the level of proficiency required to carry out even a basic conversation.

10 Barrett and Reapsome, *Seven Hundred Plans*, 36–37.

11 Carlton, "Non-Residential/Strategy Coordinator's Role," 3.

12 John D. Massey, "Wrinkling Time in the Missionary Task: A Theological Review of Church Planting Movements Methodology," *Southwestern Journal of Theology* 55/1 (Fall 2012): 115.

13 David Garrison, *Church Planting Movements: How God Is Redeeming a Lost World* (Bangalore, India: WIGTake Resources, 2007), 15. Watson's work is described as "How it all began."

14 David Garrison, *Church Planting Movements* (Richmond, VA: International Mission Board, 2000).

15 Garrison, *Church Planting Movements: How God Is Redeeming a Lost World*. The first edition was printed in 2004.

16 Jerry Trousdale, *Miraculous Movements: How Hundreds of Thousands of Muslims Are Falling in Love with Jesus* (Nashville: Thomas Nelson, 2012).

They promoted this method under the auspices of CityTeam ministries. Today, DMM is the most influential of CPM-style methods by a large margin; it differs from CPM's initial focuses by taking unique approaches to the disciple-making process. Two more methodologies are worth mentioning: Ying Kai's *Training for Trainers* (T4T)[17] and Mike Shipman's *Any-3*.[18,19] Currently, these methods are so widely followed that in many missions circles, the only question is "T4T or DMM?"[20] However, we can't embrace them simply because they're widely used. We must first examine these methods in light of Scripture.

In what follows, I'll do my best to characterize each method fairly, drawing quotes from popular resources written by the known leaders and principal designers of these methods. For example, to describe DMM, I'll generally refer to books by David and Paul Watson and Jerry Trousdale. I don't assume, of course, that every DMM practitioner agrees with Trousdale or the Watsons in every particular.

I should also note that there's much to be praised in today's most popular methods. Whenever we look at *any* ministry method, we must attempt to learn what we can. CPM-style methods tend to emphasize broad "proclamation of the gospel,"[21] rather than focusing on a few close friendships. This seems to reflect the New Testament example.

17 Steve Smith, *T4T: A Discipleship Re-Revolution* (Bangalore, India: WIGTake resources, 2011).

18 Mike Shipman, *Any 3: Anyone, Anywhere, Anytime* (Monument, CO: WIGTake Resources, 2013).

19 A fifth methodology, with some relation to CPM—the Camel Method—has been developed for use with Muslims and is described by Kevin Greeson in his book *The CAMEL: How Muslims Are Coming to Faith in Christ* (Monument, CO: WIGTake Resources, 2010). However, we will not examine the Camel Method or the controversy surrounding it in detail, since it is an evangelistic strategy rather than a full-fledged church-planting method—it does little, for example, to address issues of discipleship. In fact, Greeson writes to promote and explain CPM, suggesting that he does not see the Camel Method as a separate approach to ministry but rather as an evangelistic method that can be used within CPM techniques (Kevin Greeson, "Church Planting Movements among Muslim Peoples," *Mission Frontiers* [March/April 2011]: 22–24).

20 Steve Smith and Stan Parks, "T4T or DMM (DBS)? Only God Can Start a Church Planting Movement! - Part 2 of 2," *Mission Frontiers* (May/June 2015): 32–35.

21 Garrison, *Church Planting Movements*, 345.

Additionally, CPM-style methods attempt to evangelize in ways that won't result in new believers being forcibly extracted or expelled from their communities. While I'm not aware of any methods that idealize extraction, CPM-style methods rightly desire to avoid it. This, too, is commendable. Finally, CPM-style methods emphasize the use of inductive Bible study in which new believers learn about the Bible in discussion groups. This is a valid teaching method, and regular patterns of Bible study are vital to the Christian life.

Nonetheless, many parts of these methods are distressing. I'll discuss them below.

A. Overemphasis on Rapid Growth

Every book touting CPM-style methods begins with stories of "movements" that grew explosively. CPM-style methods tell us to expect this: movements should spread so rapidly that, ideally, they'll be primarily made up of new believers who disciple other new believers and then plant new churches. For example, in Disciple Making Movements (DMM), four generations of churches must be planted every three years for a genuine "movement" to have occurred.[22] That is, within a three-year period, a new church must plant a second new church, which in turn must plant a third new church, and that third church must also plant a fourth new church. In other words, a brand new church should plant another new church in only nine months.[23]

T4T works in the same way: "Every six months we can help the new churches to . . . double in number from 320 to 640 to 1,280 to 2,560."[24] In CPM, we find that "a Church Planting Movement might see a new

22 David Watson and Paul Watson, *Contagious Disciple Making: Leading Others on a Journey of Discovery* (Nashville: Thomas Nelson, 2014), 4.

23 In fact, leaders of the first reported movement from DMM claim to have seen "over 100 generations" of "believers and churches" in 25 years (David Coles, "A Still Thriving Middle-Aged Movement: An Interview with Victor John by Dave Coles," *Mission Frontiers* [May/June 2019]: 16)—for this to be true, churches would have had to plant new churches *every 3 months for over 100 generations!*

24 Steve Smith, "What Others Are Saying," in Ying Kai and Grace Kai, *Ying and Grace Kai's Training for Trainers: The Movement That Changed the World* (Monument, CO: WIGTake Resources, 2018).

church start every three to four months. . . . Among the Kekchi people
. . . if a church didn't reproduce itself after six months it was considered
an unhealthy church."[25] Notice: these aren't simply descriptions of what
might happen; they offer *the* benchmark of success. In fact, a new booklet vaunted as summarizing the best-practices of CPM-style methods
warns that one major reason "we are losing the battle" is that we are
"not teaching groups to become local churches (i.e., self-governing and
self-supporting) within a few short months."[26]

David Garrison sums up:

> "How rapid is rapid?" you may ask. Perhaps the most accurate answer
> is, "Faster than you think possible."[27]

Again, let me begin by affirming the good. I love CPM-style practitioners' desire for lots of people to come to Christ—and quickly. As
promoters of CPM-style methods often point out, the church *did* grow
quickly in the book of Acts, and the gospel *did* spread throughout the
entire Roman world within a few hundred years after Jesus's resurrection. I don't deny this, and I'm not interested in forbidding new
churches from starting when the Spirit moves. I'm also not interested
in forbidding excited new believers from sharing what they've learned
with their friends.

However, planting new churches goes far beyond discussing stories
about Jesus with friends, and new believers planting new churches every
6 to 9 months—as CPM-style methods suggest they should—was simply *not* the norm in the early church. Besides, such goals are impossible
to sustain for any length of time.[28] If doubling in size every 6 to 9 months

---

25 Garrison, *Church Planting Movements*, 195.

26 Wilson Geisler, *Rapidly Advancing Disciples: A Practical Implementation of Current Best
Practices* (2011), 17, accessed August 12, 2018, http://www.churchplantingmovements
.com/images/stories/resources/Rapidily_Advancing_Disciples_(RAD)_Dec_2011.pdf.

27 Garrison, *Church Planting Movements*, 21.

28 In fact, if churches in the first reported CPM—referred to as "how it all began"—had
continued to reproduce at such a rate since 1994, when it was first reported to have nearly
100 churches (Garrison, *Church Planting Movements*, 15), it would have had approxi-

had been the norm for the early church, then every person on earth would have been a believer within 8 to 12 years after Pentecost[29]—and within 20 to 30 years after Pentecost, while Jesus's original apostles were still living, the church in Jerusalem would have multiplied into more than 1 trillion gatherings! So, even though they sat under the apostles' teaching and enjoyed the apostles' shepherding, most churches in the New Testament "didn't reproduce [themselves] after six months" and could have been "considered . . . unhealthy [churches]" by CPM standards.[30] If that's the case, then there's probably something exaggerated in the so-called need for such rapid growth.

Most churches in the New Testament "didn't reproduce [themselves] after six months" and could have been "considered . . . unhealthy [churches]" by CPM standards. If that's the case, then there's probably something exaggerated in the so-called need for such rapid growth.

It is easy to forget that slow, consistent growth can still bring about tremendous results. Historian Rodney Stark finds that the early church didn't grow "at rates that seem incredible in light of modern experience."[31] He estimates population growth in the first 300 years of the church at slightly over 3 percent per year and shows how this growth

---

mately 400 billion churches by 2018. Even today, such rates of rapid growth—if they do occur—are an unsustainable exception, not a norm.

29 Assuming that the population of the world in the first century was between 170 and 330 million people, if the church had doubled in size every 6 to 9 months, then it would have taken only 8 to 12 years to grow from 5,000 people (Acts 4:4) to 327 million people! ("Historical Estimates of World Population," U. S. Census Bureau, accessed February 3, 2019, https://www.census.gov/data/tables/time-series/demo/international-programs/historical-est-worldpop.html).

30 Garrison, *Church Planting Movements*, 195.

31 Rodney Stark, *The Rise of Christianity: How the Obscure, Marginal Jesus Movement Became the Dominant Religious Force in the Western World in a Few Centuries* (San Francisco: HarperCollins, 1997), 4.

rate was sufficient for the church to spread through the Roman Empire by the mid-300s.[32] But even this rate of growth probably wasn't sustained for long: 3 percent growth per year would have caused the early church to balloon from 5,000 believers (Acts 4:4) to over 35 million in its first 300 years. In the early 300s AD, the entire world population was likely around 200 million people.[33] While the church may have formed around 10 percent of the Roman population,[34] it had little presence outside the Roman empire. So while church growth ebbed and flowed in the early years—including some rapid expansions—we can conclude that the overall trend was probably one of growth by small, consistent percentages. There's a freedom in the mathematics of compounding growth. Even slow, small gains, if they remain consistent, achieve enough momentum to eventually reach substantial goals.

Of course, my concern here isn't with mathematics. My concern is that the felt need for such obviously unsustainable growth can lead us to an excessive fascination with numbers, rather than trust in God. Let's not forget that David is judged for numbering Israel (2 Sam. 24:1–17)! An emphasis on numbers may cause us to promote faster growth than is healthy—or even possible. Consider what Paul says about the importance of a foundation: "Like a skilled master builder I laid a foundation, and someone else is building upon it. Let each one take care how he builds upon it" (1 Cor. 3:10).

What would happen if we built upward before laying a strong foundation? Can a new believer truly lay a foundation "like a skilled master builder" a few months after first hearing the message himself? Paul writes that he proclaimed Jesus by "warning everyone and teaching everyone with all wisdom, that we may present everyone mature in Christ" (Col. 1:28). According to Paul, then, the ability to teach "with all wisdom" is necessary to lead others to maturity. Until they gain this wisdom, new believers will be seriously limited in their ability to disciple others and plant new churches.

32 Stark, *Rise of Christianity*, 6.
33 "Historical Estimates of World Population."
34 Stark, *Rise of Christianity*, 6.

Foundations cannot be built in a hurry:

... whoever makes haste with his feet misses his way. (Prov. 19:2)

The plans of the diligent lead surely to abundance,
    but everyone who is hasty comes only to poverty. (Prov. 21:5)

Some things are too important to build quickly. God may sometimes ordain his people to expand at steady, sustainable rates so they have time to grow healthy and strong and root out false doctrine. Moses tells Israel,

The LORD your God will clear away these nations before you little by little. . . . lest the wild beasts grow too numerous for you. (Deut. 7:22)

Moses didn't speak this way because he lacked faith in God to make Israel grow and fill the land. He knew the people would one day out-number the stars. Rather, Moses foresaw slow, steady growth because he was more concerned with the healthy growth of God's people than with timing and numbers. We too must learn to be patient when God moves more slowly than we would hope. We need to trust him even when we have not yet "received the things promised" (Heb. 11:13).

After all, our impatience is ineffective: Abraham grows weary of waiting and fathers Ishmael, but his efforts don't make the blessing come sooner, and a lot of problems result. God's blessing cannot be hurried, and we must not despise "the day of small things" (Zech. 4:10). The same God who gives great ministry breakthroughs—like Hudson Taylor's ministry in China—also gives long years of patient plodding. For example, Robert Morrison ministered a generation before Hudson Taylor. He saw few converts, but he successfully translated into Chinese the Bible that Hudson Taylor would later use. As Jesus told his disciples just before he ascended into heaven, "It is not for you to know times or seasons that the Father has fixed by his own authority" (Acts 1:7).

We should do what we can to work toward fruitful times and seasons, but it isn't up to us to bring them about quickly through our cunning or urgency. The slow, expansive growth of a mustard seed—or of leaven seeping through dough (Matt. 13:31–33)—still characterizes kingdom growth. We can contentedly follow the pattern of Jesus; he often avoided the crowds in order to spend time with his disciples. It was only when their maturation process was complete that he committed the growth of the church into their hands. We had better not push too hard for grandchildren before the children are fully grown!

We had better not push too hard for grandchildren
before the children are fully grown!

B. DNA for Rapid Growth

CPM-style methods assume there is a "DNA" that will guarantee that churches will flourish and multiply. They use that term a lot:

Rapid reproduction starts with the DNA of the first church . . .[35]

There is a minimum DNA required for groups to replicate past the first generation.[36]

Establishing this DNA early on is vital:

Groups establish the habits and DNA for meetings very quickly—by the third or fourth meeting. . . . Consequently, group DNA must be established during your first meeting with the group.[37]

Again, we ought to begin by affirming what's good. When setting up Bible study groups—when setting up anything—we should try to establish good patterns. But is the key to missions work found simply in

---

35 Garrison, *Church Planting Movements*, 195.
36 Watson and Watson, *Contagious Disciple Making*, 145.
37 Watson and Watson, *Contagious Disciple Making*, 143.

beginning right? The assumption that Bible study groups and churches have inherently change-resistant DNA—in the way that biological organisms do!—and "will naturally transfer that DNA to their offspring" is never explained.[38]

It is worth asking: what is the "DNA" that CPM-style methods hope to instill in Bible study groups and churches? Watson states that the DNA must include elements like prayer, intercession, ministry, evangelism, obedience, Scripture, accountability, worship, learning through discovery, and more.[39] But these elements are not unique. They're emphasized in most evangelical churches and missionary endeavors. What, then, are the *distinctives* of CPM-style DNA?

Watson says this DNA is necessary "for groups that multiply."[40] This assertion alone is illuminating. The goal of CPM-style methods is rapid reproduction, and as we'll see throughout the remainder of this chapter, the core distinctives of their "DNA" are *all*—without exception—geared to enable movements to expand as rapidly as possible. David Garrison states that this DNA for "rapidly reproducing daughter churches" includes a movement having "its own internal momentum. . . . All the elements that are foreign to the church—and not easily reproduced—have been eliminated."[41]

He reiterates the point when he lists "Eliminate All Non-Reproducible Elements" as one of the "Ten Commandments for Church Planting Movements."[42] Here's what's wild about this: *Missionaries* are among the elements that are "foreign to the church—and not easily reproduced"![43] Therefore, they must play as small a role as possible. Traditional church-planting methods might suggest that churches should remain "under a missionary pastor" until pastors from within the new church can be trained.[44] But CPM-style methods see this as part of what makes

---

38 Garrison, *Church Planting Movements*, 195.
39 Watson and Watson, *Contagious Disciple Making*, 144–51.
40 Watson and Watson, *Contagious Disciple Making*, 143.
41 Garrison, *Church Planting Movements*, 196.
42 Garrison, *Church Planting Movements*, 258.
43 Garrison, *Church Planting Movements*, 196.
44 Garrison, *Church Planting Movements*, 195.

"traditional disciple-making almost impossible to rapidly reproduce."[45] In their model, there's no time for careful biblical instruction or for raising up seasoned leaders. Instead, bringing groups of seekers and new believers together is thought to be adequate "protection against bad leadership and heresy. When the authority of Scripture and the Holy Spirit is part of group DNA and group process, groups can protect themselves. . . . Groups self-correct. . . . Groups keep individuals accountable."[46]

In short, the "DNA" that makes CPM-style methods work strips ministry structures down until nothing is left but groups of people to whom the Scriptures and the Holy Spirit are available. Anything else would be considered too time-consuming, too "non-reproducible," and too top-heavy—and therefore, worthy of elimination.

We'll explore the implications of this in greater detail. For now, I simply want to note that this approach seems to lean on sociology more than theology. Its overriding concern is on which group dynamics seem easy to replicate and which do not. Of course, there's nothing inherently wrong with sociology or with studying group dynamics as long as we don't look to them before we look to Scripture. That is, we must not try to build churches on the power of sociology (group psychology and social dynamics)—which is just another way of building on the flesh and not the Spirit—even if the goals are good. We build on the Word and Spirit, not the flesh (2 Cor. 4:1–6; 10:4). Unfortunately, we will see that CPM-style methods do in fact overlook key scriptural principles in favor of planting churches with lightweight, easily replicable structures.

In reality, the "DNA" of healthy church growth isn't found in the sociology of group dynamics as applied to church structures. The "DNA" for reproduction and sustainability is *contained within the gospel message itself*. Healthy, reproducing churches will result if we impart Christ's full message. It is through the Word's intrinsic power that "the word of truth, the gospel, . . . has come to you, as indeed in the world it is bearing fruit and increasing" (Col. 1:5–6).

45 Watson and Watson, *Contagious Disciple Making*, 129.
46 Watson and Watson, *Contagious Disciple Making*, 143.

When Paul bids farewell to the Ephesian elders, he reminds them he "did not shrink from declaring to you the whole counsel of God. . . . I did not cease night or day to admonish every one with tears. And now I commend you to God and to the word of his grace, which is able to build you up and to give you the inheritance . . ." (Acts 20:27–32). It is because of Paul's in-depth teaching that he can confidently commit the Ephesian church to God's care. CPM-style methods tell us to eliminate all non-reproducible elements. But here, a clearly non-reproducible element—the ministry of a man with Paul's missionary gifting—brings great benefit to the church. The Ephesian church may not be able to replace Paul, but he has left them with a full understanding of the "whole counsel of God." This understanding is self-sustaining and will continue to "build [them] up" long after Paul is gone.

C. Aversion to Teaching

Paul's careful teaching provided a strong foundation for the Ephesian church. Unfortunately, CPM-style methods view trained teachers as a liability. Why? You guessed it. Because they're not rapidly replicable. A missionary might train leaders from a church or two. But if each church duplicates itself every six months, then the missionary will soon be unable to keep up. Before long, the only "leaders" will be brand-new believers who have been given an introductory orientation to the Word by similarly inexperienced new believers who haven't been trained to teach. Unsurprisingly, CPM-style methods downplay the role of missionaries and teachers. In their most extreme versions, they forbid teaching outright. This might sound unbelievable to you. It's not. David and Paul Watson write, "When working with lost people, we have to avoid falling into the role of explaining scripture."[47] According to the Watsons, "The disciple maker does not do any of the traditional things required by traditional disciple-making. He does not preach or teach."[48] Other CPM-style advocates agree:

---

47 Watson and Watson, *Contagious Disciple Making*, 149.
48 Watson and Watson, *Contagious Disciple Making*, 127.

The pervasive assumption . . . that trained teachers are central to the growth of the church, is something the CPM Model purposefully seeks to overcome.[49]

The church planter, as a foreigner in the culture, must remain in the background and minimize cultural transmission.[50]

Instead, CPM-style methods rely on "discovery groups" or "discovery Bible studies."[51,52,53] In these groups, seekers and new believers discover truth directly from the Word. Rather than receiving help from missionaries or teachers, they rely on the Holy Spirit to answer their questions directly. Steve Smith, a well-known proponent of T4T, whose work we introduced in chapter 2, writes, "The group learns . . . together as they ask questions of the text and ask the Holy Spirit to give them understanding."[54] Other CPM-style proponents share Smith's view:

. . . learn to go to Scripture and rely on the Holy Spirit to answer questions.[55]

. . . trust that God's Word and the Holy Spirit are enough.[56]

. . . we have to avoid falling into the role of explaining Scripture . . . when we put ourselves between the Word of God and His people, we usurp God's role.[57]

---

49 Ted Esler, "Coming to Terms: Two Church Planting Paradigms," *International Journal of Frontier Missiology* 30/2 (Summer 2013): 69.

50 Younoussa Djao, "Church Planting Movements: A Golden Key to Missions in Africa," *CPM Journal* (January–March 2006): 86.

51 Smith, *T4T*, ch. 19.

52 Garrison, *Church Planting Movements*, 61.

53 Watson and Watson, *Contagious Disciple Making*, 101.

54 Smith, *T4T*, ch. 14.

55 Watson and Watson, *Contagious Disciple Making*, 150.

56 Trousdale, *Miraculous Movements*, 183.

57 Trousdale, *Miraculous Movements*, 103–4.

In DMM especially, direct teaching and pastoring are portrayed as being so dangerous that the ideal is for missionaries and disciple-makers to be absent from Bible studies, even when curious *unbelievers* are studying Scripture together. The following quotes illustrate this:

Let the lost lead the Bible studies.[58]

If you decide that it is necessary for you to attend the group, only lead the group for 1–3 weeks, and then turn over the question-asking (facilitating) to an insider.[59]

The outsider . . . no matter if they are expat or local . . . would coach 1–2 people from the group . . . and not attend the group.[60]

Don't facilitate every group. . . . My friend facilitated the first meeting with the young man. The young man immediately went and replicated the meeting with his family. My friend never met the young man's family. From the first meeting, my friend developed the young man as the leader of the group.[61]

Coach the leader and avoid stepping into the group.[62]

Because CPM-style methods were largely developed by *nonresidential* strategic coordinators, it's unsurprising that they see no need for a

58 "Lesson 12: Plan and Implement," 1, accessed June 20, 2019, https://dmmovements.net/en/Lesson%2012%20-%20Plan%20and%20Implement.pdf. Distributed in CityTeam DMM Trainings.
59 "Process of Discovery Groups," in *DMM Training, Chiang Mai, Thailand, January 2015*, CityTeam.
60 "Lesson 8: Starting Discovery Groups," 5, accessed June 20, 2019, https://dmmovements.net/en/Lesson%208%20-%20Starting%20Discovery%20Groups.pdf. Distributed in CityTeam DMM Trainings.
61 Watson and Watson, *Contagious Disciple Making*, 135.
62 David Watson, March 16 Webinar Notes, "My Friend Just Asked, 'What About God?'—Now What?" accessed May 1, 2019, http://moredisciples.com/wp-content/uploads/2016/04/March-16-Webinar-David-Watson.pdf.

missionary to be present. Unbelievers, it is assumed, will "literally . . . lead themselves to Christ."[63] Some pastoring is recommended behind-the-scenes to ensure that Bible study groups don't fall into error. But realistically, it is impossible to keep close watch on Bible study groups when the church planter is urged to stay away from the group meetings, and when they're expected to multiply every few months. Earlier we saw just how slim such involvement can be when David Watson spoke about "627 churches started . . . [with] no evangelist, just an audio Bible."[64] Is such limited pastoring sufficient for new churches to grow in healthy ways? Again, we see that stripped-down, rapidly replicable structures form the fundamental "DNA" of CPM-style methods. Somewhat unsurprisingly—as CPM-style methods were developed in the IMB—these structures represent an extreme case of Baptist church governance: each congregation is independent from outside oversight, self-sufficient, and autonomous.

But Is This Scriptural?

Let's begin again by affirming what is good. First, it's healthy for people to grow in their understanding of God's Word until they can largely navigate it on their own. Historically, missionaries have taught those they hoped to reach. They've tried to work themselves out of a job. Second, I agree with the promoters of CPM and DMM that interactive Bible study groups provide a wonderful way to learn about Scripture.

However, these groups are not—as is sometimes implied[65]—the only alternative to boring lectures. In fact, many styles of teaching can be effective as long as learners remain engaged.[66] I doubt that many missionaries in history have preferred to teach in monologues;

---

63 "David Watson's Testimony," narrated by David Watson, *Accelerate Training*, accessed January 3, 2019, https://www.acceleratetraining.org/index.php/resources/61-david-watson -s-testimony-90-min-mp3/file.

64 "David Watson's Testimony."

65 David Watson, "What about Teaching and Preaching in Disciple-Making Movements?" Accessed March 10, 2017, https://www.davidlwatson.org/2013/08/27/what-about-teaching -and-preaching-in-disciple-making-movements/.

66 David Sousa, *How the Brain Learns*, 4th ed. (Thousand Oaks, CA: Corwin, 2011), 101.

those I know seek to teach in the most participatory settings possible. Sure, teaching *can* be pursued in boring, unengaging ways. But that doesn't mean all teaching is unnecessary, or that learning should happen entirely through self-discovery. In any endeavor—following Christ included—it takes a good deal of hand-holding in the basics to gain enough independence and mastery to guide our own learning. Children must be taught how to count—slowly and painstakingly—before they're able to do algebra or perform geometric proofs on their own. Might this be true of new believers as well?

Somewhat surprisingly, Watson quotes Jesus to validate DMM's aversion to teaching: "'And they will all be taught by God.' Everyone who has heard and learned from the Father comes to me" (John 6:45).[67] But what kind of guidance does God give? Does he help us to interpret the Scriptures correctly when we are confused? In fact, when we examine this passage, Jesus isn't claiming that God will *always* show us how to correctly interpret Scripture. Instead, Jesus is responding to a group of people who doubt him by pointing out that only those who have been "taught by God" (v. 45) will be able to believe in him. This passage shows that God enables our belief in Christ, but it doesn't say that he will give us correct answers when we try to interpret the Scriptures on our own.

At numerous points in my spiritual life, I have interpreted Scripture incorrectly when studying the Bible with friends. I've done this even as I've prayed for God to guide us into truth. I'm sure you have, too. Church history shows us that Spirit-led believers are perfectly capable of misinterpreting the Bible! Peter warns that *"the untaught* and unstable distort, . . . the Scriptures, to their own destruction"* (2 Pet. 3:16, NASB).[68] A lack of teaching can be a dangerous thing. I'm so thankful I wasn't left to exegete the book of Romans with a few of my friends at the beginning of my spiritual development! By putting new believers

---

67 Watson, "March 16 Webinar Notes," 3.

68 Here, I quote the NASB ("untaught and unstable") rather than the ESV ("ignorant and unstable"). Either translation is adequate, but the Greek word—*amatheis*—is related to the verb *matheteuo* (to teach, to make a disciple). In the ancient world, a learner or disciple (*mathetes*) learned from a teacher, so the NASB's rendering ("untaught") may capture the meaning more fully.

in such a situation, the "obsession with rapid reproducibility" of CPM-style methods "effectively abridges the teaching process in a way that does not sufficiently appreciate the doctrinal depth of the Word and the time needed to ground new believers in it."[69]

Watson would disagree. He assures us that Bible study groups "lead themselves to Christ" and "within weeks, these groups are more orthodox than most Christian Bible studies."[70] But we must remember: Watson prefers to be absent from these Bible studies after the first few meetings. He cannot have attended more than a handful of the thousands of Bible studies that he claims were born from his ministry. So how would he even know if they find their way to orthodoxy? What's more, many national leaders seem to disagree with Watson's assessment. Indian pastor Harshit Singh warns against untaught churches which are "Christianized" but have little understanding of the gospel:

> Any young church needs biblical and theological training. . . . But here's the problem. Theological training and education takes time. Christianization says that we are in a warlike situation and we do not have time because we have to reach millions, and time is running out. They are alarmists. Any structured formal or informal theological education . . . is looked down upon as . . . a time-consuming, resource-wasting, movement-slowing, terrible Western influence.[71]

Missiologist John Massey reports that other national pastors and leaders share these concerns:

> One IMB field leader responsible for developing a training program for pastors in East Asia surveyed twenty-one pastors of large churches and networks of churches regarding their greatest need.

---

69 George A. Terry, "A Missiology of Excluded Middles: An Analysis of the T4T Scheme for Evangelism and Discipleship," *Themelios* 42/2 (2017): 351.

70 "David Watson's Testimony."

71 Harshit Singh, "How Western Methods Have Affected Missions in India," 9Marks' First Five Years Conference, Columbus, OH, August 4, 2017. Accessed May 3, 2019, https://www.9marks.org/message/how-western-methods-have-affected-missions-in-india.

They all said without hesitation, "Our pastors need training!" They also commented, "Our churches are under attack by cults and false teaching. Our pastors don't have a good understanding of how to apply theology." . . . One seminary president in Southeast Asia heavily invested in training pastors in this same East Asian country and thoroughly acquainted with the church situation there stated, "We are losing 10,000 churches a year to the cults."[72]

According to Massey, mission boards persuaded by CPM-style methodologies argue that such training is unnecessary. They refuse to send missionary teachers, even though this refusal is "contrary to the felt needs of the nationals."[73] Surely it is unwise to impose our convictions on nationals unless we have a scriptural imperative to do so. In fact, Scripture leans in the opposite direction. Direct teaching is a clear New Testament tradition:

- Jesus taught directly throughout his ministry (e.g., the Sermon on the Mount; Matt. 4:23; 11:1; 11:7–30; 12:25ff.; 13:3–52; 15:10–11; 18:1–35; 23:1–39; 24:4–25:46; Luke 5:16–22; 9:11, etc.).
- The apostles taught publicly (Luke 9:6; Acts 2; 3; 5:42).
- Paul's pattern in any new city was to first go and teach publicly in the synagogues or other public places of prayer (Acts 13:5, 14, 44; 14:1; 16:13; 17:1–3; probably 18:5). He taught publicly in Athens (Acts 17:22ff.) and in the school of Tyrannus (Acts 19:9). He taught Lydia's family directly—explaining enough that after a single session with them, baptism was appropriate (Acts 16:13–15). In Acts 20, when he looks back over the years at Ephesus, Paul says he "went about preaching the kingdom" among them (v. 25 NASB) and "did not shrink from declaring to you the whole purpose of God" (v. 27) and was "teaching you publicly and from house to house" (v. 20).

---

72 John David Massey, "Theological Education and Southern Baptist Missions Strategy in the Twenty-First Century," *Southwestern Journal of Theology* 57/1 (Fall 2014): 6.

73 Massey, "Theological Education and Southern Baptist Missions Strategy," 7.

- Stephen (Acts 6:10), Philip (Acts 8:5–6), and Apollos (Acts 18:28) taught publicly.
- Paul exhorts Timothy to teach (1 Tim. 6:2; 2 Tim. 2:2; 4:2).
- Paul exhorts Timothy to entrust the message to others who are "able to teach" (1 Tim. 3:2).

Throughout the Scriptures, we never see groups of seekers or new believers left to "discover" truth on their own through the help of the Holy Spirit. Even Jesus's parables involve direct teaching. The truth is hidden in riddles from those whose ears are closed, but Jesus directly provides both stories and their explanations to his disciples. When his disciples ask for explanations (see, for example, Matthew 13), he doesn't ask leading questions ("What do you think it means?") and leave them to discover truth, as CPM-style methods would advise. He simply tells them what the parables mean.

Why, Then, Do CPM-Style Methods Try to Restrict Teaching?

In fairness to those who advocate newer methods, we must examine some of their specific concerns about missionaries teaching. Perhaps New Testament patterns of teaching aren't prescriptive for us today. Is there reason to believe missionaries will damage the church by teaching in ways New Testament missionaries did not? Proponents of CPM-style methods voice two major concerns.

First, they worry that if missionaries teach or answer questions, this may lead new churches to depend on the missionaries rather than on God. Thus, new believers should be "led to study directly from God's word and find their own answers. So we don't lecture or teach them. We just ask questions. Practice NOT answering questions."[74] Trousdale concurs: "We have to avoid falling into the role of explaining Scripture. . . . When we put ourselves between the Word of God and His people, we usurp God's role."[75]

---

74 "Lesson 8: Starting Discovery Groups," 5.
75 Trousdale, *Miraculous Movements*, 103–4.

Second, proponents of CPM-style methods worry that missionaries may introduce foreign cultural elements. This "[forces] new believers to exchange their cultural forms for alien ones" and "[injects] foreign elements into the life of the church that cannot be locally reproduced. . . . These alien invaders can cripple a Church Planting Movement."[76]

Of course, immature and egotistical missionaries can teach churches to depend on them in damaging ways. Furthermore, unwise cross-cultural missionaries can introduce their own cultural forms to a new church, and with devastating effects. But that doesn't mean we should assume this will necessarily happen.

CPM-style methods make three key errors in the diminished role they give to missionaries.

First, they fail to see teaching as a gift of the Spirit through which the Spirit generally works. Instead, CPM-style methods consistently see teachers in the church as selfishly usurping the role of the Holy Spirit. As one major proponent of CPM-style methods wrote, one major reason "we are losing the battle" is because of "pastors and leaders who are selfish and try to keep control over God's Kingdom . . . [by] not delegating authority or empowering New Believers."[77] Somehow, teaching in the church is placed in direct competition with the work of the Holy Spirit:

Paul . . . left behind maturing, spreading, multiplying groups of believers. How? He trusted the Spirit to be their teacher, not Paul.[78]

Any discipleship program that creates a dependence on the human teacher rather than the ever-present Teacher of the Spirit is doomed.[79]

But there is no indication in Scripture that we must choose be-tween listening to a "human teacher" and listening to "the Spirit."

76 Garrison, *Church Planting Movements*, 253.
77 Geisler, *Rapidly Advancing Disciples*, 17.
78 Smith, *T4T*, ch. 4.
79 Smith, *T4T*, ch. 4.

The Spirit gives human teachers to his church (Eph. 4:11). Rather than working directly, apart from human agents, the Spirit's power flows through his people. The Spirit didn't reveal the meaning of Isaiah 53 to the Ethiopian eunuch. He sent Philip to explain it to him. Similarly, the angel didn't explain the gospel to Cornelius. God sent Peter to share the gospel with him. Just as the Spirit worked through Jesus's humanity—through his human words, his human presence, his human touch (1 John 1:1–2)—so today we are Christ's body in the world, and the Spirit works to reveal God through us. Teachers aren't trying to "usurp God's role."[80] They're individuals in whom and through whom God is at work.

. . . there is no indication in Scripture that we must
choose between listening to a "human teacher"
and listening to "the Spirit." The Spirit gives
human teachers to his church (Eph. 4:11).

Second, CPM-style methods overlook the Scriptures' heavy emphasis on sound teaching. Jonathan Leeman reminds us,

> Paul, no doubt, is interested in "sound" teaching and doctrine. He uses the term five times with Timothy and five times with Titus (1 Timothy 1:10; 6:3; 2 Timothy 1:7, 13; 4:3; Titus 1:9, 13; 2:1–2, 8).[81]

Paul's repeated insistence on elders being able to give "sound" teaching shows that there are qualities teaching must possess before it can edify the church. Not all teaching will do—sound teaching requires providing *insight* into the Scriptures. Leeman explains:

80 Trousdale, *Miraculous Movements*, 104.
81 Jonathan Leeman, *Don't Fire Your Church Members: The Case for Congregationalism* (Nashville: B&H Academic, 2016), 137.

What exactly is sound teaching? Is it simply reading the biblical text? No, Paul tells Titus to teach "what accords" (ESV) or "things that are consistent" (HCSB) or "what is appropriate to" (NIV) or "what befits" (RSV) sound doctrine. A man doesn't just read a text. He explains, interprets, gives the meaning (see Neh. 8:8), and, to some extent, applies a text. D. A. Carson helpfully describes faithful preaching as "rerevelation."[82] The apostles and prophets revealed God's Word a first time. A faithful sermon does not say something new; it re-reveals that same Word to a new audience.[83]

Third, CPM-style methods overstate the importance of cultural differences. They see missionaries as *cultural outsiders*, inherently unable to fully enter into or understand another culture, and not *cultural immigrants*, who are on a journey into another culture and who will over time learn to understand and interact with it in largely seamless ways.

This is why CPM proponent Younoussa Djao can say, "The church planter, as a foreigner in the culture, must remain in the background and minimize cultural transmission."[84] But there's a problem with this: it doesn't match New Testament data. Paul taught Gentiles without culturally contaminating them. Was Paul a cultural insider? Paul spoke Greek fluently, but many of the cities and areas Paul visited, such as Perga (Acts 2:10; 13:13), Asia Minor (Acts 2:9), and Lycaonia (Acts 14:11) had their own languages, as did Rome (Latin). Though Paul had grown up in a pagan-dominated world, the Roman Empire's cultures and religious systems were too varied for him to be familiar with them all.[85] Gentile culture didn't come naturally to Paul, but he

82 D. A. Carson, "Challenges for the Twenty-First Century Pulpit," in *Preach the Word: Essays on Expository Preaching: In Honor of R. Kent Hughes*, ed. Leland Ryken and Todd A. Wilson (Wheaton, IL: Crossway, 2008), 176–77, quoted in Leeman, *Don't Fire Your Church Members*, 137.

83 Leeman, *Don't Fire Your Church Members*, 137.

84 Djao, "Church Planting Movements," 86.

85 See John Bostock and H. T. Riley, eds., *The Natural History of Pliny the Elder* (London: Taylor & Francis, 1855), 7:24. The Roman Empire was far more culturally heterogeneous than the Mediterranean and North Africa are today. Rome expanded in a short time over a vast area that was primarily made up of small states and city states, far more fragmented

still taught Gentile believers. Similarly, the Jewish apostles in Jerusalem gave teachings for Gentiles to follow (Acts 15:19–21). As Christ's ambassadors, we shouldn't assume our teaching will introduce cultural pollution into the church. Instead, we should learn how to reach across cultural barriers, as Paul did (1 Cor. 9:21–23), and teach in ways that are culturally appropriate.[86]

A Warrant to Teach

We shouldn't be afraid to teach. CPM-style proponents like Watson warn that when missionaries teach, "a church will depend on the disciple-maker. This is unhealthy. It severely limits a church's potential and in the worst cases can kill a new church before it has a chance to develop."[87]

But the book of Proverbs says the teaching of the wise helps us grow into mature, independent adults. Wise people know when to let us find answers on our own and when to provide answers for us. In some cases, direct instruction from the wise is *essential* to our well-being; we don't leave our children alone with their friends to discover how to relate to sex or alcohol. In the same way, some parts of new believers' spiritual lives are dangerous if mishandled, and we shouldn't leave them to discover these dangers on their own. We need to remember Proverbs 13:14: "The teaching of the wise is a fountain of life." We need to remember Proverbs 9:9: "Give instruction to a wise man, and he will be still wiser." The man who listens to instruction is blessed, not limited or overly dependent.

If we're tracking with the pattern of Scripture, then we'll see missionaries as ambassadors through whom the Spirit works and teaches, giving the new church an unbreakable foundation (Matt. 7:24–25). As missionaries teach in wise, mature ways, the gospel will sink deep into

---

than today's nation-states. For example, in the region of Pontus—now a part of the Black Sea region of Turkey—at least twenty-two languages were spoken.

86 As we'll discuss in greater detail in chapter 6, some caution is necessary when our teaching touches on people's cultural practices. However, even in these cases, teaching may be necessary.

87 Watson and Watson, *Contagious Disciple Making*, 173.

new believers' hearts, preparing them to depend on God long after the missionary—and other "irreproducible elements"—are gone.

D. The *Oikos* and the Person of Peace

Because missionary involvement is "foreign to the church and not easily reproduced,"[88] CPM-style methods draw heavily from *oikos evangelism*, first popularized by Thomas Wolf, a professor of missions and evangelism at the Southern Baptist–affiliated Gateway Seminary.[89,90] *Oikos evangelism* avoids evangelizing isolated individuals and it also avoids mass evangelism. Instead, Wolf contends that the New Testament pattern is to evangelize within the *oikos*—which is simply the Greek word for "household." He expands this word a bit to mean an individual's existing social network. The key to reaching the *oikos* is for missionaries to discover a "person of peace" who will then spread the good news within his existing social network. According to Wolf, the "person of peace" must satisfy three criteria: he must be *receptive* to the messenger; he must have a *reputation* that helps the message to spread;[91] and he must provide *referrals*—that is, he must introduce the missionary to his wide social network of relationships.[92,93] In every group of new believers, it is the person of peace who functions as the primary conduit of church growth. Here's how Watson describes it:

> The disciple-maker has one job—find the Person of Peace. . . . If there is no Person of Peace, you move on. . . . We are told to pray for

---

88 Garrison, *Church Planting Movements*, 196.

89 Thomas A. Wolf, "Oikos Evangelism: The Biblical Pattern," in Win Arn, ed., *The Pastor's Church Growth Handbook* (Pasadena: Church Growth Press, 1979), 110–17.

90 Dan White Jr. and J. R. Woodward, *The Church as Movement: Starting and Sustaining Missional-Incarnational Communities* (Downers Grove, IL: InterVarsity Press, 2016), 100.

91 In some cases, even a strong bad reputation can suffice. For example, the Gerasene demoniac's bad reputation helps people to take note when Jesus frees him from several demons.

92 White and Woodward, *Church as Movement*, 100.

93 Some CPM-style methods use a different set of criteria to identify the person of peace. DMM, for example, changes the criteria to *open*, *hungry*, and *sharing* (Watson and Watson, *Contagious Disciple Making*, 135). But generally, as is the case with DMM, the criteria used are similar to Wolf's criteria.

harvesters. The Person of Peace will be this harvester. We equip this person to be the disciple-maker for his or her community.[94]

Another CPM proponent agrees with Watson about the preeminence of this task: "God has given you an assignment—find the person of peace."[95]

When we remember how CPM-style methods insist on rapidity and downplay the role of the missionary, this emphasis on the person of peace makes sense. It's almost unavoidable. It is important to note: the person of peace isn't initially a believer. In fact, he *may never become one*.[96] In order to qualify as a person of peace, the person need only open up his or her social network to the gospel. But due to the demand for rapid growth, even if the person of peace *does* become a believer, he'll have little time to mature before being encouraged to become the "disciple-maker for his or her community."[97]

Finding the person of peace is so imperative that we're told *not* to minister to people with limited relational networks:

Leaving when you don't find a Person of Peace is something no one wants to talk about. Yet . . . if we don't leave, we might not find the Person of Peace waiting in the next family, affinity group, community.[98]

Avoid focusing so much time on relationships with other believers and lost "non-persons-of-peace" that you cannot prioritize searching for persons of peace among those you know and those you meet.[99]

---

94 Watson and Watson, *Contagious Disciple Making*, 128.

95 Kevin Greeson, "Jesus on Entry Strategies," Church Planting Movements, accessed August 10, 2018, http://www.churchplantingmovements.com/index.php/vert5parts/vertentry /103-jesus-on-entry-strategies#comment-6.

96 For example, see "Lesson 7: Finding Households of Peace," 2, accessed June 20, 2019, https://dmmovements.net/en/Lesson%207%20-%20Finding%20Households%20of%20 Peace.pdf. Publius is referred to as a person of peace because he seems to open his social network to Paul, but Publius does not seem to become a believer (Acts 28:7–10).

97 Watson and Watson, *Contagious Disciple Making*, 128.

98 Watson and Watson, *Contagious Disciple Making*, 138.

99 "Lesson 7: Finding Households of Peace," 4.

If [Jesus's disciples] did not find a person of peace, they were to leave and go on to another town rather than staying in an area that was unproductive for ministry.[100]

Again, let's begin by affirming what is good. First, missionaries have always known that gifted evangelists from within a culture are often more effective than they are. They've also known that their own time and efforts are limited. So we should rejoice when cultural insiders receive the message and spread it among their social networks. Second, Jesus does tell both the apostles and the seventy-two to seek out "[sons] of peace" (Matt. 10:12–3; Luke 10:5–7) and to lodge with them.[101]

Unfortunately, the search for persons of peace as practiced and encouraged among CPM-style missionaries goes far beyond Jesus's instruction. It makes at least four unfounded assumptions:

1. A person of peace will play a central role in both opening his community to the gospel and discipling his community after they believe the gospel.
2. We are able to identify up front who will and who will not be persons of peace.
3. We should be wary of investing heavily in people whom we don't identify as persons of peace.
4. We should quickly encourage persons of peace to begin teaching and discipling their communities.

Let's consider each of these assumptions.

With regard to the first, the Gospels simply describe a person of peace as someone who provides a roof to Jesus's disciples and is open to hearing their message. There's no hint that these people will play a

---

100 Jerry Trousdale and Glenn Sunshine, *The Kingdom Unleashed* (Murfreesboro, TN: DMM Library, 2015), ch. 7.

101 "Whatever house you enter, first say, 'Peace be to this house!' And if a son of peace is there, your peace will rest upon him. But if not, it will return to you. And remain in the same house, eating and drinking what they provide, for the laborer deserves his wages. Do not go from house to house" (Luke 10:5–7).

key role in opening their social network to the gospel. There's absolutely nothing that says they will help to disciple churches that form in response to the apostles' preaching. It's simply nowhere to be found in the biblical witness.

Second, it's dangerous to assume that we can know whom God will choose to work through. We're told that "you need to qualify potential Persons of Peace."[102] We're told that church planters can "usually identify the person of peace within a few hours of entering the village."[103] But first impressions can be deceiving. When Ananias is told to go and heal Saul (Acts 9:13), Ananias protests. Saul doesn't seem to be a man of peace at all! But like Ananias, we're limited in our understanding. We can't see future things. We don't know the status of people's hearts. So who's to say whom God will use or not use? Unless we are—like Ananias—prophets who receive visions from God, we may not learn we had wrong assumptions about people we've dismissed. After all, Ananias only did what was right after direct prompting from God. In short, we shouldn't trust our judgment of people we've only just met.

Third, if we bypass individuals who seem unlikely to be persons of peace, then we may devote little time and effort to the single lost sheep. This is precisely the opposite of how Jesus does ministry. He reminds us that *every* lost sheep merits an all-out search (Luke 15:1–7). Jesus was happy to meet with Nicodemus, even though he came to him alone at night, too scared to be seen by others. The last thing Nicodemus wanted was to open his social network to Jesus. But Jesus still ministered to him. Similarly, Jesus could have turned away the children whose mothers wanted him to bless them, and focused his energy more "strategically" on finding persons of peace. But he didn't. Sometimes, Jesus and the apostles ministered to those who opened doors for the gospel in their communities (e.g., Jesus and the woman at the well; Peter and Cornelius). But *they're never recorded as trying to discern who might*

---

102 Watson and Watson, *Contagious Disciple Making*, 135.

103 David Watson and Paul Watson, "A Movement of God among the Bhojpuri of Northern India," in *Perspectives on the World Christian Movement: A Reader*, ed. Ralph D. Winter and Steven C. Hawthorne (Pasadena, CA: William Carey Library, 2009), 697–700.

be a gatekeeper to a community and then exclusively working with those people. They simply share the gospel with whoever will listen. Some of these people may share within their communities; some may not. Jesus and his disciples aren't in a hurry. They don't need to find effective social networkers in order for the gospel to move forward. Their message has its own power to move forward; it doesn't need the help of social engineering (Col. 1:5–6).[104] They entrust the spread of the gospel to the sovereignty of God, so they're free to minister to whomever he brings across their path.

Fourth and finally, Scripture indicates that we shouldn't appoint new believers to leadership, but should wait for them to grow in faith, knowledge, and character (1 Tim. 3:1–13; Titus 1:5–9). I'll talk about CPM-style methods' strange interpretation of these verses below.

E. Obedience-Based Discipleship

Advocates of CPM-style methods acknowledge that the New Testament requires church leaders to be mature (1 Tim. 3:1–13; Titus 1:5–9). They also argue that *time in the faith* has no relation to maturity. According to Watson, "Maturity as a believer is defined by obedience, not by time."[105]

In CPM-style methods, a new believer may be considered mature provided that he or she seems to obey. That's why CPM-style methods dismiss traditional paradigms, characterizing them as ineffective iterations of "knowledge-based discipleship." They hope to introduce "obedience-based discipleship" instead.[106,107] This isn't surprising. Remember: the core "DNA" of CPM-style methods focuses on rapid replicability. Giving new believers time to grow in their knowledge of God through the Scriptures is simply not feasible. Instead, CPM-style methods hope that spiritual maturity can be engineered immediately

---

104 ". . . the gospel . . . has come to you, as indeed in the whole world it is bearing fruit and increasing" (Col. 1:5–6).

105 David Watson, "Let's Bake a Cake," *CPM Journal* (January–March 2006): 30.

106 Smith, *T4T*, ch. 4.

107 Similarly, David and Paul Watson state that the church's problems today result from "teaching knowledge, not obedience" (Watson and Watson, *Contagious Disciple Making*, 46).

through an initial "commitment to die to self" that results in obedi-ence.[108] This obedience, it is hoped, creates opportunities for God to move: "When people obey—even lost people—the Holy Spirit begins to validate the truth of the Bible," which leads to greater faith and obe-dience.[109] So for CPM-style advocates, obedience *initiates* the process of spiritual growth. Faith and knowledge of God are the result.

Again, we must affirm what is good. Obedience is a part of the Chris-tian life: "No one born of God makes a practice of sinning, for God's seed abides in him; and he cannot keep on sinning, because he has been born of God" (1 John 3:9). Additionally, when we obey God—as Naa-man did, when he washed in the Jordan (2 Kings 5:14–15)—he proves faithful, and our own faith in him grows.

But does this mean that discipleship *begins* with obedience or is *based on* obedience? Critics of obedience-based discipleship are con-cerned that it "is not gospel-based or grace-based discipleship. The basis for our discipleship relationship with the Lord Jesus, according to OBD [obedience-based discipleship], is our own obedience."[110] This, they worry, confuses the role of grace and works in the Christian life. It forgets that "righteousness and salvation are freely given by God, merely of grace, only for the sake of Christ's merits."[111]

Promoters of CPM-style methods disagree. They argue that the concept of obedience-based discipleship is built on the premise that "salvation has two parts, justification and sanctification. . . . Our jus-tification comes by God's grace alone; we have absolutely no part in

108 Watson and Watson, *Contagious Disciple Making*, 46.

109 Trousdale and Sunshine, *Kingdom Unleashed*, ch. 15.

110 This concern is exacerbated by confusing quotes from promoters of CPM-style methods. David and Paul Watson state that "faith is defined as being obedient" (Watson and Watson, *Contagious Disciple Making*, 15), leaving critics concerned that

> they consistently argue . . . that this "faith" is "obedience." They have turned the gospel, unintentionally, we trust, into "justification by grace through obedience to Christ." (Chad Vegas, "A Brief Guide to DMM," Radius International, accessed January 7, 2019, https://www.radiusinternational.org/a-brief-guide-to-dmm/)

111 *Heidelberg Catechism: Revised according to the Originals* (Sioux Falls, SD: Pine Hill Press, 1979), Q&A 21, quoted in Chad Vegas, "A Brief Guide to DMM," Radius International, accessed January 7, 2019, https://www.radiusinternational.org/a-brief-guide-to-dmm/.

it. . . . But our sanctification is very different. . . . [Our obedience] is integral to the process of personal sanctification. . . . We become like Christ by obeying the Father."[112] As the title *obedience-based discipleship* suggests, they believe that "obedience is the foundation of discipleship" and spiritual growth.[113]

Here we step into complicated territory, but it's critical that we understand clearly the error of obedience-based discipleship. In the Scriptures, faith—not obedience—is the foundation of both our justification *and* our spiritual growth. Paul rebukes the Galatian church for forgetting this:

> Let me ask you only this: Did you receive the Spirit by works of the law or by hearing with faith? Are you so foolish? *Having begun by the Spirit, are you now being perfected by the flesh?* (Gal. 3:2–3)

In the Scriptures, faith—not obedience—is the foundation of both our justification and our spiritual growth.

When we "hear with faith" through the power of the Holy Spirit, we grow. Though we never become fully perfect this side of eternity, the Spirit has begun in us a process of "being perfected," to use Paul's phrase. In other words, obedience in the Christian life comes through Spirit-wrought faith in God. This is why Paul calls us to the "obedience *of faith*" (Rom. 1:5). This is why Hebrews 11 states that "by faith Abraham obeyed" (Heb. 11:8), and "by faith Rahab the prostitute did

---

112 Trousdale and Sunshine, *Kingdom Unleashed*, ch. 15. When Trousdale and Sunshine mention "personal sanctification," we must assume from the context that they are referring to ongoing growth in Christian maturity, not—as New Testament writers usually use the term "sanctification"—to the already completed act by which God has set his saints apart for himself ("you were washed, you were sanctified . . ." [1 Cor. 6:11]). I do not point this difference out in order to be fastidious but because we must understand their intended use of the term if we are to interact with what they are trying to say.

113 Trousdale and Sunshine, *Kingdom Unleashed*, ch. 15.

not perish with those who were disobedient" (Heb. 11:31). And perhaps most poignantly, "By faith, Abraham, when he was tested, offered up Isaac. . . . He considered that God was able even to raise him from the dead" (Heb. 11:17, 19).

This last example helps us understand why faith must precede obedience. Abraham would not have been able to offer up Isaac if he hadn't believed God would do right and come through on his promise regarding Isaac. The same is true for us: if we don't trust God to care for us—both here and in the hereafter—we won't be able to obey him when the cost is high. Until God grows faith in our hearts, we may have "the desire to do what is right" but we don't have "the ability to carry it out" (Rom. 7:18). Obedience isn't the foundation of our discipleship; faith is.

What is faith? It is not a blind leap into the dark, as is often suggested. Rather, faith finds its foundation in the knowledge of God. We reasonably trust him because we *know* him. Paul can cheerfully trust God in the face of death because he knows whom he has believed (2 Tim. 1:12). Jesus's "sheep follow him, *for they know his voice*" (John 10:4).

In the Scriptures, then, maturity in faith comes as we "grow in the . . . knowledge of our Lord" (2 Pet. 3:18). We learn to trust God by knowing God, just as we learn to trust new friends by knowing them. What does he love? What does he despise? What is he like? What does he want from us and for us? It takes time for us to learn answers to these questions. We must listen as God reveals himself to us. This is why our maturity is tied so strongly to our knowledge of his Word. As the author of Hebrews says,

> For though by this time you ought to be teachers, you need someone to teach you again the basic principles of the oracles of God. You need milk, not solid food, for everyone who lives on milk is unskilled in the word of righteousness, since he is a child. But solid food is for the mature, for those who have their powers of discernment trained by constant practice to distinguish between good and evil.
>
> Therefore, let us leave the elementary doctrine of Christ and go on to maturity. (Heb. 5:12–6:1)

Notice that maturity comes from "constant practice" in the "word of righteousness." Constant practice takes time, of course. It involves knowing more than "elementary doctrine."[114] Notice, too, that it is "by this time" that "you ought to be teachers." Put another way, *time* is assumed to be a component of maturity.

Maturity cannot be reached simply by stressing the importance of obedience, or even by setting up strong accountability structures to help us obey. Many religions have attempted to bring about obedience in these ways, and the results always fall short of what we hope for in Christian discipleship. The temptation to rely on our own works was a snare to New Testament churches, and it has remained a snare throughout church history. Obedience-based discipleship will weaken people's defenses against this temptation. Our standing before God is based entirely on the finished work of Christ, and as we saw earlier, we mature in our Christian lives just as we began: through faith, by the power of the Spirit (Gal. 3:2–3).

Now, the Spirit doesn't simply bypass our humanity as he matures us. Rather, the Spirit empowers us to grow through our human faculties as we learn about God. Again, this learning takes time. We can't commit to obey and suddenly become mature Christians any more than a child can commit to grow up and suddenly become a mature adult. What's more, our will to obey may be sincere, but it's shaky. Christ warns Peter that "the spirit indeed is willing, but the flesh is weak" (Matt. 26:41). Though Peter earnestly desired to stand with Jesus (Matt. 26:35; John 13:37)—though he even took risks, like attacking the temple guard with a sword (John 18:10)—in the end, he denied Christ three times.

---

114 In fact, almost everywhere that the New Testament speaks of maturity in the faith, it assumes that scriptural thinking or knowledge are a key part of maturity. For example:

Him we proclaim, warning everyone and teaching everyone with all wisdom, that we may present everyone mature in Christ. (Col. 1:28)

Let those who are mature think this way . . . (Phil. 3:15)

Brothers, do not be children in your thinking. Be infants in evil, but in your thinking be mature . . . (1 Cor. 14:20)

Until we all attain to . . . the knowledge of the Son of God, to mature manhood. (Eph. 4:13)

Both the Galatian and the Ephesian churches obeyed impressively at the beginning, but their obedience petered out:

> I am afraid I may have labored over you in vain. . . . What then has become of your blessedness? For I testify to you that, if possible, you would have gouged out your eyes and given them to me. (Gal. 4:11, 15)

> Repent, and do the works you did at first. (Rev. 2:5)

Basing our spiritual growth on an intense commitment to obey puts the cart before the horse. It risks promoting "zeal for God, but not according to knowledge" of God (Rom. 10:2). But knowledge of God is what's truly valuable. Even Paul counted his "zeal" and "blameless" obedience as "loss." Why? "Because of the surpassing [value] of *knowing* Christ Jesus" (Phil. 3:6–8). Such knowledge takes time to grow, and CPM-style methods don't have time to waste. Their "DNA" insists on rapid growth, because churches must multiply.

F. Promotion of New Believers and Unbelievers to Leadership

Because maturity is thought to be immediately possible, CPM-style advocates make another error: they appoint new believers to pastor and lead other new believers. Watson writes, "Maturity as a believer is defined by obedience, not by time. . . . Leadership training begins from the moment a Church Planter starts a Discovery Bible Study. Every new believer is expected to be a leader."[115]

Leadership roles are assigned organically, reflecting how people naturally relate to each other: "Every oikos has natural leaders. We don't choose the leaders. We simply identify them."[116] But without watching people as they mature, how can we distinguish a group's

---

115 Watson, "Let's Bake a Cake," 30.
116 James Nyman, *Stubborn Perseverance: How to Launch Multiplying Movements of Disciples and Churches among Muslims and Others* (Mount Vernon, WA: Missions Network, 2017), 39.

social leaders from its spiritual leaders? It's not easy, especially early on, to discern whether apparent believers will in fact be good soil, or whether they will dry up in the harsh sunlight or be choked by the weeds. Would any of us want brand-new believers to pastor our churches at home? Would we allow our churches to appoint new believers who *seemed obedient* to shepherd our youth? We know all too well what tragedies might result!

The problems inherent in appointing new believers to leadership are only exacerbated when, as is the case in CPM-style methods, the missionaries appointing them struggle with "significant language limitations."[117] How can missionaries possibly gauge new believers' maturity if they can't understand most of what is being said? We will see just how significant their language limitations often are in chapter 6.

Finally, promoting new believers to leadership "seems to contradict what Paul says about the qualifications of overseers."[118] He writes to Timothy that an overseer "must not be a recent convert, or he may become puffed up with conceit and fall into the condemnation of the devil" (1 Tim. 3:6).

Steve Smith and Steve Addison address this passage by contending that Paul's criteria for leadership in 1 Timothy 3:1–13 apply only to mature churches. To prove this point, they claim that Titus 1:5–9 gives a more relaxed set of criteria for leaders in new churches.[119] Curiously, this distinction is nowhere indicated in the text, and even Titus includes such qualities as "able to give instruction in sound doctrine" and "above reproach." It is difficult to imagine these being qualities of new believers.[120] So shifting authority "within the first month" to the "natural spiritual leader of the group," as CPM-style methodologies

---

117 David F. Hunt, "A Revolution in Church Multiplication in East Africa: Transformational Leaders Develop a Self-Sustainable Model of Rapid Church Multiplication" (DMin diss., Bakke Graduate University, 2009), 129.

118 Steve Smith and Steve Addison, "The Bible on Church Planting Movements," *Mission Frontiers* (March/April 2011): 1.

119 Smith and Addison, "Bible on Church Planting Movements," 1.

120 How would they have had time to learn "sound doctrine"? How, without observing them over time, would we know that their lives were "above reproach"?

suggest,[121] is both premature and unwise. The same ought to be said of expecting new believers to disciple other new believers and plant new churches a few months after their conversion.

I'm not sure why CPM-style methods make such a glaring oversight. Perhaps they have a meager understanding of what "able to give instruction in sound doctrine" means. As long as new believers can explain to their friends that forgiveness comes through Jesus's death, CPM-style methods assume that they're qualified to lead. One CPM-style manual counsels sending new believers out to plant new churches after just three Bible studies: "Go and tell everyone you meet the Good News so that they also might receive God's free gift of salvation and escape judgment."[122] Their ability to proclaim the good news is based upon their having learned the "2-3-4 method,"[123] which attempts to explain the gospel in five minutes or less and which treats "escaping judgment" as the sum total of salvation.[124,125] But the message of the good news has more to it. Yes, through Jesus's death and resurrection we escape judgment. Hallelujah! But there's more. Through Jesus's death and resurrection, we're also freed from the power of sin over our financial lives, our family lives, our emotional lives, our sexual lives, and our social lives. How will new believers plant churches when they've *not*

---

121 Watson and Watson, *Contagious Disciple Making*, 130.

122 Geisler, *Rapidly Advancing Disciples*, 9, 42.

123 The 2-3-4 method attempts to help new believers explain the atonement in basic terms (judgment, repentance, Jesus's death, resurrection) in five minutes or less (Geisler, *Rapidly Advancing Disciples*, 41). It provides no further guidance into the substance of the gospel, nor does it attempt to disciple new believers. Nevertheless, it is clearly seen as an adequate foundation to begin planting churches, as it assumes that "if they say yes," the evangelist will immediately "start the church in their house . . ." (9, 42).

124 Indeed, in contexts in which people have never heard Christ's message, it is unlikely that a five-minute presentation would be enough for most people to understand even the basics of Christ's atonement. People will initially have little idea—or will have mistaken ideas—of what the Scriptures mean when they speak of God, of sin, of sacrifice, of Jesus, of forgiveness, of eternal life, etc. As we explain each concept, we will need to interact with people and answer their questions so that they will be able to understand. If we do not take time to answer these questions, can we really imagine that we will be able to send them out as enthusiastic and effective evangelists?

125 Geisler, *Rapidly Advancing Disciples*, 38.

*yet heard Jesus's teaching—let alone come to trust in it—in many areas
of their lives?*

Sadly, it gets worse. CPM-style methods even encourage *unbelievers*
to lead if they seem intent on obeying Scripture. James Nyman tells the
story of Aysha, a woman who has read some stories about Jesus and
the prophets and reports having obeyed the Bible by arguing less with
her husband.[126] Aysha is not even asked whether she has trusted Christ
as her Savior—or if she even knows what it might mean to trust Christ
as her Savior—before she is asked to coach Wati, another unbelieving
woman, as Wati leads Bible studies with her family. As a part of this
arrangement, Aysha must decide if Wati's family "has misconceptions
about faith in Jesus" in order to determine which Bible stories Wati's
family should study.[127] The problem with all this ought to be obvious:
Aysha herself hasn't professed faith in Jesus and is unfamiliar with
most of the Bible.[128] How can she assess whether Wati's family has
"misconceptions about faith in Jesus"? Because Aysha reports having
"obeyed" Scripture by arguing less with her husband, she's assumed to
be well on her way to maturity, even though there's no indication she
has obeyed Jesus's more fundamental command to repent of a sinful
life lived apart from God. Maybe she stopped arguing with her husband
simply because she was tired of it. Who knows? One can only wonder
why such an enormous oversight goes unnoticed. Would it take too
much time to look into such details? I suppose waiting until Aysha
professes faith would slow down the movement, and the movement
must proceed at all costs.

Conclusion

I believe in evangelistic movements. I believe in the Spirit's power to
propel the gospel through society and turn multitudes to Christ. Acts

126 Nyman, *Stubborn Perseverance*, 122–24.

127 Nyman, *Stubborn Perseverance*, 320.

128 Lest readers imagine Nyman's approach to be unusual among CPM-style practitioners,
it is important to note that his book receives high praise from David Garrison, David
Watson, Steve Smith, Steve Addison, Kevin Greeson, Stan Parks, Curtis Seargant, and
many other promoters of CPM-style methods.

records the beginning of a movement that would eventually spread throughout the Roman empire. But even movements in the early church—with their accompanying miracles and firsthand accounts of Jesus—didn't grow at the dizzying, unsustainable speeds that today's missions methods demand. They came about largely through steady, responsible growth. When we try to engineer rapid multiplication, we risk too much. Instead, we must focus first on planting healthy churches and only secondly on each church's capacity to multiply. CPM-style methods race past critical steps in this process, "wrinkling time"[129] to bring future goals closer than they actually are. If we use their metrics as the test of success, then missions history is littered with failure after failure. Missiologist Jim Massey agrees:

> If missiologists were to evaluate William Carey and Adoniram Judson according to CPM strategy, then the two would receive failing grades. Both men expended their lives with a great sense of urgency in fulfilling God's calling, but it took years to produce their first converts. They did not short-circuit the long, slow and arduous task of learning the language, adapting to their culture, developing relationships, making disciples, translating the Bible into the language of the people, planting churches, and training leaders. They trained leaders not in rapid multiplication principles but in principles that enabled them to know, teach, and contextually preach the Bible, develop a Christian worldview that undermined the pagan one of their own culture, and plant real churches with real leaders. Can these critical components of a holistic mission strategy ever be wrinkled? . . . Wrinkling time for the missionary appears to be an overly pragmatic and even impatient approach to church planting designed to achieve the maximum results over the shortest period of time. . . . When

---

129 Garrison, *Church Planting Movements*, 243. Garrison uses this phrase "wrinkling time" in a reference to Madeleine L'Engle's famous science fiction novel *A Wrinkle in Time*. In L'Engle's novel, time normally flows in a straight line, but by "wrinkling" this line, the present can be brought close to events in the distant future, allowing us to bypass the tedious process of waiting for time to pass.

driven by speed and pragmatism . . . quality and sustainability . . . will always be sacrificed. In CPM methodology, quick results take short-term precedence over long-term sustainability.[130]

He's right. As we'll see in greater depth in the following chapters, the Scriptural pattern doesn't focus on speed and numbers at all costs. It doesn't minimize the importance of language, culture, and other human factors in ministry. It doesn't race new believers through the discipleship process, or push trained missionaries and teachers out of the way because they can't be easily replicated. Instead, the New Testament pattern depicts missionaries as ambassadors from Christ who know his message deeply and have the necessary wisdom to communicate it clearly across cultural boundaries. This wisdom cannot be reproduced rapidly, but over time it will reproduce and sustain itself. Wise teaching that applies the "whole counsel of God" (Acts 20:27) to the hearts and minds of new believers is the scriptural "DNA" of healthy reproducibility.

Unfortunately, most young missionaries today aren't being groomed to teach deeply and slowly. Those who do so may find themselves accused of having "talking head syndrome,"[131] that is, being in love with the sound of their own voice! It's little wonder that few seriously pursue the acquisition of professional skills. What would be the point, when they're taught to see themselves in such self-deprecating ways— more-or-less bumbling figures who desperately need to "get out of the way"[132] of what God is doing and whose involvement must be carefully guarded so that it doesn't introduce dangerous dependency or cultural pollution to the church? With such an outlook, why would missionaries trouble themselves by pursuing scriptural training, or by going through years of nose-to-grindstone language and culture acquisition?

---

130 Massey, "Wrinkling Time in the Missionary Task," 110–11.
131 Watson, "What about Teaching and Preaching in Disciple-Making Movements?"
132 Steve Addison, "David Watson Author of Contagious Disciple Making," *Movements with Steve Addison*, podcast audio, November 16, 2015, https://podcastaddict.com/episode /65667146.

In the following chapters, we'll explore just how much time and effort missionaries may need to invest in order to minister with excellence. For now, it's enough to note that in all this, there's a potential for self-fulfilling prophecy. Missionaries with little depth of scriptural insight and little linguistic ability to express the insight they do have are less likely to even be able to communicate "the whole counsel of God" (Acts 20:27). Such men and women may indeed prove to be as ineffective in deep, long-term discipleship as they're imagined to be.

Of course, the tragedy is not just that missionaries may be afraid to minister but that they may foist their church-planting responsibilities on new believers—or even unbelievers—who don't yet have any solid foundation in the faith. Again, this is a failure of professional responsibility. What happens when we push people to build upward before laying a strong foundation? Buildings collapse, and people get hurt or even die. Likewise, when we don't take the time to disciple young believers toward maturity, we make them easy prey for false teachers, whose deceptive ideas may snare not only these new believers but everyone who follows them. The missionary might report exponentially explosive statistics back home. Yet what he's actually produced may be a burned-over district for the gospel, or, worse, a circus of heresies where a generation of people are now inoculated against the real gospel because they were fooled by a substitute.

CPM-style methods have many flaws. Does this mean that God can't work through missionaries who use them? Of course not. God can work through *any* method, and we should rejoice wherever we see him at work. But God can work through *anything* we do: good or evil, wise or unwise. So, the fact that God can work through a method isn't a good enough reason to build our ministry strategies on it. We can't afford to take shortcuts under the assumption that the Holy Spirit will "correct our flawed . . . church planting"[133] approaches. In reality, God may not be pleased to pick up the pieces if we naively depend on meth-

133 Tom Steffen, "Flawed Evangelism and Church Planting," *Evangelical Missions Quarterly* 34/4 (1998): 428–35.

ods that promise success while bypassing scriptural responsibilities. A wiser and humbler course of action is simply to build our churches and ministry strategies on the things God has explicitly instructed us to build on in his Word. So let's take up these responsibilities diligently and professionally, embracing the task in all its fullness. We shouldn't worry if there's no fruit right away. "We walk by faith, not by sight" (2 Cor. 5:7). What's more, Jesus told us that the kingdom of heaven grows like a mustard seed. Today it's small and slow-growing, but one day it will fill the whole garden.

PART TWO

―――――――――

CORRECTING
OUR COURSE

4

Ambassadors for Christ

WE'VE SPENT THE LAST two chapters looking at what can go wrong when we strip missionaries of their responsibilities and pursue speed and numbers at all costs. I'd like to change gears now. What would be a healthier approach? In chapter 1, we saw that God is at work in missionaries' efforts as they accomplish a set of very human tasks. We shouldn't buy into the fears of CPM-style advocates that missionaries will slow down or contaminate God's work by sticking with these tasks until they are accomplished. Instead, we should encourage them to look at the Bible and then to fulfill their responsibilities professionally and well. What would it look like to do this? Let's start at the beginning by examining how Scripture defines the missionary task. If we want missionaries to work responsibly and professionally, then what is their job description?

The apostle Paul gives us an excellent definition of the missionary task when he says that "we are ambassadors for Christ" (2 Cor. 5:20). But before we can understand what Paul means, we will have to address some common misinterpretations of this passage. What does it mean to be an "ambassador for Christ"?

Many Christians imagine that when Paul wrote 2 Corinthians 5:20, he was addressing all believers and was calling them to be something like a "brand ambassador"—a person appointed by a company to make its products more appealing by identifying with its brand. Is that what Paul is getting at? Is our job to make Jesus more appealing—to build his brand—by being good, decent, likeable people who identify with him? Now, I'm sure Paul would have wanted us to be good, decent, likeable people. But that's not what he's talking about in 2 Corinthians.

In fact, Paul doesn't say that *all* Christians are "ambassadors for Christ." Instead, Paul uses the term "ambassadors for Christ" specifically to describe himself and his team of missionaries. And he's not telling us to build Jesus's brand—he's claiming authority. In essence, he's saying, *We are Christ's ambassadors. We come in his authority with his message. You had better listen to us!*

This is evident when we read 2 Corinthians more closely. The context is clear: a group of "false apostles" have infiltrated the Corinthian church. They want to usurp Paul's authority and alter his message:

> If someone comes and proclaims another Jesus than the one we proclaimed, or if you receive a different spirit from the one you received, or if you accept a different gospel from the one you accepted, you put up with it readily enough. Indeed, I consider that I am not in the least inferior to these super-apostles. . . . Such men are false apostles, deceitful workmen, disguising themselves as apostles of Christ. (2 Cor. 11:4–5, 13)

Throughout the letter, Paul contrasts the genuineness of his apostleship with the duplicity of the false apostles[1] in an effort to convince the Corinthians to reject their "different gospel." In 2 Corinthians 5, Paul

---

1   See, for example:

> We are not, like so many, peddlers of God's word, but as men of sincerity, as commissioned by God, in the sight of God we speak in Christ. (2 Cor. 2:17)

> . . . we have renounced deceitful, underhanded ways. We refuse to practice cunning or to tamper with God's word . . . (2 Cor. 4:2)

> Are they servants of Christ? I am a better one . . . (2 Cor. 11:23)

> For I was not at all inferior to these super-apostles, even though I am nothing. The signs of a true apostle were performed among you . . . (2 Cor. 12:11–12)

hopes that reminding the Corinthians who he and his team are will call them back to the true gospel. He writes,

> What we are is known to God, and I hope it is known also to your conscience. . . . so that you may be able to answer those who boast about outward appearance and not about what is in the heart. (2 Cor. 5:11–12)

> Christ . . . gave us the message of reconciliation; . . . God was reconciling the world to himself, . . . and entrusting to us the message of reconciliation. (2 Cor. 5:18–19)

Paul claims to be an ambassador because God has entrusted him with this message. He continues with his heartfelt plea:

> Therefore, we are ambassadors for Christ, God making his appeal through us. We implore you on behalf of Christ, be reconciled to God. . . . Working together with him, then, we appeal to you not to receive the grace of God in vain. (2 Cor. 5:20; 6:1)

"We" refers to Paul and his missionary team, and "you" to the Corinthian church. Paul wants the Corinthians to see that his message contains the King's true terms of peace and reconciliation—and the Corinthians had better pay attention.

In summary, the term "ambassadors for Christ" applies to Paul's missionary team, not to all Christians, and Paul uses it to indicate that he comes in Jesus's authority with Jesus's message.

Ambassadorship in the New Testament

Ambassadorship is a major New Testament theme. We miss this because, when we read that Jesus called the twelve his *apostles* (*apostolos*, in Greek), we imagine that he must have been inventing a brand-new word to describe a spiritual gift or an office that existed only in the church. But the Greek word *apostolos* had existed long before

Jesus's birth; it was a perfectly secular word until Jesus used it. It connoted something along the lines of an ambassador,[2] one who was sent (*apostellō*) to represent a nation, with the power to negotiate on its behalf.[3] For example, the Greek historian Herodotus writes,

> Then, when the Delphic reply was brought to Alyattes, straightway he sent a herald to Miletus, offering to make a truce with Thrasybulus and the Milesians. . . . So the envoy [from Greek *apostolos*] went to Miletus.[4]

The envoy is sent with power to negotiate a truce. Similarly, Josephus writes,

> For a delegation of the Jews was come to Rome . . . that they might petition for the liberty of living by their own laws. Now, the number of the ambassadors [from Greek *apostellō*] that were sent by the authority of the nation was fifty.[5]

The apostles are sent by a nation and have the authority to represent it and negotiate on its behalf. Apostles, then, are similar to ambassadors, and the message Jesus gives to these apostles focuses on God's coming kingdom: "The kingdom of heaven is at hand" (Matt. 10:7). Jesus sends his ambassadors to negotiate peace. His terms of peace must be accepted, or destruction will follow.

This is why, in 2 Corinthians, when Paul appeals to his own authority, he seems to treat his status as an "ambassador for Christ" (2 Cor. 5:20) and a "true apostle" (2 Cor. 12:12) somewhat interchangeably.

---

2 Liddell and Scott define *apostolos* as "a messenger, ambassador, envoy" (Henry George Liddell and Robert Scott, *An Intermediate Greek English Lexicon* [Oxford: Clarendon, 2000], 107).

3 David Hesselgrave, *Paradigms in Conflict: 10 Key Questions in Christian Mission* (Grand Rapids, MI: Kregel, 2005), ch. 5.

4 Herodotus, *The Persian Wars: Volume 1*, trans. Alfred Denis Godley (Cambridge, MA: W. Heinemann, 1920), book 1, 21.

5 Josephus, *Antiquities*, trans. William Whiston (Grand Rapids, MI: Kregel, 1999), 579.

His duty as an ambassador to bring the "message of reconciliation" to the Corinthians (2 Cor. 5:19) is no different than his "apostleship to bring about the obedience of faith for the sake of his name among all the nations" (Rom. 1:5).[6]

This helps us make sense of the apostles' unique ministry giftings. They've been given miraculous powers (2 Cor. 12:12), they have firsthand knowledge of Jesus's message (Acts 1:21–23), and they're eyewitnesses of the risen Christ (Acts 1:21; 1 Cor. 9:1). These characteristics validate the apostles as ambassadors. They can believably say, "I have been sent by God!" because they come with clear signs from God. They can believably claim to know Christ's message because they've been there "during all the time that the Lord Jesus went in and out among us" (Acts 1:21). And most importantly, they can believably proclaim the resurrection because they've seen him with their eyes and touched him with their hands (1 John 1:1). Why did early Christians collect the writings of the apostles and those who worked directly with them? Why did they treat those writings as Holy Scripture? Because as Christ's direct ambassadors, the apostles could be fully trusted to deliver his authentic message.

Once we view the apostles as ambassadors, some of Jesus's unusual statements begin to make sense. For example, Jesus tells his apostles,

As the Father has sent me [from Greek *apostellō*], even so I am sending you. . . . If you forgive the sins of any, they are forgiven them; if you withhold forgiveness from any, it is withheld. (John 20:21–23)

This doesn't mean that Peter could have an argument with his wife and threaten to withhold God's forgiveness until she did what he wanted. Instead, Jesus is entrusting the apostles as his ambassadors to faithfully determine who has accepted his terms of peace and thus

6 Additionally, though the Greek word in 2 Cor. 5:20, *presbeuō* (*to be an ambassador*), is used only twice in the New Testament, its use mirrors that of the term *apostle*. It is used once to apply to Paul (Eph. 6:20) and once to apply to Paul and his missionary team (2 Cor. 5:20). In the same way, the word *apostle*—while it refers most often to Paul and the twelve—is also extended to describe Paul's missionary teammates (Acts 14:14; 1 Thess. 2:6).

116 PART TWO: CORRECTING OUR COURSE

who is to be forgiven. Elsewhere, Jesus says, "Whoever receives you receives me, and whoever receives me receives him who sent me" (Matt. 10:40). Jesus equates receiving the apostles with receiving him because as ambassadors, they come with his message in his authority.

The Gospels tell the story of Jesus bringing his kingdom near and then sending out special ambassadors with his terms of peace. Consider Jesus's Great Commission:

> Go therefore and make disciples of all nations, baptizing them in the name of the Father and of the Son and of the Holy Spirit, teaching them to observe all that I have commanded you. And behold, I am with you always, to the end of the age. (Matt. 28:19–20)

Missionaries as Christ's Ambassadors Today

What does this have to do with missions today? Jesus sent the apostles as ambassadors to the nations two thousand years ago—what does that have to do with us?

God knew that Jesus's eleven apostles wouldn't fulfill the Great Commission by themselves. Today, the wider church carries on their ambassadorial task. Missionaries among the unreached are at the forefront of these efforts. In saying this, I'm not equating missionaries with the apostles. I sincerely hope no one will collect *my* writings and revere them as Scripture! However, even without the New Testament apostles' unique gifting, we can act as ambassadors in smaller, subsidiary ways.[7]

Understanding missionaries as ambassadors is helpful because it suggests a definition for the missionary task. In chapter 1, I suggested that the missionary's goal is "establishing Christ-centered churches that are sufficiently mature to multiply and endure among peoples who have had little or no access to Jesus's message." The missionary's

---

7   Today's missionaries may act as ambassadors to the nations, but our ambassadorship is only legitimate to the extent that our message conforms with the apostles' original message, as recorded in their New Testament writings. The ambassadorship of missionaries today, then, is only a smaller, subsidiary extension of the apostles' work and is "built on the foundation of the apostles . . ." (Eph. 2:20).

task, then, *is to go in Christ's authority as ambassadors of his kingdom, to communicate his message to the nations.*

Like any king, Christ sends ambassadors to communicate on his behalf. In fact, communication is the sum total of the missionary task. David Hesselgrave writes,

> If the Christian mission were something to be played, communication would be the name of the game. As it is, the Christian mission is serious business—the King's business! In it, missionaries have ambassadorial rank. Their special task is to cross cultural and other boundaries in order to communicate Christ.[8]

Like any king, Christ sends ambassadors to communicate on his behalf. In fact, communication is the sum total of the missionary task.

Do you see how markedly this differs from CPM-style methods? As we saw, CPM-style methods restrict missionary communication and teaching because they worry that missionaries are inherently prone to *miscommunicate* Christ's message across cultural lines. Hesselgrave reminds us that missionaries are ambassadors and communication is their primary job. Sure, cross-cultural communication has difficulties. All ambassadors have to learn how to communicate cross-culturally despite these difficulties. If missionaries serve as Christ's ambassadors, they must see this as a professional responsibility.

Communicating and teaching are not optional. The oft-quoted[9] line that "we must preach always, and when necessary, use words" is the death knell of missionary work. We must never downplay the necessity of words. Certainly, missionaries *should* live righteous, attractive

---

8   David Hesselgrave, *Communicating Christ Cross-Culturally: An Introduction to Missionary Communication*, 2nd ed. (Grand Rapids, MI: Zondervan, 1991), 20.

9   Though commonly misattributed to St. Francis of Assisi, this quote is modern.

lives that "preach" the word (see Titus 2:10). But that's not enough for missionaries to fulfill their role as Christ's ambassadors. If ambassadors don't communicate their message, then they're not doing their job.

The Centrality of Communication in the Missionary Task

There are many ways Christians can serve God cross-culturally, but not all of them focus on serving Christ as *his ambassadors*. We can participate in many worthwhile Christian ministries, such as drilling wells, providing dental care, and overseeing micro-loans; the list is endless. But we can do all of those things well without ever sharing Jesus's message or even knowing the language well enough to be able to do so. To be sure, such ministries may meet urgent needs. But if we want to maintain our focus as ambassadors, we need to be wise as to how we address these pressing, felt needs around us.

Consider this common mission-field quandary: In their early years, should a team of missionaries focus less on language learning in order to provide humanitarian services to the poor? If they pull back on language learning, they may hamstring their ability to communicate the message of Christ later on. But if they spend the bulk of their time learning the language, they will be less able—at least for a time—to serve the poor in tangible ways. The question is simple: which calling is primary?

Different Christians will answer this differently, according to their different callings. But missionaries whose ministry and giftedness revolves around serving *as Christ's ambassadors* should prioritize communicating the gospel message over all other ministry activities. To be sure, they should still show compassion for the felt needs of those around them, but they should engage in *ongoing ministries*[10] to meet those needs only when doing so doesn't hinder their ability to effectively proclaim the gospel, or when it's necessary to open doors for their message.[11]

---

10 Here, it may be helpful to distinguish between showing compassion to the sick (e.g., taking a sick neighbor to the hospital) and establishing an *ongoing ministry* of compassion for the sick (e.g., regularly devoting several hours of one's day or week to transporting sick people to hospitals).

11 For example, many missionaries gain access to restricted areas by engaging in humanitarian work. In such cases, they are responsible to do the humanitarian work they have

Am I advocating a "turn or burn" approach to missions? Am I trading the holistic love of Jesus for a crude salvationism that's indifferent to human suffering around us? No and no. Let me explain.

First, Jesus's love *is* holistic, but my ministry is limited, and so is yours. In the underdeveloped nations in which I have worked, a truly holistic ministry would have provided education, dentistry, optometry, water treatment, medical care, mental health services, public health services, infrastructure development, and marriage and family counseling—and much, much more. No missionary or team of missionaries should deceive itself by believing it is able to meet every need. Christian love requires that we stand ready to do what we can to meet the needs of those around us. But in order to do so, we must recognize that what we can do is limited, and we must prioritize which needs we will attend to. For example, when widows are overlooked in the daily food distribution, the apostles conclude that "It is not right that we should give up preaching the word of God to serve tables" (Acts 6:2). Did the apostles not care that widows were suffering? Of course they cared! They found the most responsible men they could to look after them. But as ambassadors of Christ, their primary ministry was to preach Jesus's message. And because knowing Jesus is people's deepest need, they refused to let other needs get in the way.

It's hard for some of us to treat Jesus so unapologetically as people's deepest need. A Christian humanitarian argues in an opinion article that we should "show up for people in need . . . [and] seek their well-being, flourishing, and justice, whether they ever convert to our religion or not."[12] Certainly, we should care about people regardless of whether or not they become believers. But since ultimate well-being is possible only through faith in Jesus, why not phrase this in the opposite way? Why not say, unapologetically, that we "show up for people in need,

---

promised to do, but their primary ministry as missionaries must still be to proclaim the gospel.

12 Jeremy Courtney, "Why Missionaries Shouldn't Pose as Aid Workers," *CNN*, August 17, 2016, accessed January 22, 2019, https://www.cnn.com/2016/08/17/opinions/declassified-covert-missionaries/index.html.

simply seeking for them to know Jesus, whether or not they ever attain our Western standards of well-being, flourishing, and justice"? If we could somehow meet all of people's this-world needs without introducing them to Jesus, then their greatest need would be left unmet. Sharing Christ's message must take priority over other acts of mercy and justice—it's the only act that can meet their eternal needs. Tim Keller explains:

> Evangelism is the most basic and radical ministry possible to a human being. This is true not because the spiritual is more important than the physical, but because the eternal is more important than the temporal.[13]

John Piper sums this up: "We Christians care about all suffering, *especially eternal suffering.*"[14]

Second, when I say that missionaries' primary ministry is to proclaim the gospel, I'm not arguing that they should ignore people's humanitarian needs. Christians care about all suffering. And while the relationship between evangelism and other acts of mercy is "asymmetrical"—evangelism takes priority—Keller reminds us that it is still an "inseparable" relationship.[15] Nor are missionaries likely to forget this! After all, the straw-man portrayals of "traditional missionaries" who want only to convert people and neglect their tangible needs are just that: straw-man portrayals. Let's not forget that William Carey is best known in Kolkata today for promoting literacy among Bengalis, and that Hudson Taylor himself was a doctor! Compassion is an indispensable part of the Christian life.

That being said, Christians of most vocations—from engineers to ambassadors of foreign nations—shouldn't structure their *vocational*

---

13 Timothy Keller, *Generous Justice: How God's Grace Makes Us Just* (New York: Penguin, 2010), 139.

14 John Piper, "Making Known the Manifold Wisdom of God through Prison and Prayer," speech, Third Lausanne Congress for World Evangelization, Cape Town, South Africa, 2010, accessed February 1, 2021, https://www.desiringgod.org/messages/making-known -the-manifold-wisdom-of-god-through-prison-and-prayer. Emphasis added.

15 Keller, *Generous Justice*, 139.

lives around meeting the most tangible humanitarian needs of people around them. Of course they should give to the poor and help their neighbors when needs arise. But an engineer's vocational life is structured around serving society by designing roads well, and an ambassador's vocational life is structured around serving society by negotiating peace between nations. Similarly, missionaries should help the poor, but they shouldn't structure their vocational lives around this. They already have a vocation as Christ's ambassadors. They've been sent to deliver his message and set people free from eternal suffering. They'll serve those around them best by staying focused on that.

Conclusion

Just before he ascended into heaven, Christ told his apostles, "You will receive power when the Holy Spirit has come upon you, and you will be my witnesses in Jerusalem and in all Judea and Samaria, and to the end of the earth" (Acts 1:8). Jesus is clear: the Holy Spirit will inhabit our message and witness, rather than work apart from it. As we saw in chapter 3, the Spirit doesn't explain the gospel to the Ethiopian eunuch; he leads Philip down the Gaza road to do so (Acts 8:28–40). The angel that appears to Cornelius doesn't explain the gospel to him; he tells him to seek out Peter (Acts 10:22, 34–43). Throughout the New Testament, the most common result of the Spirit coming on people or filling people is that they *speak*.[16] Rather than bypassing ordinary, human means of communication, the Spirit communicates through

---

16 See, for example, the following Scriptures:

> For it is not you who **speak**, but the Spirit of your Father speaking through you. (Matt. 10:20)

> David himself, in the Holy Spirit, **declared**, "'The Lord said to my Lord, "Sit at my right hand . . ."'" (Mark 12:36)

> And Elizabeth was filled with the Holy Spirit, and she **exclaimed with a loud cry** . . . (Luke 1:41–42)

> And his father Zechariah was filled with the Holy Spirit and **prophesied, saying** . . . (Luke 1:67)

> The Spirit of the Lord is upon me, because he has anointed me to **proclaim** . . . (Luke 4:18)

God's people, and communication is "the missionary problem, *par excellence.*"[17] God sends missionaries as ambassadors. He is "entrusting to us the message of reconciliation" (2 Cor. 5:19). As Hesselgrave has helpfully summarized, "Whatever else the missionary is, he is a persuaded man persuading others."[18]

This task is the missionary's guiding star.

And they were all filled with the Holy Spirit and began to **speak** in other tongues as the Spirit gave them utterance. (Acts 2:4)

. . . on my male servants and female servants in those days I will pour out my Spirit, and they shall **prophesy.** (Acts 2:18)

. . . they were all filled with the Holy Spirit and continued to **speak** the word of God with boldness. (Acts 4:31)

But they could not withstand the wisdom and the Spirit with which he was **speaking.** (Acts 6:10)

. . . the believers . . . who had come with Peter were amazed, because the gift of the Holy Spirit was poured out even on the Gentiles. For they were hearing them **speaking** in tongues and **extolling** God. (Acts 10:45–46)

But Saul . . . filled with the Holy Spirit, looked intently at him and **said** . . . (Acts 13:9–10)

. . . the Holy Spirit came on them, and they began **speaking** in tongues and **prophesying.** (Acts 19:6)

17 David Hesselgrave, *Communicating Christ Cross-Culturally*, 23.
18 David Hesselgrave, *Communicating Christ Cross-Culturally*, 87.

5

New Testament Missionary Communication

MISSIONARIES ARE SENT to communicate on Christ's behalf as his ambassadors. But once they get there, how can they complete their task? This chapter will explore this question by examining how New Testament missionaries communicated Christ's message. In the next two chapters, we'll explore what missionaries today can learn from their example.

First, New Testament Missionaries Communicate Clearly

New Testament missionaries explain the gospel message *clearly* so that it may be understood. This insistence on clarity dates back to the Old Testament. When God's Word is reintroduced to the people after the exile, Ezra and the priests "helped the people understand the Law. . . . They read from the book, from the Law of God, clearly, and they gave the sense, so that the people understood the reading" (Neh. 8:7–8).

This emphasis on clarity is reflected in New Testament missionary work. Take the apostle Paul, for example. In Thessalonica, he spends three Sabbath days "*explaining . . .* that it was necessary for the Christ to suffer and to rise from the dead" (Acts 17:3). He asks the Colossians to "pray also for us, that God may open to us a door for the word, to declare the mystery of Christ, on account of which I am in prison—*that I may make it clear, which is how I ought to speak*" (Col. 4:3–4). In letter after letter, Paul explains theological truths in an orderly fashion so that his meaning will be clear.

Clear communication marks nearly every New Testament teacher and missionary.[1] Luke, a member of Paul's missionary band, is concerned to write "an orderly account" of the life of Christ (Luke 1:3) so that it may be clear to Theophilus. Luke tells us in Acts, the sequel to his Gospel, that when Peter shared the gospel with the Gentiles for the first time, he "explained it to them in order" (Acts 11:4). Acts is full of such examples: Priscilla and Aquila took Apollos aside and "explained to him the way of God more accurately" (Acts 18:26). The Spirit sends Philip on the road to Gaza to find an Ethiopian eunuch who is confused by the Scriptures. Here's what happens next: "Philip ran to him . . . and asked, 'Do you understand what you are reading?' And he said, 'How can I, unless someone guides me?'" (Acts 8:30–31). Philip then clarifies for the eunuch what the passage means.

Over and over again in Scripture, we see that God does not bypass the ordinary rules of communication. He expects us to understand what is communicated clearly, not what is unclear and indistinct. And God works through ordinary human communicators to make his gospel clear. As we saw earlier, God sends an angel to Cornelius, but it's not the angel who explains the gospel to him directly. Instead, the angel tells Cornelius to go and find Peter (Acts 10:22).

---

1   I say "nearly every" because an apparent exception to this trend is the fact that Jesus himself conceals his message during part of his ministry by teaching in parables. However, it is important to note that Jesus is not concealing his message in order to evangelize. Quite the opposite! Jesus speaks in parables in order to *stop* hard-hearted people from understanding his message (Matt. 13:13–15; Mark 4:11–12). Jesus may be attempting to conceal his message and identity from hard-hearted people because he knows some want to use him for their own political purposes (John 6:10–15), and also because by this point in his ministry, many who do not believe are attempting to antagonize him and drive his followers away (Matt. 12:22–45; Mark 3:22–30). At times, we may need to be less clear in order to avoid provoking our enemies, but we should not expect our unclarity to lead them to Christ!

A reader unfamiliar with the present state of missions might be forgiven for asking why I'm emphasizing the New Testament's call to communicate clearly. It might seem too obvious to mention. But today's wider missions community has largely neglected the call to clear gospel communication. In the next chapter, we'll explore in more detail how this has happened, particularly as missionaries have downplayed the importance of language acquisition. We'll also explore what a healthier approach might look like and what it might take for missionaries to master the languages in which they minister.

God does not bypass the ordinary rules of communication.
He expects us to understand what is communicated
clearly, not what is unclear and indistinct.

Second, New Testament Missionaries Communicate Credibly

Missionaries strive to communicate *clearly* so that the message can be understood. They also strive to communicate *credibly* so that the message can be believed. The message becomes credible to people as missionaries present it persuasively. Paul tells the Corinthians that he wants to "persuade others" (2 Cor. 5:11). And we see him laboring to demonstrate the credibility of the gospel throughout the book of Acts:

- Paul's preaching "confounded the Jews who lived in Damascus by proving that Jesus was the Christ" (Acts 9:22).
- In Thessalonica, Paul enters the synagogue "as was his custom, and on three Sabbath days he reasoned with them from the Scriptures, explaining and proving that it was necessary for the Christ to suffer and rise from the dead. And some of them were persuaded" (Acts 17:2–4). They believe Paul's message at least in part because he makes a credible case from Scripture.

- In Corinth, Paul "reasoned in the synagogue every Sabbath, and tried to persuade both Jews and Greeks" (Acts 18:4).
- Demetrius says of Paul that "not only in Ephesus but in almost all of Asia [he] has persuaded . . . a great many people . . . that gods made with hands are not gods" (Acts 19:26).
- Agrippa realizes that the purpose of Paul's speech is to "persuade me to be a Christian" (Acts 26:28).

Every sermon, every spiritual conversation, and every instance of evangelism is at least in part a battle of ideas. This is what Paul means when he writes, "For the weapons of our warfare are not of the flesh but have divine power to destroy strongholds. We destroy arguments and every lofty opinion raised against the knowledge of God" (2 Cor. 10:4–5). So, to quote J. I. Packer, "When Paul preached the gospel, . . . what he did was to teach—engaging attention, capturing interest, setting out the facts, explaining their significance, solving difficulties, answering objections, and showing how the message bears on life."[2]

Paul isn't the only New Testament missionary who uses persuasive teaching to convince people that his message is credible. Other missionaries and New Testament evangelists also sought to persuade:

- Apollos "powerfully refuted the Jews in public, showing by the Scriptures that the Christ was Jesus" (Acts 18:28).
- Luke appeals to the testimony of eyewitnesses (Luke 1:2; Acts 1:3) and "many proofs" (Acts 1:3) to show the credibility of his message.
- Stephen's opponents cannot "withstand the wisdom and the Spirit with which he was speaking" (Acts 6:10).

Of course, in order for the message to be credible, the messenger must also be credible. In his letters, Paul gives evidence for his own

---

2   J. I. Packer, *Evangelism and the Sovereignty of God* (Downers Grove, IL: InterVarsity Press, 2012), 51.

credibility: he has seen the resurrected Lord (1 Cor. 9:1); he has done "signs and wonders and mighty works" like a "true apostle" (2 Cor. 12:12); and his character is above reproach (2 Cor. 11:7–10). Paul isn't afraid to trot out his credentials when they're called into question: "Whatever anyone else dares to boast of—I am speaking as a fool—I also dare to boast of that" (2 Cor. 11:21). He builds strong relationships where people know they can trust him (1 Thess. 2:11–12). His entire lifestyle—whether he eats or doesn't eat, whether he observes special days or doesn't observe special days—is carefully calculated to increase the credibility of his message. When seeking to reach Jews, Paul becomes "as a Jew" (1 Cor. 9:20). When seeking to reach Gentiles, he becomes "as one outside the law. . . . I have become all things to all people, that by all means I might save some" (vv. 21–22). Paul not only works to persuade people that his message is credible; his lifestyle choices and social identity are strategically and proactively crafted to help his credibility. This ought to be true of all ambassadors.

It bears repeating: it's the Spirit, not our persuasive rhetoric or upright living, that brings people to faith. And yet, rather than working *apart* from Paul's and other New Testament evangelists' efforts to persuade, the Spirit inhabits their words (Eph. 6:17). Luke tells us that Stephen's opponents "could not withstand the wisdom and the Spirit with which he was speaking" (Acts 6:10). The Spirit doesn't bypass Stephen's wisdom. Quite the opposite—the Spirit *works through* Stephen's wisdom and quickens his listeners' reasoning to recognize it until his opponents are overcome with jealousy. People who haven't heard the gospel message before will naturally have questions. But like the Bereans in Acts 17, those who earnestly seek answers are commended. As they seek, the Spirit works through ordinary, human reasoning and persuasion to convict them of the truth of the gospel.

Again, readers might be wondering why I emphasize the need for a credible witness. Is this really worth mentioning? In fact, today's missions community has largely dismissed the need to present the gospel credibly. Most missionaries are diligent enough in their efforts to tell stories about Jesus, but make little effort to address the sincere questions and objections that stop their listeners from believing. They're often unaware of what these questions are, and may not even imagine that wise, persuasive answers to these questions are necessary. We'll discuss why this is, and how missionaries can begin providing a more credible witness, in chapter 7.

Third, New Testament Missionaries Communicate Boldly

New Testament missionaries preach *clearly*, so that their message may be understood, and *credibly*, so that their message may be believed. They also preach *boldly*, so that as many as possible may hear. Hostile authorities try to stop the gospel message from circulating, but the apostles "continued to speak the word of God with boldness" (Acts 4:31). Paul asks the Ephesians to pray for him "boldly to proclaim the mystery of the gospel, for which I am an ambassador in chains" (Eph. 6:19–20). Paul's preaching is described as bold on seven different occasions.[3] Twice he reminds the Ephesians that he "did not shrink" from declaring the whole message to them (Acts 20:20, 27). Even Barnabas, whom we typically think of as a soft-spoken cheerleader due to his moniker ("son of encouragement"), engages in vigorous debate and speaks "boldly" alongside Paul (Acts 13:46; 14:3).

This boldness has casualties. Stephen is martyred when he denounces the Sanhedrin. Accused of speaking against the temple and the law (Acts 6:13), Stephen responds with an accusation himself: the men of the Sanhedrin have forgotten that the temple is too small for God (Acts 7:48–50), and that they themselves don't keep the law (Acts 7:53). Understandably, the Sanhedrin are enraged by this. Years later, Paul also boldly denounces the Sanhedrin, which leads to prolonged imprisonment and plots on his life.

Of course, New Testament ministers aren't just looking for trouble. Paul is generally happy, when persecuted in one place, to "flee to the next" (Matt. 10:23; see Paul follow this pattern, for example, in Acts

---

3   Acts 9:27–28; 13:46; 14:3; 19:8; 26:26; 28:31.

14:19–20; 20:1), but he never stops preaching, and when the time for confrontation arrives, he speaks boldly (Acts 22:30–23:11).

New Testament Christians are bold because they no longer have anything to fear. The greatest weapon their opponents had was the power to put people to death. Simply put, after the execution and resurrection of Jesus, this no longer terrified Christians because it *didn't work*. Jesus didn't stay dead, and the Word spread further. In the same way, when Christians are martyred in Acts, the Word only gathers momentum. When Stephen is executed, for example, we read, "And falling to his knees he cried out with a loud voice, 'Lord, do not hold this sin against them.' And when he had said this, he fell asleep. And Saul approved of his execution" (Acts 7:60–8:1). Luke mentions Saul after Stephen's prayer because he wants us to see that Saul's conversion was the answer to Stephen's prayer. Stephen gained everything—he was beckoned into glory by Christ himself. His persecutors, on the other hand, gained nothing. Executing Stephen was intended to stop the spread of the early church. Words cannot describe how colossally this failed. Saul became the greatest missionary in history. Bold preaching of the gospel is a win-win situation for Stephen; the worst that can happen to him after he is executed is to "be with Christ"—and that, as we know, is "far better" (Phil. 1:23). And nothing can stop his message.

It is with this unshakable hope that Peter and John answer the Sanhedrin's threat: "Whether it is right in the sight of God to listen to you rather than to God, you must judge, for we cannot but speak of what we have seen and heard" (Acts 4:19–20).

One can imagine them wondering: *Do you really expect to intimidate us? Death no longer has any power over us. What are you going to do anyway? Kill us? That doesn't seem to work so well anymore.* To be sure, New Testament believers feel fear at times—the church prays for boldness when the chief priests and elders threaten Peter and John (Acts 4:29–31)—but they're not driven by it. In the same way, we need not be driven by fear that harm will come to us or to new believers on account of bold truth-telling at appropriate times. New believers may be persecuted or expelled from their communities. We certainly don't *seek* such outcomes, but we must remember that even this will not hinder the work of the Spirit.[4]

Conclusion

Proclamation plays a central and necessary role for any missionary. Clarity, credibility, and boldness worked together to move the gospel message forward in the ministry of New Testament missionaries. Because the message was taught clearly, it could be understood. Because the message was taught credibly, it could be believed. Because the message was taught boldly, many people could hear. Missionaries who neglect any of these aspects will only hinder their own work.

New Testament missionaries communicated as wisely and capably as they could because they knew they played a central and necessary role. The Holy Spirit is pleased to work through missionary efforts and to use human tools—wise communication, persuasive reasoning, bold proclamation—to propel the message forward. We too must embrace the centrality of our task: "Him we proclaim, warning everyone and teaching everyone with all wisdom, that we may present everyone mature in Christ. For this I toil, struggling with all his energy that he powerfully works in me" (Col. 1:28–29).

That our role is central is no reason to boast. Our labor is necessary because God has chosen to work through us, not because of any particular strengths we bring to the table. We're weak, and it's only through God's blessing that our labor bears fruit: "I planted, Apollos watered, but God gave the growth" (1 Cor. 3:6). Or, as Paul says elsewhere, "the surpassing power belongs to God and not to us" (2 Cor. 4:7).

Here's why that's great news: once we have communicated the gospel message clearly, credibly, and boldly, we can happily leave the outcome

---

4   It is important not to romanticize or downplay the challenges persecution causes. It's largely because of past persecution that the church *isn't* spreading quickly in many countries around the world. But sometimes, persecution is inevitable. When we're living wisely and maturely and persecution comes, we have to trust God that even if it slows down our work in one area, his kingdom will benefit in other ways. In Acts, when the church was persecuted, the spread of the gospel slowed in Jerusalem, but it sped up elsewhere (Acts 8:1–5).

of our work in God's hands. We must remember this, so that we don't become overwhelmed. Our message comes "not only in word, but also in power and in the Holy Spirit and with full conviction" (1 Thess. 1:5).

We see an example of how this works in Acts 13. After Paul spoke "boldly" (Acts 13:46) in Pisidian Antioch and reasoned carefully from Scripture, Luke concludes that "as many as were appointed to eternal life believed" (Acts 13:48). Paul proclaimed the gospel faithfully and left the rest up to God. God's Word is sufficient on its own to sort out the saved from the perishing. Isaiah describes its efficacy in this way:

> For as the rain and the snow come down from heaven
>   and do not return there but water the earth,
> making it bring forth and sprout,
>   giving seed to the sower and bread to the eater,
> so shall my word be that goes out from my mouth;
>   it shall not return to me empty,
> but it shall accomplish that which I purpose,
>   and shall succeed in the thing for which I sent it. (Isa. 55:10–11)

6

Communicating Clearly Today

IN MOST VOCATIONS, some degree of preparation or training is necessary. But for some reason, we tend to think of missions as requiring far less training than other vocations. Sure, doctors and dentists and mechanics need to formally prepare. But missionaries? Not so much.

On one level, this makes sense. Much of our training will occur "on the job." You can't replicate it until you get there. But if we want to be capable missionaries, we need to master a substantial skill set. Remember: we've been sent out as ambassadors. In the secular world, ambassadors are usually highly intelligent people. Their preparation includes developing a detailed knowledge of their own nation's interests, the interests of the nations to which they are sent, and how—in a language and culture not native to them—they can communicate their nation's message in the most persuasive and winsome way possible.

As we saw in the previous chapter, New Testament missionaries strove to communicate with clarity, credibility, and boldness. In this chapter, we'll look at how we can prepare ourselves to communicate *clearly* today. Then in the next chapter, we'll look at what it means for us to communicate *credibly* and *boldly*.

The Challenge of Clear Communication

When my great-grandfather first came to the United States from Italy, he didn't know a lick of English. Not long after arriving, he got very sick and had to be hospitalized. He didn't know what was happening, and was terrified that the doctors might operate on him, so he decided to simply answer "No" to everything he was asked.

This plan would have worked quite well, except . . . there was a friendly nurse who came into his room every morning and asked him a series of questions. "No . . . no . . . no," he would respond, over and over again. He had no idea what she was saying. Each morning, she seemed more concerned, and he soon learned why—after several days marking "Still no bowel movement" in his chart, she brought in a doctor to give him an enema!

In today's world, we face increasing challenges as we try to communicate clearly. The nurse had studied to become a specialist. She needed to ask important questions and relay important information. She *knew* what she needed to communicate—this is key before clear communication can occur! But a language barrier stood in her way. The same thing happens to missionaries. In our increasingly multicultural world, we must handle these challenges effectively if we want to communicate our message.

Knowing the Message

Before we can share Jesus's message clearly, we must know what his message actually is. As we saw in the first chapter, Christians today tend to see Jesus's message as a fairly simple message of love and the forgiveness of sins through Christ's death and resurrection. Indeed, the fundamental parts of the gospel message are simple. However, this doesn't mean it comes without nuance or complexity, nor does it mean that people's objections are simple or easily addressed.

In the Gospels, Jesus doesn't speak only of love and forgiveness. He also engages in extensive, nuanced teaching. He answers difficult questions that arise from his listeners' culture. He helps them through the complexities of learning how the gospel relates to the law. Similarly, Paul's letters have "things in them that are hard to understand, which the ignorant and unstable twist to their own destruction" (2 Pet. 3:16). Did you catch that? Ignorance of the complexities of the Scriptures can lead not only to wayward teaching, hurt, and syncretism but even to destruction. We have no choice but to strive for a careful understanding of the Word.

We should expect that disentangling people's lives and beliefs from sin and deception may be a complicated process. At each step, then, we need answers that are profound—not glib. For example, people in the West often object to Christianity with questions like,

- Why does God forbid sexual activity in some situations when people are in love?
- How could a loving God send people to hell?
- How can there be only one true religion?
- How could a good God allow suffering? How could he have allowed the specific suffering I've endured?
- Does the Bible contradict clear scientific evidence?

Those who do come to faith may also have to sort out complicated questions about what following Jesus looks like:

- How do I now relate to my unbelieving significant other, spouse, or family member?
- How do I change deeply ingrained patterns in my speech, spending, sexuality, or use of substances?
- If I'm not saved by works, what role does obedience play in my walk with Christ?
- How do I turn the other cheek without enabling people to be abusive?

In other cultural contexts, the questions will be different. In the part of North Africa where I work, people considering the claims of Christ may struggle with questions like,

- Isn't it a sin to doubt Islamic teaching? Should I be even considering the Christ of the New Testament at all?

- If God is one, then why should I worship Father, Son, and Holy Spirit?
- Why do Christians deny the prophethood of Muhammad when Muslims acknowledge all the prophets—even Jesus?

People from such a culture who put their faith in Christ may ask,

- How does Christ want me to relate to my multiple wives?
- What will I do if the wider community takes my family away from me?
- How do I share with my family and community what has happened? How do I handle rejection and violent mistreatment?

Wherever you live, you'll come face-to-face with difficult questions that require careful answers. Both seekers and new believers will struggle—and simplistic, flippant answers will not be helpful. We must deeply understand Jesus's teaching in order to answer people's questions in wise, Scriptural ways. We are ambassadors, and ambassadors need to understand their nations' terms of peace fully enough to clarify how exactly they're meant to play out in the complexities of life.

This includes understanding that the *good news* as defined in the Gospels is a message of reconciliation with God. But this reconciliation is more than God simply agreeing not to hold our sins against us. Rather, the Gospels define the *good news* as "the kingdom of heaven is at hand" (Matt. 4:17). What does this mean? Among other things, it means that God's kingdom—his generous sovereign reign—has come near and is available to us through Christ.

Of course, if we're still under the weight of our sins, then it could hardly be *good* news that God's power is at hand. This explains why Jesus's atonement for our sins is a key part of the Christian gospel. He makes salvation possible. But the good news isn't merely that Jesus shows up, and we're simply forgiven and left to fend for ourselves until one day we die and find ourselves in heaven. Rather, our salvation also includes being rescued from the power of sin in our everyday lives. Starting now, we can enter a new life in which we know God (John

17:3) and live as he created us to live. This will bring freedom and transformation to all areas of our lives: our finances, our family lives, our sexuality, our friendships, and even our sufferings.

Indeed, Jesus's plan to save the nations includes our "teaching [disciples] to observe all that I commanded you" (Matt. 28:20). We must teach people how Jesus wants them to live, and how good this way of life has always been for those who follow him. We must help them see that, though following Jesus is sometimes painful, it will never make our lives more anemic, fragile, or empty. Instead, following Jesus is *deeply good for us, is best for us* in all areas of our lives—in the real lives in which we work, conduct relationships, marry, raise children, engage in conflict, and pay taxes.

Life is messy. How do we learn to trust that Jesus will be with us in the messiness, and that his way will always be good for us? By reading and understanding his Word more deeply. Missionaries must have a deep knowledge of the Scriptures in order to "rightly [handle] the word of truth" (2 Tim. 2:15), correctly applying it amid thorny issues of doctrine and discipleship that inevitably surface. For many missionaries, this will involve formal Bible school or seminary training on the way to the field. These steps slow us down, but the investment is worth it—both for the sake of the lost and for the sake of the message we hope to proclaim.

Knowing the Language

On July 26, 1945, as World War II was drawing to a close, the Allies met in Potsdam, Germany, and issued an ultimatum. The now-famous Potsdam Declaration promised Japan's "prompt and utter destruction" if Japan did not surrender immediately. This threat had teeth: the United States had recently finished constructing operational nuclear weapons. Some historians, like Kazuo Kawai, argue that Japan took the ultimatum seriously.[1,2] So why, merely two weeks later, did the United States destroy Hiroshima and Nagasaki with nuclear weapons?

1 Kazuo Kawai, "Mokusatsu, Japan's Response to the Potsdam Declaration," *Pacific Historical Review* 19/4 (1950): 409–14.

2 David Hesselgrave, *Communicating Christ Cross-Culturally: An Introduction to Missionary Communication*, 2nd ed. (Grand Rapids, MI: Zondervan, 1991), 343.

Because American ambassadorial staff mistranslated a single word in Japan's response. The Allies believed the word *mokusatsu* meant that the Japanese government planned "to ignore" the Potsdam Declaration; in reality, Kawai tells us, a better translation would have told the Allies that Japan planned "to refrain from comment" while deliberating over it.

As ambassadors, we also cross language barriers with an ultimatum, and we should be haunted by the danger of miscommunication. If we're not, we might mistakenly assume that people have rejected Christ. Or we might mistakenly assume that others have accepted Christ. What if it isn't Christ's message that they've either accepted or rejected, but only our badly stammered version of it? It can be hard enough to explain the gospel to our friends at home. In unreached places where our ability to communicate is hampered by linguistic and cultural differences, the task of communication only gets more difficult.

As ambassadors, we also cross language barriers with an ultimatum, and we should be haunted by the danger of miscommunication. If we're not, we might mistakenly assume that people have rejected Christ. Or we might mistakenly assume that others have accepted Christ. What if it isn't Christ's message that they've either accepted or rejected, but only our badly stammered version of it?

Shared languages have always been necessary for communication (see 2 Kings 18:26ff.; Ezra 4:7). In Nehemiah's day, the scribes translated the law from Hebrew into Aramaic to help the people understand (Neh. 8:8). In Jesus's day, rabbis provided *targums*, translations of the Hebrew Old Testament into Aramaic.[3] After Jesus's resurrection, it is significant

---

3   Philip S. Alexander, "Targum, Targumim," in *The Anchor Bible Dictionary*, ed. David Noel Freedman (New York: Doubleday, 1992), 6:320–21.

that the Spirit empowers the apostles to "be my witnesses in Jerusalem and in all Judea and Samaria, and to the end of the earth" (Acts 1:8), and the first miracle he performs is enabling the disciples to preach in other languages (Acts 2). Though Paul and other New Testament missionaries are fluent Greek speakers who don't struggle with language barriers in their ministries, they do reach across other cultural barriers to communicate clearly and to meet people on their own terms as much as possible (see 1 Cor. 9:19–23). And Paul recognizes the futility of speaking to people in languages they don't understand:

> . . . if with your tongue you utter speech that is unintelligible, how will anyone know what is said? . . . if I do not know the meaning of the language, I will be a foreigner to the speaker and the speaker a foreigner to me. (1 Cor. 14:9, 11)

It shouldn't surprise us, then, when we encounter language barriers in our ministries, that we must reach across those barriers to communicate the gospel clearly.

Missionary statesmen of previous generations understood this. They placed a high value on language acquisition, believing fluency was a professional skill without which one could not effectively minister. Here are a few examples:

- For **William Carey**, one of the great "impediments in the way of carrying the gospel" to the unreached was "the unintelligibleness of their languages."[4] Carey is still known today in Kolkata and the surrounding area for his work in the Bengali language, including literacy promotion and the publication of a Bengali dictionary.
- Upon their arrival to Burma, **Adoniram and Ann Judson** spent twelve hours a day studying Burmese.[5] Ann also learned Siamese

---

4   William Carey, *An Inquiry into the Obligation of Christians to Use Means for the Conversion of the Heathen* (Leicester, UK: Ann Ireland, 1792), 67.

5   Vance Christie, *Adoniram Judson: Devoted for Life* (Fearn, Scotland, UK: Christian Focus, 2013), ch. 10.

while Adoniram learned Pali and Talaing.[6] His Burmese reached such a level that more than fifty years later, another missionary would write of his tract "the Golden Balance" that it "has probably more powerfully influenced the thinking of the Burmese people, and caused them to see the insufficiency of Buddhism, than anything else ever written by a foreigner."[7] His Burmese translation of the Bible was "free from all obscurity to the Burmese mind. It is read and understood perfectly. Its style and diction are as choice and elegant as the language itself . . . and [it] conveys . . . the mind of the Spirit effortlessly."[8] It wasn't surprising that Judson bemoaned the limited effectiveness of medium-term missionaries who served for only a few years: "As usual, they could not be of much real use until they became fluent in the language; and that would be a matter of years."[9] When Judson returned to the United States, he had worked in Burmese for so long that he no longer felt articulate in English and asked to be excused from preaching.[10]

• **John Paton** operated in the Aniwan language for so long that when he returned home, like Judson, he sometimes struggled with English. He recalls one visit to Dundee: "I was asked to close the forenoon meeting with prayer. . . . I offered prayer, and then began— 'May the love of God the Father' but not another word would come in English; everything was blank except the words in Aniwan, for I had long begun to think in the Native tongue, and after a dead pause, and a painful silence, I had to wind up with a simple 'Amen'!"[11]

6   Christie, *Adoniram Judson: Devoted for Life*, chs. 12, 26.

7   Stacy Warburton, *Eastward! The Story of Adoniram Judson* (Warwick, NY: Round Table Press, 1937), 158.

8   Edward Judson, *The Life of Adoniram Judson*, vol. 3 (Philadelphia: American Baptist Publication Society, 1883), 416.

9   Courtney Anderson, *To the Golden Shore: The Life of Adoniram Judson* (King of Prussia, PA: Judson Press, 1987), 409.

10   "Having devoted himself exclusively to the Burmese language for over thirty years, his facility in English had been greatly diminished. He considered himself incapable of adequately carrying out public speaking in America" (Christie, *Adoniram Judson: Devoted for Life*, ch. 34).

11   John G. Paton and James Paton, *John G. Paton: Missionary to the Hebrides: An Autobiography* (New York: Revell, 1907), 360.

- **Hudson Taylor** advised newcomers to "consider six or eight hours a day sacred to the Lord and His work and let nothing hinder your giving this time (to language study and practice) till you can preach fluently and intelligibly."[12] He turned down Henry Guinness's application to China Inland Mission because Guinness had a wife and three children and there was "little likelihood of his being able to learn the language sufficiently well as to be as useful in China as he was at home."[13] Taylor rebuked C. T. Studd and Arthur and Cecil Polhill for praying for the gift of tongues so that they could skip language study: "How many and subtle are the devices of Satan . . . to keep the Chinese ignorant of the gospel. If I could put the Chinese language into your brains by one wave of the hand, I would not do it."[14] In what may have been a nod to Carey's "obligation to use means," Taylor referred to language study as "a necessary means."[15]

- **Jim Elliot** asked Elisabeth to marry him under one condition: "not until you learn Quichua." He didn't want their marriage to distract them from studying their new language and culture.[16]

These men and women experienced success in their missionary work at least in part because of their remarkable devotion to language acquisition. We might do well to note that Hudson Taylor pursued fluency in a way that his contemporaries did not.[17]

12 A. J. Broomhall, *Hudson Taylor and China's Open Century, Book Five: Refiner's Fire* (London: Hodder & Stoughton, 1985), 230.

13 Alvyn Austin, *China's Millions: The China Inland Mission and Late Qing Society, 1832–1905* (Grand Rapids, MI: Eerdmans, 2007), 96.

14 Austin, *China's Millions*, 222.

15 Austin, *China's Millions*, 222.

16 Elisabeth Elliot, *Love Has a Price Tag* (Ann Arbor, MI: Servant, 1979).

17 Taylor began getting up at 5 a.m. to study Mandarin even before leaving for China. Upon arriving, he was happy to live in a dangerous neighborhood—rather than among other missionaries and expatriates—so that he could be surrounded by the Chinese language (Howard Taylor and Geraldine Taylor (Mrs. Howard Taylor), *Hudson Taylor's Spiritual Secret* [Peabody, MA: Hendrickson, 2008], 9, 37). His attitude contrasted with that of other missionaries who feared "that the Chinese would 'lose respect' if foreigners 'descended to their level'" (Austin, *China's Millions*, 2).

But language acquisition isn't easy. In fact, its drudgery is so over-whelming that those who have not endured it have trouble understand-ing or even imagining what it's like. Missiologist and church historian Gary McGee describes the difficulty of language learning:

> One missionary to China said, "It is dull work to pass the day saying Ting, Tang, in a hundred different tones." Indeed, "to thoroughly master the Chinese language would require a head of oak, lungs of brass, nerves of steel, a constitution of iron, the patience of Job, and the lifetime of Methuselah." Another missionary . . . groaned, "No white man could ever get his tongue round the long Indian words which seemed to have been growing since the [flood of Noah] itself, so long and so immense are they in size."[18]

I've lived through this. Having learned two dialects of Arabic and a tribal language, I can tell you that—as bad as they sound—the quotes above don't even come close to conveying the mind-numbing grind of my many years of language study. J. C. R. Ewing, a prominent nineteenth-century missions leader in what is now Pakistan, cautioned new missionaries that learning Asian languages would be "a lifetime's work. No person with less than five years of hard study can speak to the peoples of oriental lands as he should."[19] If Ewing is correct, then English speakers learning Asian languages should imagine that mastering these languages may take more hours of study than finishing medical school.

Of course, learning a language related to one's own mother tongue—an English speaker learning Spanish, for example; or an Arabic speaker learning Hebrew—is easier. But even this requires a substantial amount of study. Most missionaries today are plunged into linguistic contexts quite different from their own. Increasingly, they must master two languages in order to communicate. Not surprisingly, their language learning often plateaus long before they acquire even low levels of

18 Gary McGee, "Shortcut to Language Preparation? Radical Evangelicals, Missions, and the Gift of Tongues," *International Bulletin of Missionary Research* 25/3 (2001): 118.
19 McGee, "Shortcut to Language Preparation," 118.

proficiency. Few missionaries that I've encountered pursue language learning as if their ministries depended on it. The vast majority spend one to two years of part-time study before they're expected to move on to other, more "important" responsibilities.

Clearly, times have changed. In the first chapter, we saw how David Garrison describes "sequentialism": "Missionaries naturally think in sequential steps. First, you learn the language, then you develop relationships with people, then you share a witness, then you win and disciple converts, then you draw them into a congregation."[20]

This approach, Garrison concludes, is "deadly" to church-planting efforts.[21] In fact, Garrison's preferred approach is to send "nonresidential missionaries" who live at a distance from the people they hope to reach and therefore *cannot* learn their languages well:[22] Garrison writes,

> Early indications are that the "nonresidential" missionary is able to change an evangelistically stagnant situation with remarkable alacrity. . . . The healthier and more diverse the world of Christian resources becomes, the more vital the nonresidential missionary approach will be.[23]

Of course, Garrison isn't *against* language learning. In fact, I've never met a missionary who doesn't at least nominally affirm its importance. All the same, in North Africa where I serve, the vast majority of missionaries fail to achieve the proficiency of a seven-year-old.

You might be wondering: But why? The answer is as simple as it is disheartening: most missionaries see language learning as "important," but not vital. Useful, sure, but nonessential. Few missionaries understand—as we saw in chapter 4—that as ambassadors, communication is their primary task. Previous generations of missionaries believed it would

---

20 Garrison, *Church Planting Movements*, 243.

21 David Garrison, *Church Planting Movements: How God Is Redeeming a Lost World* (Bangalore, India: WIGTake Resources, 2007), 243.

22 V. David Garrison, *The Nonresidential Missionary*, vol. 1 of Innovations in Mission (Monrovia, CA: MARC, 1990).

23 David Garrison, "An Unexpected New Strategy: Using Nonresidential Missionaries to Finish the Task," *International Journal of Frontier Missiology* 7/4 (1990): 107.

be unrealistic and unprofessional to expect God to fill in the gaps of communication when they'd gained only a cursory familiarity with the languages they work in.[24]

I experienced this firsthand. In my first term overseas, I served on a team that ran a center teaching English and computer courses. After several months there, my Arabic was functional but certainly not strong; I'd reached the proficiency of a six-year-old. At this point, however, I was asked to pull back from language study in order to help teach English. When I declined, a senior leader in my organization told me that devoting myself so fully to language study was morally wrong. He explained that his Arabic wasn't strong and God didn't need mine to be strong either. He then told me that it wasn't right for me to spend so much time learning Arabic when there were English learners at the team's center whom I might be able to evangelize. Such pressure to move on only grows more intense after a missionary learns enough language to "function" in daily life. Ultimately, I was allowed to continue in language study,[25] but many new missionaries aren't given that option. I've known more than one couple whose leaders refused to let them stay on the field unless they sharply reduced their language study. Choosing to enter ministry prematurely may result in short-term gains, but only at the cost of long-term effectiveness.

Again, the leaders in the stories above probably would acknowledge that language acquisition is important. But lip service is not enough. Because of the intense drudgery involved in learning language, nothing short of whole-hearted, sacrificial support for language learning—making concrete plans and expecting intense commitment until high-level mastery of the language is achieved—will enable new missionaries to master their languages of ministry.

As we saw in chapter 3, today's most popular missions methods seem to pursue speed at all costs. Thus, it isn't surprising that they

---

24 Tom Steffen, "Flawed Evangelism and Church Planting," *Evangelical Missions Quarterly* 34/4 (1998): 428–35.

25 This was partly due to field leaders' deference to my sending church, which insisted that I continue with language study until achieving a high level of fluency.

have little patience for language learning. It is deeply concerning that they give language learning only halfhearted support at best. I'll list a few examples below. As I do, compare this list of missionaries to the one above:

- Steve Smith describes the birth of his *Training for Trainers* (T4T) methodology this way: "In my limited language, I poured out my heart about the Great Commission. . . . I helped them come to the realization that it was their responsibility to take the gospel to other Ina valleys."[26] Smith never balances this story out by mentioning that mastering the local language could also be helpful, nor does he explain how—in the context of his "limited language" and a short-term relationship with the people he was addressing—he could know whether the realization the Ina had come to was deep or genuine, or whether they would even be able to "take the gospel" to others.
- A popular booklet discusses "best practices" in *Church Planting Movements* (CPM). The writer describes working with men "from each of the 4 major mother tongue languages in our region."[27] This raises questions because it simply is not possible for missionaries to acquire high levels of proficiency in four languages. So we must assume that these missionaries worked through a *trade language*.[28] Statements such as these are not balanced anywhere by affirmations of the necessity of language acquisition.
- David Watson is the principal designer of *Disciple Making Movements* (DMM). In his book, he admits, "I didn't have . . . the

---

26 Smith, *T4T*, ch. 5.

27 Wilson Geisler, *Rapidly Advancing Disciples: A Practical Implementation of Current Best Practices* (2011), 89, accessed August 12, 2018, http://www.churchplantingmovements .com/images/stories/resources/Rapidily_Advancing_Disciples_(RAD)_Dec_2011.pdf.

28 A *trade language* is a "bridge language" which native speakers of different languages may use to communicate with each other, particularly in commercial situations. However, because it isn't the speakers' native language, they may have very limited proficiency in it. For example, Tok Pisin serves as a trade language between the tribes of Papua New Guinea.

inclination to keep the clothes new, and the language perfect. I had to learn another way."[29] He reports spending only eighteen months living in India.[30] Furthermore, he lived in Delhi[31]—not among the Bhojpuri speakers his ministry focused on. We can reasonably conclude that he might have acquired limited conversational ability in Hindi, but he couldn't have made much progress with Bhojpuri, and his study would have been further slowed down by the fact that he reports having simultaneously pursued a doctoral program in Sanskrit, while also learning Hindi and Bhojpuri![32,33]

- Another prominent DMM author, Jerry Trousdale, tells of a couple "handcuffed by language and cultural barriers" who saw more than a hundred people come to Christ in their first year on the field.[34] His two books never mention the importance of language learning.[35,36] Such silence, as they say, is deafening.

- In a widely publicized DMM success story, David Hunt moved to Ethiopia in 2005 and almost immediately began overseeing church planting workshops.[37] Hunt didn't see the need to study local languages because "it takes years for someone to learn to communicate in the heart language of another people." This loss

29 David Watson, in David Watson and Paul Watson, *Contagious Disciple Making: Leading Others on a Journey of Discovery* (Nashville: Thomas Nelson, 2014), 11.

30 David Watson, "David Watson: My Journey with Disciple Making Movements," *Movements with Steve Addison*, podcast audio, August 29, 2016, accessed January 3, 2019, http://www.movements.net/blog/2016/08/29/121-david-watson-my-journey-with-disciple-making-movements.html.

31 Victor John and David Coles, *Bhojpuri Breakthrough: A Movement That Keeps Multiplying* (Monument, CO: WIGTake, 2019), 8.

32 "David Watson's Testimony," narrated by David Watson, *Accelerate Training*, accessed January 3, 2019, https://www.acceleratetraining.org/index.php/resources/61-david-watson-s-testimony-90-min-mp3/file.

33 David Watson, "David Watson: My Journey with Disciple Making Movements."

34 Jerry Trousdale, in Trousdale and Sunshine, *Kingdom Unleashed*, ch. 13.

35 Jerry Trousdale, *Miraculous Movements: How Hundreds of Thousands of Muslims Are Falling in Love with Jesus* (Nashville: Thomas Nelson, 2012).

36 Trousdale and Sunshine, *Kingdom Unleashed*.

37 David F. Hunt, "A Revolution in Church Multiplication in East Africa: Transformational Leaders Develop a Self-Sustainable Model of Rapid Church Multiplication" (DMin diss., Bakke Graduate University, 2009), 58.

of time can be avoided "if the church planter with significant language limitations disciples the insider and the insider takes the message to the people."[38] Unfortunately, Hunt does not explain how the church planter will be able to successfully "disciple the insider" or verify the success of the insider's ministry without knowing the insider's language. Indeed, as we'll see in chapter 8, working with national believers can be an extremely effective ministry strategy. But at other times, it can create illusions of success. After all, without knowing their language, it will be difficult to evaluate what's happening.

- Mike Shipman, designer of the Any-3 method, doesn't encourage language learning. In its place, he advocates using "a translator . . . to bridge language barriers."[39] But working through translators is cumbersome, and usually far more error-prone than we might imagine. Translators in many parts of the unreached world have a limited familiarity with the missionary's mother tongue, rendering nuanced communication mostly impossible. Indeed, unless the translator himself is a mature believer, he may not understand the concepts the missionary is trying to communicate and will be unable to explain them in his own tongue. In addition to all of that, communicating via a translator makes relationships difficult. It's slow and unnatural. It can't be done privately. This makes it hard to establish close relationships.

Something is awry when the most widely published missions thinkers happily tell stories of ministering with "limited language" and working through translators, but never stress the importance of language learning in normal situations. Language learning requires costly self-discipline, and missionaries who don't understand its importance will have little motivation to persevere. The stories above are told as if we should *assume* that God works through missionaries who never learn the languages.

38 Hunt, "Revolution in Church Multiplication in East Africa," 129–30.
39 Mike Shipman, *Any 3: Anyone, Anywhere, Anytime* (Monument, CO: WIGTake Resources, 2013), ch. 7.

But let's apply this assumption to other situations. Let's say you're going through some marriage or family problems. Wouldn't you want to see a counselor who spoke your language? After all, conversations about relationship problems are often complicated and confusing. Or, let's say you're investing in setting up a business overseas. If you had a lot of money on the line, wouldn't you hire customer service representatives who understood your customers' language and culture? After all, conversations about business problems are often complicated and confusing. Do you see what I'm getting at? I take it for granted that discipling new believers will be *at least* as complex as counseling struggling marriages or serving unhappy customers. After all, discipleship includes dealing with family problems and business practices . . . which are often complicated and confusing!

Of course God *can* work through our "limited language"—and God *can* work through translators. I'm not writing to condemn the authors above, or to imply that God did nothing through them. I'm merely suggesting that *we cannot actually know what God is doing in the lives of people we minister to* if we're unfamiliar with their language and culture.

We don't need to look far for illustrations of this. A friend who worked in Papua New Guinea for several years once told me of a Catholic priest who would occasionally travel up-river to minister the sacraments to tribes along the way. This priest knew only the people's trade language and was unaware that these tribal people had simply added the Catholic saints to the list of spirit beings in their animistic worldview. On many occasions, they hoped to steal objects from him because they believed the objects would grant them spiritual power or protection. In their worldview, the priest had spiritual power. His statues of Mary had spiritual power. But so did the trees, and so did the spirits who filled the surrounding jungle's sky, rivers, and animals. Don't get me wrong: the priest had communicated some new spiritual ideas to these people. But he lacked the linguistic ability to help them resolve the tension these ideas presented to their previously held belief systems. In this case, the priest's doctrine didn't subvert their pagan worldview; it became subsumed by it. Where linguistic depth is absent, syncretism is often present.[40] People are capable of an enormous amount of doublethink, and it's not enough just to tell them to let go of old beliefs— we need the linguistic ability to learn and explain where those views differ from the Scriptures and why the Scriptures are more believable.

At this point, I often hear an objection: "Wait a second. Are you saying missionaries shouldn't *try* to share the good news about Jesus until they reach a high level of language ability?" No, I'm not saying that. In fact, I'm actually making a more startling claim: for all practical purposes, we simply *cannot* communicate the good news about Jesus until we reach a high level of language ability. It isn't a question of *should*, but *can*; not propriety, but ability. Similarly, the primary issue is not whether first-year medical students *should* be practicing medicine, but whether they *can* with any sort of effectiveness. Of course they can't. Because they don't yet know how.

———————

At this point, I often hear an objection: "Wait a second. Are you saying missionaries shouldn't try to share the good news about Jesus until they reach a high level of language ability?" No, I'm not saying that. In fact, I'm actually making a more startling claim: for all practical purposes, we simply cannot communicate the good news about Jesus until we reach a high level of language ability.

———————

40 One result of this that has a powerful effect on today's missions world is the common Muslim belief—alleged in the Qur'an (5:116)—that Christians worship God, Jesus, and Mary. As a young man growing up in a polytheistic culture, Muhammad had interacted with Christians and seems to have believed that this reflected trinitarianism. It is possible that local sects of Christians did actually include Mary as a member of the Trinity—if so, trinitarian doctrine had become syncretized with the polytheistic worldview of the day. However, no historical evidence can be found for such a claim. More likely, Muhammad simply misunderstood the teachings of local Christian communities. If so, then his culture's polytheistic worldview had clearly influenced his own perception of Christian teaching. In either case, the lack of clear Christian teaching and of available Christian Scriptures in Arabic allowed a syncretized understanding of Christianity to emerge. Islam rightly rejects this syncretized understanding, but does so only to replace it with a newer, fatally syncretized understanding of Jesus, in which Christian traditions about Jesus are combined with Muslim anti-trinitarian monotheism. The reinvented Jesus that emerges is a mere prophet who denies his own divinity.

I fear yet another misunderstanding. I'm not saying missionaries without language fluency should never speak of spiritual things in their first months and years. Generally, they should feel free to communicate whatever spiritual truths they can communicate clearly. But for those who haven't struggled to master a foreign language, it might be hard to imagine just how limited these missionaries will be in their early and intermediate stages. "God is big" and "Jesus is nice" might honestly be the best they can do. They likely won't be able to engage in any deep conversations at all.

Simply put, we need more than introductory language skills if we're going to explain the gospel in an understandable way. The sentence "Jesus died for your sins" won't help our listeners if we can't follow it up—in ways they understand—with answers to the following questions: Who is Jesus? What are sins? And why did this Jesus have to die for these sins?

In my early months and years of language study, I spoke often about God. I spoke of my gratitude to him. I spoke of his love and goodness. I like to think that my friends and neighbors knew I was a spiritual person. But saying "Thank you, Lord" when something wonderful happens to you is not the same as sharing the gospel. God may choose to use us in these early stages. Sometimes, we may meet people who are simply *ready*, like fruit waiting to be plucked. My friend "Ahmad" became a believer when two missionaries who spoke neither Arabic nor his tribal language gave him an Arabic Bible. But this happened only after Ahmad had already become deeply disillusioned with Islam and was searching for answers. Most people will need *significantly* more help than he did! And even in cases like this, our lack of fluency poses real dangers. Ahmad was left in a spiritually dangerous place. His spiritual growth was seriously hindered and he suffered as he wrestled, alone and sometimes unsuccessfully, with false teaching and temptations of the flesh that sought to destroy his soul.

If we hope to minister professionally and well, we must not use stories like Ahmad's as a pattern for ministry. Cutting corners and hoping for God to mop up the mess is a bad idea. Too many missionaries never put in the effort to reach high levels of fluency because they overestimate how regularly God works apart from language fluency. They've heard one too many stories where Missionary A showed up to Unreached People B and—somehow, against all odds—God worked a miracle. I wish these stories weren't so alluring, because they paint an unrealistic picture and set unrealistic expectations.

Certainly, there are some niche roles on the mission field for those who never master the language. Missions efforts in various settings will depend on the work of pilots, aircraft mechanics, boarding school staff, doctors, and logistics coordinators. These roles are crucial to the success of the wider ministry, and we should honor those who fill them. But they're still *niche roles*. People who fill them are essential precisely because they enable others to concentrate on proclaiming the gospel. Other missionaries should take full advantage of this and focus on attaining high levels of proficiency in the languages they minister in. In much of today's mission field, we see the opposite trend; those who do acquire high levels of proficiency are the exception to the rule.

How Fluent Is "Fluent"?

Let's talk about fluency for a moment. How fluent should missionaries be before shifting their primary focus from language learning to ministry?

Fluency is a slippery concept. It's related to the word "fluid," meaning that speech *flows* without the speaker having to stop and think about each word. The truth is, however, that whether someone is *fluent* is something of a grey area. After a few months in a new language, a missionary may be able to fluently negotiate prices in the market. After a year, she may be comfortable navigating certain more complex topics with close friends.[41] But it may take years before she can fluently

---

41 Language learners' fluency when speaking with close friends is usually stronger than it is when speaking with people they do not know. This is because spending extensive time together allows them to become far more familiar with their friends' *idiolects* (personal dialects, which are made up of an individual's personal speech patterns, preferred vocabulary, expressions, and grammar) than they are with the language in general.

negotiate humor, feelings, and spiritual concepts in less controlled situations—like in a group of friends where people speak quickly, colloquially, and with much emotion.

In order to dependably evangelize and disciple unreached peoples, we should be not only fluent but also adept in their languages. We may never have the facility of native speakers, but we should aim to routinely be able to handle a range of situations—from rapid, everyday banter to the thorniest and most personal of topics. Our language ability should never be the limiting factor in an important conversation. We need not only to know the meaning of words; we need to have a sense for their nuance. We need to be able to interact humorously. We need to understand body language and cultural symbols—what is and is not appropriate; what communicates disappointment, aggression, and respect. We need to be able to take control of a conversation when it's our turn to speak—and to know *when* it is in fact our turn to speak. We need to understand how stories are told. We need to be able to replicate the proper cadence of the language.

It is outside the scope of this book—indeed, it would take its own book—to explain how to learn a language efficiently and what an adequate level of fluency might look like. But for now, I want to make three critical points.

First, immersive language-learning strategies with a heavy focus on vocabulary enrichment and listening comprehension are ideal. Those unfamiliar with such strategies could begin by examining the *Growing Participator Approach*[42] or *Becoming Equipped to Communicate*.[43] Well-designed, immersive language-learning approaches allow new missionaries to develop deep familiarity with the culture even as they study language.

Second, immersion on its own—even immersion with a trained tutor—won't be enough to bring most adults to a high level of proficiency. Most missionaries will also benefit from training in language

---

42   Growing Participator Approach, https://www.growingparticipation.com.
43   Mike Griffis and Linda Mac, *Becoming Equipped to Communicate: A Practical Guide for Learning a Language and Culture* (Baulkham Hills, New South Wales: AccessTruth, 2015).

acquisition before going to the field, or from detailed input in the grammar, speech patterns, and phonetics of the language they're learning.[44] Third, many missionaries will never reach native-speaker fluency. So I'm not counseling that we wait that long before withdrawing from full-time language learning focus to pursue ministry more fully. Instead, I'd advise that before pulling back from full-time language learning, missionaries should aim for a level of at least *Advanced Mid* proficiency according to ACTFL guidelines.[45] Focused language learning wouldn't cease at this point, and it's essential that language ability does not plateau here. However, pulling back from full-time study can be strategic

---

44 Contrary to popular belief, most adults will not automatically learn a language well simply from being surrounded by it. While adults are capable of learning other languages, their brains are less flexible than children's brains, and the environments they can immerse themselves in don't provide the same type of nurture or instruction that parents give to children. Missionaries may benefit from language-acquisition training, including training in grammar, discourse analysis, and phonetics. This is because we cling unknowingly to patterns we are familiar with. Training in these areas helps because:

- Other languages often have profoundly different grammatical patterns than our own, and simply immersing ourselves in a new language is not enough to help most adults master a new grammar. Grammatical help specific to the language being studied—or training in how to analyze grammar—is needed.
- It's also difficult to master new patterns of discourse: how do stories begin and end? What's the cadence of a language? How do I know when it's my turn to speak?
- See Christophe Pallier, Laura Bosch, and Nuria Sebastian-Galles, "A Limit on Behavioral Plasticity in Speech Perception," *Cognition* 64 (1997): B9–B17. Our perception of sounds hardens in childhood, and many adults struggle to perceive sounds that are not present in their native languages. For example, many Chinese immigrants to the West struggle to differentiate between "l" and "r" sounds, though they are entirely different sounds to a native English speaker. Similarly, native English speakers learning Arabic will struggle to distinguish between ت and ط.

45 *ACTFL Proficiency Guidelines 2012* (Alexandria, VA: American Council on the Teaching of Foreign Languages, 2012). To provide a basic idea of what *Advanced Mid* level language ability looks like, I quote below from descriptions of *Advanced Mid* level speaking abilities. For a fuller idea of *Advanced Mid* level—including descriptions of *Advanced Mid* level listening, reading, and writing—readers can consult ACTFL guidelines:

> Speakers at the Advanced Mid sublevel are able to handle with ease and confidence a large number of communicative tasks. They participate actively in most informal and some formal exchanges on a variety of concrete topics relating to work, school, home, and leisure activities, as well as topics relating to events of current, public, and personal interest or individual relevance.

as a high enough level of language has been achieved to allow the missionary to minister freely. At this level, language development will naturally continue as the speaker uses the language in a wide variety of circumstances in everyday life.

If this level of fluency is the goal, then language study will likely last many years, and Hudson Taylor's estimation of the daily time commitment—six to eight hours per day in a well-designed immersive study program—is a good indication of the type of dedication that will be required. In my own experience, language study really begins to accelerate when a missionary spends more than eight hours per day immersed in the "growth-zone" level interaction with the language.[46]

This is more difficult than it sounds. Many missionaries who have experienced field life will throw their hands up in despair. I'm not trying to criticize or to weigh missionaries down with impossible tasks. I'm trying to provide a reminder that, one way or another, we *must* attain a high level of linguistic proficiency if we want to share the gospel clearly. I know there are many obstacles. Steady language tutors can be hard

---

Advanced Mid speakers demonstrate the ability to narrate and describe in the major time frames of past, present, and future by providing a full account, with good control of aspect. . . .

Advanced Mid speakers can handle successfully and with relative ease the linguistic challenges presented by a complication or unexpected turn of events that occurs within the context of a routine situation. . . . Communicative strategies such as circumlocution or rephrasing are often employed for this purpose. The speech of Advanced Mid speakers performing Advanced-level tasks is marked by substantial flow. Their vocabulary is fairly extensive although primarily generic in nature, except in the case of a particular area of specialization or interest. Their discourse may still reflect the oral paragraph structure of their own language rather than that of the target language.

Advanced Mid speakers contribute to conversations on a variety of familiar topics, dealt with concretely, with much accuracy, clarity and precision, and they convey their intended message without misrepresentation or confusion. . . . When called on to perform functions or handle topics associated with the Superior level, the quality and/or quantity of their speech will generally decline.

46 When we are in our "growth-zone," we are using the language at or near the limits of our abilities. Thus, after a year of language study, greeting a store-keeper and purchasing sugar is not a growth zone activity. Sitting down with a friend and having a conversation over tea is likely to be.

to find. We may have to travel unexpectedly due to war or civil unrest, or to renew our visas, or to deal with family crises. Some of us face seasons of business development that force us to reduce our weekly hours of language-acquisition focus. We can address these obstacles when they arise, and we shouldn't feel guilty about doing so. Life is complicated, and even our best-laid plans can fall apart. At points, we'll have to content ourselves with what is possible, not what is ideal. But within the limits of reasonable flexibility, we must do what we can to keep our nose to the grindstone.

Full-time language study may be especially difficult or impractical for mothers, particularly when their children are young. We need to allow for special flexibility here. Mothers will sometimes take considerably more time to master the language, and in places where ministry would ideally be conducted in more than one language, mothers may need to focus most of their energy on whichever language is more important. Most mothers on the field will greatly appreciate whatever we can do to encourage them in these situations.

Because some countries don't give language study visas, full-time language study may not always be possible. So in some cases, it may be important for missionaries to make significant progress in their language learning before entering the country.

Motivation wanes as the years press on. It's highest in the first years of ministry. So those who don't make progress in language acquisition immediately will easily settle into a "slow-drip approach," where they learn only little by little. Additionally, few other ministry activities can be entered into as effectively before we acquire language as they can be afterward. So wherever possible, language study should be front-loaded and entered into aggressively at the beginning of ministry.

Few people—missionaries included—have the internal motivation to continue full-time language study for years on end. Some accountability may be necessary to cultivate growth. Team leaders will help their team members by asking them to log the hours they intend to study. This suggestion often grates on people; it feels overbearing to ask missionaries to "report their hours." Such objections only heighten my concern. It isn't a matter of motivation but of discipline, and we have no reason to chafe against it. Some kind of accountability is normal in the professional world. Why would we imagine we're above this?

A missionary once complained to me that tracking her hours made her feel like "the number of hours I study per day is all that matters." Well, it isn't *all* that matters. But when trying to learn a language, the number of hours spent studying matters a good deal—just as the number of miles run matters when training for a marathon! Hours spent studying language are not *the point*, of course. They're the discipline that carries us to our actual goal. We may have the best of motivations, but once we're overseas—a little sleep, a little slumber, a little surfing of the internet . . . and before we know it entire days will disappear into a vortex.

Translation

In addition to learning a language and culture well enough to share the gospel, it may be necessary, in many cases, to translate Scripture into that language. Translation itself is a task that requires months of technical training and years of slow, careful work. In some cases, doing so may require creating an alphabet and promoting literacy. There are still languages with tens of thousands of speakers that have no written alphabet.

Providing an accurate, readable translation of the Bible is of the utmost importance. We know from history that small mistranslations can cause enormous problems. Increasingly, missionaries are relying on mother tongue translation strategies in which a missionary who speaks only a trade language simultaneously manages several teams of local translation helpers who translate the Scriptures into their own languages.[47] But these translation helpers are rarely tested for bilingual proficiency in the trade language used for communication with the

---

47 Karl J. Franklin, "Bible Translation and Small Languages in the Pacific: Ten Years Later," *International Journal of Frontier Missiology* 29/2 (Summer 2012): 82–89.

missionary; they're not always believers; and they often lack familiarity with crucial Christian concepts.

In such cases, they'll inevitably struggle to accurately translate ideas they don't fully understand. Of course, translators try to screen out major inaccuracies, but the potential for both error and opaqueness increases when the missionary can only use a trade language to check the final translation. Nuances will be missed, and strange ideas will often creep in. Even when a translation is grammatically correct, if its ideas and stories are not told smoothly, then native readers may lose interest and leave their Scriptures on the shelf. Quality matters more than quickness, and in any Bible translation—certainly in translations into languages that have never before had the Bible translated—we must value professionalism over productivity.

Conclusion

Clear communication matters. Ultimately, it's God's Spirit who convicts people of sin. And yet, in order to do so, he works through our very human abilities to communicate. Past generations of missionaries understood this and pursued mastery of the languages they worked in so that they could communicate the gospel clearly. Today's missionary force has largely forgotten this. We are happy, for the most part, to work through translators—who may not even understand the ideas they are translating!—and to stumble through the few stories about Jesus our limited language abilities will allow. Our neglect of language learning is intended to save time and energy, to maximize efficiency. But while our slapdash approach may be well-intended, it is ill-advised and unprofessional. Maximizing efficiency—communicating to as many people as we can, as quickly as possible—risks communicating unclearly and compromising the message itself. God has sent us as ambassadors to communicate his gospel to the lost. For their sake and for the sake of the gospel, we must communicate it as fluently and clearly as possible.

7

Credibility and Boldness Today

THERE ARE MOMENTS in life when everything changes. When a missionary can finally function at a high level in the language and culture she lives in, her life goes through a significant transition. She begins to feel more secure, more at home. She can handle the situations she finds herself in far more easily than before. Her friendships deepen as she has the tools now to know and be known more deeply. Her ministry expands. Now, rather than simply making spiritual *comments*, she's able to have spiritual *conversations*. She can navigate confidently into worldview-level themes and values. Her language isn't perfect—she's painfully aware of that—but it isn't an obstacle when she addresses spiritual matters. She's no longer an obvious cultural outsider, though her appearance still marks her as a foreigner. She has largely immigrated—or moved into—the culture so that for the most part, she can participate in it seamlessly.

She has a far-reaching web of relationships and is increasingly accepted by those around her. Her ministry changes. Increasingly, rather than being trained by others, she is ministering *to others* as God provides opportunities. As this happens, she is able to share her faith clearly and—if the Lord opens hearts to believe—to disciple new believers. Amid all the change, her primary task remains the same. She is still, first and foremost, an ambassador who bears Christ's message. But now she's able to communicate that message more clearly.

And yet, as we saw in chapter 5, clarity by itself is not enough. Clarity allows people to understand Christ's message. That's vital. But if she wants people to hear and believe Christ's message, then she must also share it boldly and present it in credible ways.

Credibility

Culture and Worldview

Years ago, an older woman living in the desert just south of the Sahara grew to love my coworker "Beth" like a daughter.

"One day," she told Beth, "I'm going to travel to America to meet your family."

Beth laughed. "America is a long way. I don't think you can make it all the way there."

"I'll ride my donkey," the woman responded.

"But there's an ocean in between—a whole lot of water!"

The woman thought about this. She then concluded, "I'll wait till dry season!"

Clearly, Beth and this woman from the South Sahara were operating from different worldviews. What made complete sense to Beth's friend made no practical sense to Beth.

For many, Jesus's message makes no practical sense. It isn't believable. We need to be aware of this so that we can present it credibly and deal with various objections and misunderstandings.

Here are important questions for missionaries to consider:

- Where does Jesus's message contradict ingrained assumptions and deeply cherished beliefs?
- Where it does contradict, will the story be so foreign that it seems laughably false to all but the most open of hearers?
- How can we help people through these impasses when they occur?

We can answer these questions only when we're familiar enough with the culture and worldview to understand and interact with its beliefs.

Because of the intense focus that language acquisition requires, I've addressed it on its own, with little reference to cultural learning. But language and culture are always intertwined. Language is a part of culture. It's the best means to learn about a culture. Now, that word "culture" gets thrown around a lot. But what does it mean? Broadly speaking, a culture is comprised of all the different ways different groups of people live and see the world around them. It covers "linguistic, political, economic, social, psychological, religious, national, racial, and other differences."[1] Without deeply understanding a culture, it is nearly impossible to build deep and trusting relationships. After all, we need to learn a laundry list of things:

- how friendships work
- what causes offense
- what communicates respect
- how opinions are presented
- how conflict gets handled
- how men and women relate to each other
- what people fear
- what they hope for
- how gifts are given and received
- how respectable people dress and eat, and how they groom themselves

I could go on, but you hopefully get the point. Every interaction and every conversation carries with it various cultural overtones and assumptions. We rarely think about this when we're "at home." But when you are on the field, the cultural dissonance can become overwhelming. Until we know instantly and intuitively what each of our behaviors will communicate across a wide variety of situations, we'll unwittingly be a source of awkwardness or even offense.

---

1   David Hesselgrave, *Communicating Christ Cross-Culturally: An Introduction to Missionary Communication*, 2nd ed. (Grand Rapids, MI: Zondervan, 1991), 100.

We want to grow in our cultural fluency for one main reason: to share the gospel in understandable ways. This means that as we learn about a people's culture, we need to focus especially on learning their worldview. That word "worldview" gets thrown around a lot, too. When I say it, I'm referring to the set of more-or-less unquestioned assumptions that determine a group of people's beliefs and values. Discerning someone's worldview means asking questions like: Is there a God or gods? Is there a spirit world? How did the world we know come to be? What are humans? What "ought" we do? What makes life good?

Most people go about life substantially unaware of their worldviews. David Hesselgrave defines worldviews as "thought systems; assumptions about the nature of the world; the ways in which various peoples 'see' the world."[2] Theologian N. T. Wright says worldviews are "that *through* which, not *at* which, a society or an individual normally looks."[3] Like a pair of tinted glasses, worldviews enable people to process everything around them. We all have these "glasses," and the fact that we can navigate the world more or less successfully with these glasses on only strengthens our confidence that we're accurately seeing what's actually there. We don't realize that our reality may be substantially colored by the lenses we're wearing. This is unfortunate, because worldview "embraces all deep-level human perceptions of reality, including the question of whether or not gods exist, and if so what he, she, it, or they are like, and how such a being, or such beings, might relate to the world."[4] We rarely question our deepest beliefs about the world.

Importantly, worldviews aren't simply a set of abstract beliefs ("there is a God"; "God is good"), since the world itself isn't abstract. The world is concrete and real, and so the most foundational parts

2   David Hesselgrave, "Worldview, Scripture, and Missionary Communication," *International Journal of Frontier Missiology* 14/2 (April–June 1997): 79–82.

3   N. T. Wright, *The New Testament and the People of God*, vol. 1 of Christian Origins and the Question of God (London: Society for Promoting Christian Knowledge, 1992), 125.

4   N. T. Wright, *New Testament and the People of God*, 123.

of our worldviews are concrete stories that tell us why things are the way they are. Tim Keller writes that "All people are living out some mental world-story that gives their lives meaning."[5] These stories shape our lives in profound ways. They drive our actions. Satan didn't deceive Eve by telling her that God was evil but by telling her a story in which God was trying to oppress her. Similarly, in Hosea, Israel turns to idols because she has been tricked into believing a false story:

> For she said, "I will go after my lovers,
>   who give me my bread and my water,
>   my wool and my flax, my oil and my drink." . . .
> And she did not know
>   that it was I who gave her
>   the grain, the wine, and the oil,
> and who lavished on her silver and gold,
>   which they used for Baal. (Hos. 2:5, 8)

From couples in love to nations at war, everyone is driven by a story.

The biblical story tells how God created the world to be good; how mankind fell into sin; how God chose a special people for himself and gave them the law; how he loved those people even though they walked away from him; and how he finally sent his Son to die for them and rise again so they could live with him forever. By contrast, a secular story might tell us that matter and energy came together somewhat arbitrarily, and that the world we know developed entirely through mechanical, scientific processes without any higher purpose or spiritual meaning. Stories like these shape people's beliefs and attitudes about themselves, God, and the world around them. As missionaries, our job is to subvert the deceptive stories people have believed in with the true story of Scripture.

---

5   Timothy Keller, *Every Good Endeavor: Connecting Your Work to God's Work* (New York: Penguin, 2012), 157.

In order to do this, we need to take people's stories and world-views seriously. The ideas that stand between people and belief in God are not *merely* excuses. Often, people are genuinely deceived. They simply cannot believe in God until these deceptions are addressed. Our job, then, is to help people see the inconsistencies in their beliefs, and to see how the stories they're following will lead them to a lack of fulfillment and eventually even to ruin. In Hosea, for example, God subverts Israel's story that idol worship had led her to prosperity:

> I will take back
>   my grain in its time,
>   and my wine in its season,
> and I will take away my wool and my flax,
>   which were to cover her nakedness.
> Now I will uncover her lewdness
>   in the sight of her lovers
>   and no one shall rescue her out of my hand. (Hos. 2:9–10)

Once Israel has realized how deeply she was deceived, she is able to listen to God's story:

> Therefore, behold, I will allure her,
>   and bring her into the wilderness,
>   and speak tenderly to her. (Hos. 2:14)

The process of subverting people's false stories and beliefs with truth is often called *pre-evangelism*. How might it work for us today? In the West, for example, we might help people see the inconsistencies of moral relativism. We might show how it sucks human life dry of purpose and how it destroys relationships and people. We might also need to challenge preconceived ideas and stories that paint the Christian message as foolish, cruel, or irrelevant. For example, consider these commonly held claims that need to be addressed:

- Science has disproved the miraculous stories in the Bible.
- Christianity teaches that we should hate gay people.
- Jesus's teachings are no different than any other religion's teachings.

In the Muslim world, we might ask whether a holy God is really likely to dismiss sin as lightly as people imagine. We might need to challenge other preconceived ideas. Here are some I often hear:

- The New Testament was changed.
- Human life is too profane for God to involve himself in it.
- Christians aren't monotheists; they worship God, Jesus, and Mary.
- Christianity permits promiscuity.

It is very difficult to challenge others' worldviews before we've taken them seriously enough to understand them. New Testament missionaries and teachers ought to be able to interact with their listeners' ideas adeptly. We catch a glimpse of what this may have looked like when Paul preaches against idolatry in Athens:

1. Paul identifies polytheism as a fundamental area where the Athenians' worldview differs from Scripture.
2. Paul points out the dangerous inconsistencies of polytheism: how could a god need humans to serve or build temples for him, when in fact God created all things (Acts 17:24–25)? God will not overlook such ignorance forever (vv. 30–31).
3. Paul presents the biblical story as an alternative: God isn't an idol fashioned by human hands. Instead, he created mankind. People are his children, and one day, he will raise the dead and judge all humanity. Paul makes his case in a way that the Athenians are well-positioned to understand. He argues from what they already know—that there may be an unknown God or gods (v. 23)—and he even borrows words from a Greek poet (v. 28) whose writings would have been part of the Athenians' "wisdom

texts." His familiarity with Greek culture allows him to address their worldview in ways that Greeks would find persuasive, or at least plausible.

We can follow a similar pattern by striving to understand how people's beliefs contrast with Scripture, by pointing out inconsistencies and dangers, and by presenting the truth in ways that our listeners are well-positioned to understand.

Unfortunately, modern missions thinking tends to dismiss all this. Many say it is unnecessary to learn people's culture and beliefs in detail before sharing the gospel with them. In fact, we're warned that it may even be detrimental. I've quoted this already but it's worth repeating. One of today's prominent missionary leaders contends, "We find being a bit 'dumb' better than being too smart, as expertise in the local culture can provoke defensiveness."[6] But until we understand what people believe, how can we engage with them or answer their questions? As the proverb says, "If one gives an answer before he hears, it is his folly and shame" (Prov. 18:13).

The late Nabeel Qureshi writes of how deeply convinced he was of his Muslim beliefs. But then his Christian friends first began sharing the gospel with him. Here's how he described what happened next:

The more I shared my views, the more I felt confirmed in my faith. . . . I realized no one had anything to rebuff my views.[7]

I can recall many *jumaa khutbas*, classes at youth camps, religious education books, and Quran study sessions dedicated to rebutting the Trinity. They all taught the same thing: the Trinity is thinly veiled polytheism.[8]

---

6 Mike Shipman, "Any-3: Lead Muslims to Christ Now!" *Mission Frontiers* (July/August 2013): 22.

7 Nabeel Qureshi, *Seeking Allah, Finding Jesus: A Devout Muslim Encounters Christianity* (Grand Rapids, MI: Zondervan, 2014), 88.

8 Qureshi, *Seeking Allah, Finding Jesus*, 191.

Everyone I loved and respected taught me to reject the Trinity, and that, combined with the inability of Christians to explain it, makes it easy to see why a repulsion to the Trinity was part and parcel of my Islamic identity. The same thing is true for almost all practicing Muslims.[9]

He then describes his feelings about the Bible: "I knew in my very core that the Bible had been altered."[10] And later:

I was convinced the Quran would stand up to scrutiny. No one in the *ummah*[11] doubted its divine inspiration. . . . We knew that the Quran was so perfect and miraculous that no one would dare question it. . . . We considered our arguments incontrovertible.[12]

What emerges in the quotes above is the portrait of a young man who is deeply convinced—through "two decades of Islamic teaching"—that the Christian gospel was a deception. He is seized in his mind and in his conscience by sincere objections to Christ's message. Without help to work through these objections, he simply *could not* trust in the Jesus of the Bible. It wasn't enough to be loved by Christian friends or to hear stories illustrating the beauty of Jesus's character, just as having good pagan friends who tell nice stories about their gods wouldn't be enough to make us believe in Zeus.

Qureshi's curiosity and powerful intellect enabled him to research these questions more deeply than most people will. But almost all people will face similar questions, even if they don't spend years scouring primary sources to answer them. We must understand the intellectual and emotional barriers that stand between people and Jesus, and we must be ready to address them.

I work in Muslim North Africa. Most missionaries I've met cannot—even in their own mother tongues—explain the basics of what we *do*

9   Qureshi, *Seeking Allah, Finding Jesus*, 191.
10   Qureshi, *Seeking Allah, Finding Jesus*, 133.
11   The Islamic community.
12   Qureshi, *Seeking Allah, Finding Jesus*, 228.

understand about the Trinity, let alone present this doctrine in a way that their Muslim friends and neighbors might understand. Generally speaking, the missionaries I've met are unaware of the great differences in emphasis between Christian monotheism and Muslim monotheism. Few have even a basic familiarity with the Qur'an, the Hadiths, or the *sira*. Few even know what the *sira* are.[13] Similarly, few are aware of the local flavor of Islam in the areas in which they work. Which *imams* are most influential? Which schools of Islamic thought do they represent? Furthermore, they have little historical knowledge to back up their claims that the New Testament remains unchanged—another major stumbling block for Muslims—nor are they aware of the passages in the Qur'an that both suggest the New Testament is reliable and even encourage people to read it.

Missionaries too often waste time discussing non-fundamental issues. For example, they tend to frequently engage in dialogues about the injustice of polygamy, a practice condoned by Islam. But arguing with Muslim men about polygamy is no more helpful in sharing the gospel than demanding people stop sleeping with their girlfriends or boyfriends would be in the West. It's certainly a conversation for discipleship, but it isn't where you start introducing the gospel. I've also seen lots of missionaries chat with Muslims about whether we're saved by works or by grace. This is difficult, because Muslim views of salvation are somewhat complicated. In many forms of Islam, entry into paradise depends on our works to an extent, but God ultimately shows mercy to whomever he pleases. So Muslims struggle to perceive any conflict between salvation by works or by grace. Most missionaries don't know how to lay the necessary groundwork to help their friends understand how starkly the Christian doctrine of salvation by grace differs from Muslim teaching.

Missionaries in other parts of the world—even in other parts of the Muslim world—will face different issues that they must understand and

---

13 The *sira* are traditional biographies of Muhammad, and their stories are foundational religious texts for many Muslims.

address. But the point is clear: missionaries should invest substantial time in understanding people's beliefs before trying to convince them of Christ's message. Any ambassador sent to a foreign nation would do all he could to thoroughly understand the thinking and motives of his new home. He wouldn't see this as optional, or as going above and beyond. He would see it as his professional responsibility.

Earning the Right to Be Heard

Of course, no one needs to question the credentials of a political ambassador. When the United States, for example, sends an ambassador to Mexico, it is clear to the Mexican government who that ambassador is and by whom he is sent. But as missionaries, our claims and our credentials are more dubious. We claim to carry a message from God. Very well, but others have claimed that, too, and most of them are crazy! Why would anyone listen to us? Certainly, our *message* must be convincing, but unless we ourselves are also credible, our message may not even be heard.

Credibility isn't easily established when we share a message that confronts cultural beliefs and values. Anthropologist Paul Hiebert explains, "One of the [principal] characteristics of . . . culture is that it is particularly resistant to manipulative attempts to change it from the outside."[14] Newcomers to a culture are inherently perceived as suspicious and potentially sinister actors, especially when they offer critique. This is especially true when the critiques are aimed at parts of people's culture that are central to their sense of identity.[15]

Obviously, most missionaries are foreigners. But with time they can ultimately be perceived as "one of us"—at least to the extent of being

---

14 Paul G. Hiebert, *Transforming Worldviews: An Anthropological Understanding of How People Change* (Grand Rapids, MI: Baker Academic, 2008), 32.

15 For example, *animism* is a worldview which contradicts Christianity at multiple levels. However, many tribal *animists* do not see part of their identity as being "members of the animist religious system, which differs from the Christian system." In contrast, most Muslims or Hindus *do* see their identity, in part, as members of religious systems that are in contradiction to Christianity. This will increase the level of resistance they offer when Christians critique their worldviews.

"someone who understands us" and "someone who is on our side." This was a central thrust of Paul's ministry (1 Cor. 9:20–21).

But we must earn the right to be heard. And this takes patience. I suspect some will protest. David Garrison does. He writes that we don't need to earn "the right to share your faith. Jesus earned that right when he died on the cross for us."[16] This is true in some sense, but while Jesus earned us the right to share our faith, that may not give us the right in our listeners' minds to be taken seriously. So how do we earn the right to be heard? A few things come to mind.

We should strive to be people of character who are known and respected as such (2 Cor. 11:7–10). We should cultivate relationships of love and trust as Paul did. Here's what he said to the Ephesians: "You yourselves know how I lived among you the whole time from the first day . . . serving the Lord with all humility" (Acts 20:18–19). He wrote to the Thessalonians, "You are witnesses, and God also, how holy and righteous and blameless was our conduct toward you believers. For you know how, like a father with his children, we exhorted each one of you and encouraged you" (1 Thess. 2:10–12).

Qureshi agrees that cultivating a relationship is vital. Reflecting on "David," a Christian who shared the gospel with him, he writes, "a strong friendship is critical. A surface-level relationship might snap under the tension of disagreement."[17] David's friendship with Qureshi earned him the right to speak difficult truths without the risk of Qureshi walking away from the friendship. From Qureshi's perspective, his friendship with David gave him room to question and examine his Muslim beliefs for the first time. Qureshi describes his upbringing: "Questions are often seen as a challenge to authority."[18] And later: "The act of questioning leadership is dangerous. . . . Correct and incorrect courses of action are assessed socially, not individually. A person's virtue is thus determined by how well he meets social expectations,

---

16   David Garrison, *Church Planting Movements: How God Is Redeeming a Lost World* (Bangalore, India: WIGTake Resources, 2007), 177.

17   Qureshi, *Seeking Allah, Finding Jesus*, 190.

18   Qureshi, *Seeking Allah, Finding Jesus*, 76.

not by an individual determination of right and wrong."[19] Until he met David, Qureshi had little provocation to ask questions and follow them to their conclusions.

Second, because people tend to experience *alienation* when they encounter *alien* cultures, we embrace the cultures we minister in to whatever extent possible. In doing so, we reflect Paul's example:

> For though I am free from all, I have made myself a servant to all, that I might win more of them. To the Jews I became as a Jew, in order to win Jews. To those under the law I became as one under the law (though not being myself under the law) that I might win those under the law. To those outside the law I became as one outside the law (not being outside the law of God but under the law of Christ) that I might win those outside the law. (1 Cor. 9:19–21)

Successful missionaries throughout history have followed Paul's example. Hudson Taylor's China Inland Mission was ridiculed as "the Pigtail Mission" for its enthusiastic embrace of Chinese culture.[20] But such critiques were both shallow and short-sighted. Embracing a people's culture lets them see how well and how realistically our faith can be lived out in *their own world and their own culture.* They won't see it as an alien faith that only makes sense in an alien culture. Qureshi describes how necessary this is when he reflects on the experience of Muslim immigrants to the West:

> They expect people in the West to be promiscuous Christians and enemies of Islam. . . . Their cultural differences and preconceptions often cause them to remain isolated from Westerners. . . . On the rare occasion that someone does invite a Muslim to his or her home, differences in culture and hospitality may make the Muslim feel uncomfortable. . . . There are simply too many barriers for Muslim

19 Qureshi, *Seeking Allah, Finding Jesus*, 108.
20 Vance Christie, *Hudson Taylor: Founder, China Inland Mission* (Uhrichsville, OH: Barbour, 1999), 151.

immigrants to understand Christians. . . . Only the exceptional blend of love, humility, hospitality, and persistence can overcome these barriers.[21]

Boldness

If we strive to communicate Jesus's message clearly, so that it may be understood, and credibly, so that it may be believed, we must also strive to speak it boldly, so that as many as possible may hear. We can learn much about speaking boldly from modern methods such as *Church Planting Movements* (CPM) and *Disciple Making Movements* (DMM). These approaches emphasize looking for interested people in an ever-widening circle of relationships rather than spending years on deepening a few close friendships in the hopes that they will eventually open their hearts to our message. The apostles sowed boldly and broadly, and so must we. "How are they to hear without someone preaching?" (Rom. 10:14).

Broad evangelism will often result in intense opposition among the unreached. In the face of such hostility, we must be wise. Boldness does not mean tactlessness. Yet again, Paul's example is helpful on this point:

> Give no offense to Jews or to Greeks or to the church of God, just as I try to please everyone in everything I do, not seeking my own advantage, but that of many, that they may be saved. (1 Cor. 10:32–33)

> And the Lord's servant must not be quarrelsome but kind to everyone, able to teach, patiently enduring evil, correcting his opponents with gentleness. (2 Tim. 2:24–25)

Nor should we confuse boldness with recklessness. Both Jesus and Paul spend significant portions of their ministry avoiding opposition in order to focus on teaching their disciples. Christ himself advises, "When they persecute you in one town, flee to the next" (Matt. 10:23).

---

21 Qureshi, *Seeking Allah, Finding Jesus*, 80.

But neither Jesus nor Paul avoid opposition entirely. Nor do they ever stop preaching because of it.

Missionaries today are sometimes taught to avoid contentious issues. As I prepared for the field, I was often told, "We don't talk about the Prophet or the Qur'an; those issues are far too controversial. It's better to simply tell stories about Jesus." There's some wisdom in this. In many Muslim cultures, questioning the prophethood of Muhammad or the inspiration of the Qur'an will anger people. Critique must be offered carefully, or the results will be more damaging than helpful. Other people and other cultures will have other issues that seem too sensitive to address. Nevertheless, New Testament missionaries and teachers didn't regard any truth as "off-limits." At various points, Jesus, Peter, Stephen, and Paul angered people by confronting issues straightforwardly. Sometimes, addressing issues that anger people may be important in leading them to Christ.

We must remember that we earn the right to be heard. Before we know the culture and form vital, loving relationships with people, we won't even know when or how to address "off-limits" issues. We won't have the relational capital to do so. But over time, we'll learn to approach these issues in ways that help people through their misbeliefs, rather than just making them angry. So when people do become angry—and some will—we'll be able to have confidence that Jesus's message itself has angered them, not just our insensitive way of presenting it.

As we'll discuss in the next chapter, we're not simply outsiders to the cultures we work in; we're newcomers seeking to migrate inward. Though the transition is daunting, it is also possible. It's possible—over enough time and spurred on by eager desire—to enter into and to be able to explore even the most sensitive issues with the people to whom we are sent. And we *must* learn to do so. This is the job of an ambassador.

Conclusion

New Testament missionaries sought to communicate clearly, credibly, and boldly. So must we. This will be mostly impossible until we develop a deep fluency in the language and culture of those we serve. As we do so, we'll begin to understand the deeper beliefs and values that stand between people and a saving knowledge of the gospel. We'll know how to address those issues and how to relate to people in safe, credible ways. At each step, much more could be written, and indeed much more has been written elsewhere. But what's beginning to become clear here, I hope, is that this a monumental task. Missionaries must expend tremendous effort to develop their communication abilities—master the language, and learn the culture.

Sadly, what I'm highlighting here is given only lip service by much of the missions world today. Adequate language and cultural acquisition—that monumental, years-long, soul-crushingly-difficult, nose-to-grindstone task—is the exception, not the norm. The missions community often views real, in-depth analysis of a people's culture and worldview as stuffy, academic, and eggheaded. And as we saw in chapter 3, missionaries are not taught to see themselves as ambassadors for Christ whose teaching is essential and who must work according to the highest professional standards. Instead, they're taught to avoid teaching, to "get out of the way" of what God is doing, and to minister as indirectly as they can—to avoid contaminating God's work.

But in Scripture, God never works apart from capable human teachers when the gospel spreads to new peoples. As we saw previously, the Holy Spirit doesn't explain Isaiah 53 directly to the Ethiopian eunuch; he sends Philip. The angel doesn't explain the gospel to Cornelius; he directs Cornelius to Peter. Missionaries should be ready to play a *central role* in teaching the gospel, and they must prepare themselves to fulfill this role as competently as they can. This shouldn't stoke pride; we're still entirely dependent on the power of the Holy Spirit. But in William Carey's language, we are the *means* through which that power flows.

It will take years to learn to communicate well. Having counted the cost, are we ready? Shortcuts abound. Let's commit to avoiding them.

8

A Long-Term Path for Missionaries

IN CHAPTER 4, I suggested that the missionary task is to go in Christ's authority as ambassadors of his kingdom to communicate his message to the nations. Since then, I've added considerable detail to this definition. Missionaries should strive to communicate their message clearly, credibly, and boldly.

But what should their ministry actually look like? Based on what we've already discussed, a ministry pathway is beginning to emerge, which I'll outline below. The Lord is free to bypass various points along this path as he sees fit. Nonetheless, I mean for what follows to be a bare-bones approach, containing only the major milestones of ministry. Missionaries should seek to follow it except in the most unusual cases.

Put another way: I'm not describing a full-fledged *methodology*. I'm not trying to specify which lessons should be taught when, which techniques are most helpful in sharing the gospel, or which curriculum—if any—should be used in training elders. I'm simply offering a broad, commonsense sketch of milestones that missionaries should commit to pursuing if they want to plant churches. I also want to point out that the path I'm presenting here isn't mine; it is *not new at all*. It can be traced through the ministries of Hudson Taylor, Adoniram Judson, John Paton, and others. Were these missionaries perfect? No, but they may still have a lot to teach us. In recent years, it has become fashionable to disparage "traditional missionaries." It is true that some missionaries in the past have made regrettable errors.[1] But that doesn't mean most missionary work in the past was primarily characterized by failure. We should learn both from the mistakes of the past *and* from what was done well.

Missionary Milestones

So, following the example of those who came before, here are the missionary milestones we ought to pursue:

Milestone #1: Raise Support and Communicate Well with Your Sending Church

Missionary candidates raise financial support, recruit people to support them practically and in prayer, and dialogue with their churches about their plans. Churches unfamiliar with missionary work learn about overseas ministry.

Milestone #2: Pursue Pre-Field Training in the Scriptures

There are many ways to do this. Perhaps go to a good Bible school or seminary. Or just read lots of good books on theology and hermeneutics. You don't need a degree in missions or theology, but you do need some kind of pre-field training. Regardless of the form, missionaries should possess a broad enough understanding of Scripture to think flexibly and

---

1   The phrase "traditional" is used almost exclusively in modern evangelical missions literature to refer to the ways in which people—rightly or wrongly—perceive historical missionary practice to be outdated or harmful, rather than to refer to the attributes of historical missionary practice that we find invaluable. The quotes below serve as examples of many others:

"... traditional missionaries will never be able to complete the Great Commission by themselves" (Danny D. Martin, "The Place of the Local Church in Tentmaking," *International Journal of Frontier Missiology* 14/3 [July–September 1997]: 131).

"the traditional missionary practice has been to require Muslim believers to renounce their religious cultural identity, to apostatize" (Rick Brown, "Response to 'A Humble Appeal to C5/Insider Movement Muslim Ministry Advocates to Consider Ten Questions,'" *International Journal of Frontier Missiology* 14/1 [Spring 2007]: 9).

"In traditional missions one talks about 'closed countries' and 'restricted access countries,' but there are no closed doors for real business people doing real business" (Issue Group on Business as Mission, *Business as Mission* [Pattaya, Thailand: Lausanne Committee for World Evangelization, 2004], ch. 3.).

as a result appreciate the merits of certain denominational distinctives with which they might not agree. They should also be able to think critically as they apply biblical principles in foreign situations and cultures.

*Milestone #3: Don't Forget Pre-Field Training
That Covers Practical Skills*

Pre-field training should cover most of what we've already discussed: language acquisition, team ministry life, cultural analysis, and various life skills the missionary will need in his or her location on the field.

*Milestone #4: Insist on Several Years of Full-Time Language
and Culture Acquisition upon Arriving on the Field*

No matter how long it takes, the missionary should see this as his primary task until he reaches a high level of linguistic proficiency. Communication shouldn't be impeded by inability with the language or lack of cultural awareness. Whenever possible, new missionaries must be protected from other responsibilities that would intrude on their years of language and culture acquisition (e.g., working in a clinic, teaching English, helping run a team business, etc.). While there's some subjectivity in language proficiency, full-time language learning should generally continue at least until a missionary reaches a level similar to *Advanced Mid* proficiency according to ACTFL guidelines.[2] Some focused language learning should continue after this point, even as language ability continues to grow on its own as the missionary uses language in a variety of circumstances.

*Milestone #5: Develop a Deep Understanding
of Your Target People's Worldview*

This includes the following:

- Learning how their worldview contradicts a biblical worldview.
- Learning how to address deceptions in their worldview clearly, persuasively, and respectfully.

2 *ACTFL Proficiency Guidelines 2012* (Alexandria, VA: American Council on the Teaching of Foreign Languages, 2012). See the discussion in chapter 6, including note 45.

- Earning the right to be heard in the wider community by cultivating relationships of respect and trust, by establishing a good reputation, and by learning how to interact appropriately within cultural norms.

Milestone #6: Communicate the Gospel Widely and Boldly in Culturally Understandable Ways

This typically involves *pre-evangelism*, in which we address inconsistencies in the prevailing worldview and beliefs that will serve as stumbling blocks to Christ's message, and always involves *evangelism*, in which Christ's message is presented.

Milestone #7: Baptize New Believers and Bring Them Together into a Church[3]

The new church should meet regularly—unless geographical obstacles or extreme security threats make this impossible—for teaching, prayer, worship, and the Lord's Supper. We'll spend some time later on in this chapter looking at characteristics of a mature church.

Milestone #8: Disciple New Believers until Their Christian Worldview Has Subverted Other Ways of Looking at the World

The goal is for new believers to be "transformed by the renewal of your mind" (Rom. 12:2). This will result in Christlike character, and their new, Spirit-wrought identity in Christ will supersede all other identities: ethnic, political, religious, or cultural.

Milestone #9: Appoint Leaders from within Churches Once Both Local Churches and Local Believers Have Reached Maturity

Elders and church leaders need a substantial foundation in scriptural knowledge so that they are "able to teach" (1 Tim. 3:2) all parts of the

---

3 Some believers will be ready to meet together before they are ready to be baptized, particularly if baptism is likely to result in persecution. We shouldn't pressure people to be baptized if they are not ready. Quite the opposite! It is the Spirit's work to grow people's faith to where they are ready to face their fears. However, we should disciple and teach with the expectation that baptism will be their initiatory rite into the Christian life; believers who refuse to be baptized cannot be seen as being stable or mature in their faith.

biblical narrative. When leaders have been trained and appointed, churches begin to govern themselves. As they've always intended, the missionaries have worked themselves out of a job.

Milestone #10: Where the Scriptures Are Not Available,
Translate the Scriptures and Promote Literacy
So That New Believers Are Able to Read

Recorded oral translations are helpful, but ultimately a church's leadership will benefit from being able to compare and cross-reference scriptural passages. Some level of literacy will be greatly advantageous. Accurate, readable Bible translations require training and may take a translator several years.

I hope it's obvious: these ten milestones will take many years, and this path differs sharply from modern missions approaches that expect churches to multiply every few months. It will require a daunting level of commitment. That's part of why missionaries need to know what they're getting into before they leave for the field. As we saw in chapter 1, part of ministering professionally and well is "avoiding shortcuts by allocating adequate time, energy, and resources to the task." In chapter 9, we'll discuss how to find and equip missionaries for the task. But for the remainder of this chapter, I simply want to add detail to the pathway described above. It is impossible for all members of a missionary team to be equally involved in every part of the task. Some may be gifted evangelists; others may be gifted teachers or translators. Nevertheless, as a ministry team helps new churches move toward maturity, there are key ingredients that must be part of their work. We've already briefly examined pre-field training, language and culture acquisition, and some aspects of pre-evangelism and evangelism. How do we continue to minister professionally in later phases of ministry?

Discipleship

Jesus doesn't just command his disciples to "go and baptize." He also commands them to go and "[teach] them to observe all that I have commanded you" (Matt. 28:19). Everything Jesus said is part of the message we carry. Indeed, the salvation Jesus offered does more than simply cancel our guilt so that we get to go to heaven when we die. Jesus delights to save people so they can walk with God and experience freedom from the power of sin. Certainly, this involves canceling our guilt—we couldn't very well live and walk with God if he didn't forgive us. But we'd also have no idea *how* to walk with God apart from Jesus's teaching.

According to missiologist Paul Hiebert, missionaries often succumb to the "flaw of the excluded middle."[4] In other words, they address people's "lower" needs—things like disease that are seen, felt, and experienced—and their "highest" needs—things like answers to life's most important questions. In doing so, however, they ignore a vast "middle" of people's worldviews. For example, what about things like "mana, astrological forces, charms, amulets and magical rites, evil eye, evil tongue"?[5] On these topics, people are generally left undiscipled. It isn't difficult to imagine a similar situation in which one's "highest" beliefs about God and the afterlife were more or less correct, but one's fundamental "middle beliefs" about money, power, sexuality, other ethnicities, alcohol, and the worth of women were confused, at best, and downright depraved at worst. Perhaps we don't even have to look too far in some of our own churches to find such cases.

Discipling toward Maturity

Cases like these should not be the norm. Every believer—no matter their background or upbringing—can grow into maturity. Such is the power of the Holy Spirit. "Generational" and societal sins are not too entrenched for him. Though we shouldn't rush people through the process of maturation, we should expect real and solid progress. If Paul tells the Ephesians that he "did not shrink" from declaring the whole counsel of God to them (Acts 20:20, 27), then that's part of our

---

4   Paul G. Hiebert, "The Flaw of the Excluded Middle," *Missiology* 10/1 (January 1982): 35–47.

5   Hiebert, "Flaw of the Excluded Middle," 40.

job, too. But it takes time. There's no "abridged version" of Christian discipleship. We cannot let our modern concern for speed lead some missionaries to trim the "whole counsel of God" into an abbreviated discipleship curriculum.

One common version of this abbreviated approach to discipleship is "storying." This approach first showed up in missions in the 1980s, and it has since grown widely popular.[6,7] Such methods attempt to disciple people entirely through the retelling of summarized Bible stories.[8] These stories are sometimes shared in person. But more often, they are shared through "oral Bibles"—solar-powered MP3 players containing a few dozen recorded Bible stories. Do you remember David Watson's startling claim, in chapter 3, to have planted 627 churches by just passing out a thousand audio players?[9] Storying methods imagine that such audio players can "give the whole overview of the purpose of God."[10] Their proponents make some startling claims: "Without [a] doubt, oral Bibles are the best way forward to make disciples of the non-literate unreached peoples of the world."[11]

To be sure, telling stories is an excellent teaching technique, and recordings can be a valuable tool. But that doesn't mean that *exclusively* sharing stories is an adequate way to evangelize non-Christians or disciple new Christians. This is *especially* true if the stories are merely recorded and sent without a missionary to answer questions as people listen. Oral Bibles provide a convenient, low-cost way to circulate the gospel message.[12] But we must not overstate the usefulness of a disembodied monologue. Furthermore, we must

---

6   J. O. Terry, *Basic Bible Storying* (Seattle, WA: Amazon Digital Services, 2012).

7   Tom Steffen, "Orality Comes of Age: The Maturation of a Movement," *International Journal of Frontier Missiology* 31/3 (Fall 2014): 139–47.

8   Terry, *Basic Bible Storying*, ch. 1.

9   "David Watson's Testimony," narrated by David Watson, *Accelerate Training*, accessed January 3, 2019, https://www.acceleratetraining.org/index.php/resources/61-david-watson -s-testimony-90-min-mp3/file.

10 Rick Leatherwood, "The Case and Call for Oral Bibles: A Key Component in Completing the Great Commission," *Mission Frontiers* (September/October 2013): 38.

11 Leatherwood, "Case and Call for Oral Bibles," 39.

12 Leatherwood, "Case and Call for Oral Bibles," 38.

not let the desire for efficiency short-circuit our responsibility to teach effectively. Discipleship requires personal interaction. We must be present to ask and answer questions until we know that people understand.

There's another problem with this model: God didn't communicate everything he wants us to know through stories alone. Many essential parts of his revelation—the New Testament epistles, major sections of the Law and Prophets, and much of Jesus's teaching—aren't stories at all. So how can we obey Jesus's instruction to teach people "to observe all that I have commanded" (Matt. 28:20) without sharing these other parts of Scripture? Even the best set of stories on its own is insufficient to disciple new believers through their "middle beliefs." It will fail to provide a grounded, fully fleshed-out theology.

Naturally, proponents of storying methods disagree. They claim that non-literate peoples struggle to relate to abstract arguments in Scripture because "non-literate people do not think in abstract terms like literate people do."[13,14] Indeed, we all have different levels of abstract intelligence, but abstract thinking is not beyond the grasp of people from non-literate cultures. Indian pastor Harshit Singh rightly warns against underestimating non-literate peoples, reminding us not to assume that just because people have "an oral culture, they don't understand propositional teaching."[15] In many cases, our inability to communicate abstractly with our hearers may have more to do with our poor language skills than with their lack of abstract intel-

---

13   Leatherwood, "Case and Call for Oral Bibles," 37.

14   We should be very careful making such dichotomies. It is not the case that literate Westerners love abstraction while non-Western, non-literate people love stories. In fact, though it is argued that "Westerners find it difficult to move beyond abstract ideas such as justification by faith, love, hate, propitiation, and so forth" (Tom A. Steffen, *Reconnecting God's Story to Ministry: Cross-cultural Storytelling at Home and Abroad* [Downers Grove, IL: InterVarsity Press, 2006], 126), people in the West spend billions of dollars a year following stories in books, TV, and film. All people instinctively love stories. Similarly, all people are capable of abstract reasoning.

15   Harshit Singh, "How Western Methods Have Affected Missions in India," 9Marks' First Five Years Conference, Columbus, OH, August 4, 2017. Accessed May 3, 2019, https://www.9marks.org/message/how-western-methods-have-affected-missions-in-india.

ligence.[16] Besides, most of the Roman world was non-literate,[17] and Paul still engaged in complex, abstract discussions. Similarly, literacy in Roman-occupied Palestine may have been as low as 3 percent,[18] but Jesus employed nuanced, abstract teaching all the time. His most famous block of teaching, the Sermon on the Mount, is an excellent example of this.

Sharing an abridged gospel can only call people to an abridged faith in Jesus's message. It is not enough to win people to faith in the Jesus Film or in a set of recorded Bible stories. These tools may be helpful as part of a larger process of evangelism and discipleship, but they don't share the full Christian message and story. Can the Lord use them to convert someone? Of course he can! But in the discipling of new believers, we must share God's story from creation to redemption. We must include the full range of biblical theology and teaching. We must disciple people in their views and practices relating to anger, money, sexuality, magic, alcohol, work, family, gender roles, other tribes and races, conflict resolution, the spirit world, honor and reputation, proper use of authority, and so on.

Importantly, it isn't enough to give people commands about what they must and must not do. When we teach, we must impart the fullness of the Christian worldview in each area. We must help new believers to understand that Jesus's teachings are not simply burdensome rules that we "ought" to follow. Instead, Jesus's teachings are deeply good for us, and departing from them fills our lives with ugliness and despair. For example, when we forbid the use of pornography, we do so by explaining the beauty of God's plan for intimacy, the dignity of

---

16 This is more likely than we might imagine. In early stages of language learning, abstract discussion is impossible to engage in or comprehend, but simple stories are comprehensible. Missionaries who can only understand stories might easily imagine that the people they work with have no appreciation of abstract concepts.

17 Keith Hopkins, "Conquest by Book," in J. H. Humphrey, *Literacy in the Roman World* (Toronto: Ancient World Books, 1991), 133–58.

18 Meir Bar-Ilan, "Illiteracy in the Land of Israel in the First Centuries C.E.," in *Essays in the Social Scientific Study of Judaism and Jewish Society*, ed. Stuart Schoenfeld, Simcha Fishbane, and Jack N. Lightstone (New York: Ktav, 1992), 55.

184   PART TWO: CORRECTING OUR COURSE

self-control and of celibacy, and the horror of exploitation, addiction, and self-degradation that results from sexual sin.

Put simply, discipleship is focused primarily on changing people's mindsets—on leading them to greater faith in Jesus—and only secondarily on changing their actions. It is through the renewing of our mind that we are transformed (Rom. 12:2), and it's as we teach "everyone with all wisdom" that people grow "mature in Christ" (Col. 1:28).

Indeed, the New Testament almost always speaks of maturity in relation to our thinking.[19] As we saw in chapter 3, this cuts against the pattern of "obedience-based discipleship" that is taught in many modern methods.[20,21] Discipleship is *not* based on obedience. Rather, it is based on *faith*, and our obedience flows from that faith. Abraham first believed, and then was circumcised (Rom. 4:1–11). It is the "obedience *of faith*" to which we are called (Rom. 1:5). It was the *faith* of the men and women of Hebrews 11 that inspired them to such inspiring acts of obedience. Those who truly believe that God "exists and that he rewards those who seek him" (Heb. 11:6) won't find obedience difficult. Obedience happens when people are deeply convinced that God will be with them in their obedience, and that Jesus's way is fundamentally good for them.

Discipleship is not based on obedience. Rather, it is based
on faith, and our obedience flows from that faith.

This is a more difficult step than we might imagine. Many of our forays into sin occur when we "want to be good, but we are prepared, ready, to do evil—should circumstances *require* it."[22] We lie not because

------

19 See 1 Cor. 2:6; 14:20; Eph. 4:13; Phil. 3:15; Heb. 5:14.
20 David Watson and Paul Watson, *Contagious Disciple Making: Leading Others on a Journey of Discovery* (Nashville: Thomas Nelson, 2014), 65.
21 Stan Parks, "How Your Church Can Work toward Church Planting Movements," *CPM Journal* (January–March 2006): 44.
22 Dallas Willard, *The Great Omission: Rediscovering Jesus' Essential Teachings on Discipleship* (New York: HarperCollins, 2006), 14, emphasis original.

we want to but because we feel we have to. We mistreat others when they "make us angry," leaving us no other choice—or so we think. Yet if Jesus's teaching is correct—if God is really with us—we don't have to lie. It's actually better *for us*—in our real lives and circumstances, and despite the consequences that may come—to confess our wrong. Similarly, people cannot force our anger, since we are safe in God's care and their actions cannot ultimately damage us. This is the kind of faith that leads to obedience.

Outsiders or Immigrants?

Somewhat controversially, discipling new believers through their "middle beliefs" also means helping them to evaluate their pre-Christian cultural and religious practices in light of the gospel. We are rightly warned to be careful in doing so. Most cultural practices are not either good or bad but simply cultural. The food people eat, the music they listen to, and the clothes they wear usually aren't moral issues. In such cases, we shouldn't impose our own cultural practices as biblical.

But there are many cases in which cultural practices *are* morally wrong. After all, cultures teach us not only what to eat but also how to view women, children, the sick, and the elderly. They teach us how to use money, power, and sex. They teach us who is and who is not an "honorable" person. These issues are of fundamental spiritual importance where cultural beliefs and moral teachings overlap.

Some popular missions thinkers argue that we should not address cultural practices at all, even when they have moral implications. Instead, we are taught to "trust the Holy Spirit, as the apostles did, to guide the new believers and to redeem their pagan or heretical religious practices as He chooses."[23] Remember how we saw in chapter 3 that CPM-style methods caution missionaries that their instruction will introduce cultural contamination into the church? In other words, because we are cultural outsiders, we cannot hope to understand practices

---

23 Rebecca Lewis, "Insider Movements: Honoring God-Given Identity and Community," *International Journal of Frontier Missiology* 26/1 (Spring 2009): 19.

inside the culture. Therefore, we should let people form their own verdicts about which cultural and religious practices they can bring with them into their lives with Christ.

Can I suggest a different approach? Rather than seeing ourselves as "outsiders," we should see ourselves as immigrants. Indeed, we did come from "outside," and we're in the process of migrating in. As we do, we'll inevitably grow in our understanding of the culture. We need to be careful not to overestimate how much we know about a new place. And on matters we don't understand, we should avoid making moral judgments. In most circumstances, a healthy church will eventually come to proper conclusions about its cultural practices. But especially in the early days, this process will involve indigenous church leaders working with missionaries to determine which cultural practices might be in tension with the Scriptures. Missionaries shouldn't make these decisions unilaterally, without the buy-in of local Christians. After all, it's the church that must live or die with the consequences of these decisions, and people are unlikely to follow rules they don't believe in.

But missionaries should help new Christians understand how the gospel speaks to matters of culture. Consider Paul's example. He wasn't a Gentile. He spoke fluent Greek, but not the mother tongues of many of the congregations with whom he worked (cf. Acts 2:9–11; 14:11).[24] While he had a general familiarity with Greek polytheism, the Mediterranean in Paul's day was far from culturally homogeneous. It was made up of countless city-states marked by diverse cultural and religious traditions. Paul would have experienced many of these cultures as an "outsider." And yet, Paul didn't feel inherently disqualified from giving Christian teaching on cultural issues. He spoke on any number of them: eating of non-kosher foods (Rom. 14:1–4), eating meat sacrificed to

---

24 Pliny claims that Mithridates, King of Pontus, who lived just a few decades before Paul, ". . . was king of twenty-two nations, administered their laws in as many languages, and could harangue each of them, without employing an interpreter" (John Bostock and H. T. Riley, eds., *The Natural History of Pliny the Elder* [London: Taylor & Francis, 1855], 7:24).

idols (1 Cor. 8:1–13), and immodest clothing during worship (1 Cor. 11:1–16; 1 Tim. 2:8–10).

Similarly, we're not automatically disqualified from speaking about cultural issues. At some point, we'll almost certainly have to. Those who grew up as cultural insiders will likely have a familiarity with cultural issues that we don't have. But we may also be able to bring an outside objectivity they don't have. In any case, if we're acting as Christ's ambassadors, then we ought to be—at least at the beginning of their discipleship—far more familiar with Christ's message than they are. In these situations, if we're trusted as people who respect the local culture—and if we dialogue with nationals until our observations are informed and relevant—then it won't be hard to explain our conclusions in ways that make sense to cultural insiders.

Establishing the Church

As we saw in chapter 1, our goal is to plant churches that are "sufficiently mature to multiply and endure." Such churches will have mature leaders who shepherd the immature and wayward. Our task as missionaries is to find and teach a core of such people. They will "be able to teach others also" (2 Tim. 2:2) and will continue the work where we leave off. In fact, if discipled with proper care, they will be able to minister far more effectively than we could.

But it bears repeating yet again: it will take time for a core of mature believers to grow. We must be patient. Jesus took three years to train his apostles. He didn't emphasize simplicity and rapidity. He sought to give the apostles as strong a foundation as possible so that they could build the church on the foundation of his teaching. Indeed, the church is built on this "foundation of the apostles and prophets" (Eph. 2:20), through whose writings we know God's message to us. While we don't function as apostles, and while we *certainly* won't leave behind a trove of inspired teaching, it must be our goal to leave a strong foundation in the truth. If the apostles' ministry is any indication, once we've done this, then replication will take care of itself. Our duty isn't to hurry up that replication but to carefully prepare for it. If Jesus took three years

188 PART TWO: CORRECTING OUR COURSE

to train his disciples, we should imagine we might need a timeframe of *at least* three years.[25]

Don Dent argues for more "rapid discipleship" today on the basis that "Paul, Silas and Timothy made disciples in the city of Thessalonica for a period that appears to be little more than three weeks."[26] According to this point of view, Paul's hands-off approach shows that Jesus's model of slow, careful discipleship is no longer relevant. Why? Because after Pentecost, "the Spirit is the primary discipler."[27] But rapid discipleship isn't Paul's preferred pattern. For example, he spent three years in Ephesus (Acts 20:31). Dent is right that Paul leaves Thessalonica after three weeks, but he doesn't leave of his own free will; his friends send him away for his own safety after his enemies cause a riot (Acts 17:5–10). Indeed, the pattern of Paul's ministry is that he *does not leave an area in which he is ministering until intense opposition arises*:

- Paul stays in Pisidian Antioch long enough that "the word of the Lord was spreading throughout the whole region" (Acts 13:49), leaving only after the Jewish leaders "stirred up persecution against Paul and Barnabas, and drove them out of their district" (Acts 13:50).
- The next cities Paul visits—Iconium, Lystra, and Derbe—are close enough to each other to form an interconnected community. Thus, Timothy is described as being from "Derbe and . . . Lystra," and he is known by "the brothers at Lystra and Iconium" (Acts 16:1–2). Paul "remained a long time" in Iconium until "an attempt was made . . . to mistreat . . . and to stone" Paul and Barnabas and they "fled to Lystra and Derbe" (Acts 14:5–6), remaining as close as possible in order to continue working with the same

25 Indeed, we should plan on taking a good deal more time than this, since Jesus was probably much better at pastoring his disciples than we will be! Additionally, Jesus's disciples had grown up knowing the Old Testament, and many may have had a deep life of faith with God before meeting Jesus, since they were disciples of John the Baptist before Jesus's ministry began.

26 Don Dent, "Decisive Discipleship: Why Rapid Discipleship Is Preferable and How It Is Possible," *Global Missiology* 1/13 (October 2015): 12.

27 Dent, "Decisive Discipleship," 18.

community. Paul then stays in Lystra until he is stoned and left for dead (Acts 14:19), but—clearly desiring to stay nearby—flees no further than nearby Derbe, returning to Iconium and Lystra soon after (Acts 14:21–22).

- Paul stays in Philippi with Lydia's family until he is beaten and jailed (Acts 16:14–40).
- He stays in Thessalonica until a riot breaks out (Acts 17:5–10).
- He stays in Berea until he is sent away by his friends after "the Jews . . . came there too, agitating and stirring up the crowds" (Acts 17:13).
- He stays in Corinth for a year and a half, leaving only after an enormous riot occurs (Acts 18:11–17).
- He stays in Ephesus for three years until a riot occurs (Acts 19:21–20:1).

Paul's clear pattern, then, is to continue working in an area until he is forced to leave. Even in these cases, he often returns quickly, leaves coworkers behind, writes letters when he is able, and insists that elders not be appointed until they are known to be "above reproach . . . able to give instruction in sound doctrine and also to rebuke those who contradict it" (Titus 1:7, 9).[28]

Simply put, neither Jesus nor Paul seem interested in "rapid discipleship." This is perhaps doubly surprising because they had an additional ministry advantage which enabled them to work more quickly than we will usually be able to: many of their disciples were men who had grown up steeped in an Old Testament worldview and who may have held an Old Testament faith since childhood. Lest we fail to appreciate how fully this might have prepared them to understand the gospel, let's remember that when Paul argues for the gospel in his letters, his arguments are based entirely on the Old Testament. He tells Timothy—

---

28 The letters through which Paul pastors his churches make up much of the New Testament. It is unlikely that we have an exhaustive list of Paul's—or his companions'—visits to his churches. However, from what is recorded, we know he returns at least once to Perga (Acts 14:25), twice to Iconium and Lystra (Acts 14:21–22; 16:1–2), and once to Derbe (Acts 16:1–2). He leaves Silas and Timothy to minister to the Bereans (Acts 17:14). He sends Titus to Corinth (2 Cor. 12:18), returning at least once himself and planning a second return (2 Cor. 13:1). He sends both Timothy (1 Tim. 1:3) and Tychicus to Ephesus (2 Tim. 4:12).

who mostly had only Old Testament Scripture available to him—that the Scriptures were sufficient to make "the man of God . . . complete, equipped for every good work" (2 Tim. 3:17). Men raised in the Old Testament Scriptures already had a wealth of spiritual insight and a profoundly biblical worldview. As such, they would likely need far less shepherding than most unreached people today before they would be mature enough to shepherd the church. Going slowly isn't the point, of course. The point is to "present everyone mature in Christ" (Col. 1:28). But we shouldn't deceive ourselves that it won't take time to get there.

What Is a Mature Church?

When churches reach maturity, our goal and great joy will be to have worked ourselves out of a job. We should, of course, maintain warm ties with the congregations we leave behind. We should even, as is appropriate, be ready to provide help or correction later on if need be, as Paul does in many of his letters. But by and large, these churches will be capable and grown and we can have great confidence in them.

Our goal and great joy will be to have worked ourselves out of a job.

A quick disclaimer may be helpful. When I speak of leaving "churches" behind, I'm not speaking of buildings with steeples and pews, as "churches" are often—quite critically—portrayed in missions literature. John Piper states that "a local church is a group of baptized believers who meet regularly to worship God through Jesus Christ, to be exhorted from the Word of God, and to celebrate the Lord's Supper under the guidance of duly appointed leaders."[29] Such a church can always be set up in culturally appropriate ways. Many will still object to

---

29 John Piper, "The Local Church: Minimum vs. Maximum," accessed April 30, 2019, https://www.desiringgod.org/messages/the-local-church-minimum-vs-maximum.

the term *church* because of the "baggage" it carries. For example, Herbert Hoefer claims the word was coined in England during colonial times and thus is tainted with the baggage of colonialism.[30] I'm not particularly inclined to haggle about terms, but no term is without baggage; and if any are, they will acquire baggage soon enough. A few years ago, it was suggested in the organization in which I work that we should replace the term "church" with the term "movement," which—it was imagined—had less baggage. This was debated until someone pointed out that in many of the countries in which we work, the term "movement" is associated with anti-government political uprisings. So I will trust readers to interpret me charitably. After all, the term *church* can't help having baggage—the church is made of believers who have baggage!

So let's keep the word church. What might a mature church look like? It should have a number of characteristics, which I will list below and then briefly discuss.

1. A mature church should hold to orthodox Christian doctrine and not be easily swayed by false teachings (Eph. 4:14).

2. A mature church should be full of individuals marked by renewed minds and the fruit of the Spirit. It won't be easily led into sin but should consider itself dead to sin and alive to God (Rom. 6:6–11; 12:1–2; Gal. 5:16–25; Col. 3:4–17).

3. A mature church should see the Word of God as its primary authority in all matters of life and teaching. The Scriptures should be held above cultural traditions and all other sources of authority (Matt. 15:1–9; 2 Tim. 3:16–17; Heb. 4:12). Contradictory religious texts should be discarded.

---

30 Herbert Hoefer, "What's in a Name? The Baggage of Terminology in Contemporary Mission: How Do We Deal with the Baggage of the Past?" *International Journal of Frontier Missiology* 25/1 (Spring 2008): 25–29. In fact, the word "church" was used long before the age of colonialism. It is found as far back as the 1300s in John Wycliffe's translation of the Bible.

4. A mature church should practice baptism (Matt. 28:19; Acts 2:41) and the Lord's Supper (1 Cor. 11:23–27) and should gather together regularly for teaching from God's Word, prayer, and worship (Heb. 10:23–25).

5. A mature church should be led by men who are qualified shepherds and teachers. These leaders should be people of character who are "above reproach" (1 Tim. 3:1–13; Titus 1:5–10). They should understand and be able to teach core tenets of the faith from the Scriptures.

6. A mature church will teach its people that identity in Christ should supplant any previous religious identity and should be seen as more fundamental than any familial, political, or cultural identity (1 Cor. 1:10; Gal. 3:26–29; Col. 3:10).

7. A mature church exercises an affectionate care and accountability among members, encouraging love and good deeds while also correcting sin as occasion requires (Heb. 10:24–26). It practices church discipline among members in cases of significant, verifiable, and unrepented sin for purposes of love and redemption (Matt. 18:15–17; 1 Corinthians 5).

8. A mature church should value and welcome persons from all walks of life (Gal. 3:26–29). It shouldn't be demographically homogeneous (e.g., both men and women are present, and there is some degree of diversity across age groups).

9. A mature church should understand itself as distinct from the world and as a member of Christ's larger, worldwide church (John 15:18–21; 2 Cor. 6:14–18). It should relate to outsiders with love and respect.

10. A mature church should be ready to endure hardship and persecution for the sake of Christ (Matt. 10:37–39).

11. A mature church should be committed to evangelizing the lost, discipling young believers, and equipping them for ministry (Eph. 4:11–12).

The conditions above should be generally true of a mature church's leadership—and, to a lesser extent, of the congregation. Of course, no church is perfect, and demanding exhaustive compliance with each of these conditions is unrealistic. Life is messy. Things don't go as planned, and when new churches run into problems, we don't want our lofty ideals to make us ungrateful for the complicated, real-life churches that God raises up. Paul expresses confidence and gratitude for the Corinthian church (see 1 Cor. 1:4) despite the many struggles (see 1 Cor. 5:1–13; 11:27–32; 2 Cor. 11:1–4) that cause it to need his ongoing intervention (see 2 Cor. 13:1–10). Churches take time to grow and mature, and we don't need to despair over their struggles or to hurry them to mature faster than they are able. We simply need to stick with them, if God allows, until they are mature enough to stand on their own.

Among the characteristics of a mature church described above, some involve a clear separation from one's previous religious community:

Contradictory religious texts should be discarded.

The church should understand itself as distinct from the world and as a member of Christ's larger, worldwide church (John 15:18–21; 2 Cor. 6:14–18).

Identity in Christ should supplant any previous religious identity and should be seen as more fundamental than any familial, political, or cultural identity (1 Cor. 1:10; Gal. 3:26–29; Col. 3:10).

These points will be controversial, because communities may take offense as their friends or family members claim a new identity in Jesus that supplants their current identities and allegiances. New believers may even be persecuted or expelled from their wider communities. New believers can often mitigate these consequences if they conduct themselves with wisdom and respect. But not always. The New Testament contains stories of believers being expelled from their communities (John 9:22, 34; Acts 8:1) and even martyred (Acts 7:54–60). Thankfully, the Spirit works even through these tragedies for the expansion of the church (Acts 8:1–4). In some cases, it won't be possible for new believers to simultaneously maintain strong ties with their communities of origin and embrace their new identity in Christ. In these cases, the loss of relationships and social networks isn't a failure. Consider Paul's words to the Corinthians:

> For what partnership has righteousness with lawlessness? Or what fellowship has light with darkness? . . . Or what portion does a believer share with an unbeliever? . . . For we are the temple of the living God. . . .
>
> > Therefore go out from their midst,
> >   and be separate from them, says the Lord . . .
> >   (2 Cor. 6:14–17)

We must embrace God's kingdom above all other previous allegiances. Doing so is part of what it means to put off the old self, as Paul described in Colossians:

> You have put off the old self with its practices and have put on the new self. . . . Here there is not Greek and Jew, circumcised and uncircumcised, barbarian, Scythian, slave, free; but Christ is all, and in all. (Col. 3:9–11)

This has special implications for those of us who work in culturally diverse areas. In missions circles today, there's a great deal of emphasis on working through people's preexisting social networks to establish churches.[31] Indeed, there's some real wisdom in this. We should respect

---

31 David Garrison, *Church Planting Movements: How God Is Redeeming a Lost World* (Bangalore, India: WIGTake Resources, 2007), 165.

all human relationships: new believers don't become less a part of their tribes, families, or social groups simply by virtue of following Jesus. Yet working through preexisting social networks comes with a danger: the church might end up cementing the exclusiveness that's naturally part of the world. In many unengaged areas, fierce tribalism exists between different groups that inhabit the same social contexts. Churches can easily harden along tribal lines, limiting the spread of the gospel.

In my first country of service, a group of new believers from a disadvantaged tribe grew to love Christianity, in part because they saw it as a tribal possession. Their acceptance of Christ doubled as a way for them to reject Arab culture after Arab tribes had attacked them in a brutal ethnic cleansing. Sadly, missionaries *encouraged* this tribal ownership of the gospel because it motivated people to keep attending Bible studies. Forget the fact that it limited the group's potential to open itself to Arabs and other tribes. Forget the fact that, in Jesus, there's neither Arab nor African, neither Jew nor Palestinian, neither rich nor poor, but Christ is all, and in all (see Col. 3:11).

There's a certain amount of sociological wisdom in working through preexisting social networks, but ultimately, we shouldn't let our ministry be limited by what seems—historically or sociologically—to be impossible. In the New Testament church, the gospel spread early and often across ethnic lines. This resulted in enormous complications. The largely Jewish church was soon flooded by Gentiles. It's hard to imagine a starker set of cultural differences. We go as Christ's ambassadors to the nations to bring people from all nations together under the rule of Christ. What seems impossible can and will be accomplished by his authority (Rev. 5:9–10).

Partnering with National Believers

It is worth noting that there are professing Christians in every nation in the world. Why, then, are we still sending foreign missionaries? If it's going to take foreign missionaries as many years as I have described to plant healthy churches, why not focus instead on mobilizing national believers to plant churches among the unreached peoples who already live near them? As we saw in chapter 3, new approaches have increasingly focused on hiring "nonresidential missionaries" as "strategy coordinators" whose goal is not to evangelize or to disciple but rather to catalyze movements among unreached peoples *without ever living among them*.[32,33] These nonresidential approaches were initially designed for "closed" countries that didn't give missionary visas. But now they're widely used and idealized "even in open access countries"[34] where missionaries could easily live among the people they serve. Today's most widely used missions methods—including *Church Planting Movements* (CPM), *Disciple Making Movements* (DMM), and *Training for Trainers* (T4T)—have sprung from nonresidential approaches. While missionaries who practice such methods today do sometimes live among the people they minister to, their work is still profoundly affected by the nonresidential missionary approach's emphasis on missionary noninvolvement. Thus, today's methods emphasize partnering with national believers, especially those who are insiders to the people group being ministered to. Certainly, mobilizing national believers is an attractive strategy. But it isn't always feasible—and where it can be done, it must be done *well*. What might this look like?

Let's begin by looking at the advantages of mobilizing national believers:

- National believers likely have easy access to the peoples we hope to reach. They don't need visas.

32 V. David Garrison, *The Nonresidential Missionary*, vol. 1 of Innovations in Mission (Monrovia, CA: MARC, 1990).

33 "The convergence of various factors within the evangelical Christian community created a ripe environment for the development of the nonresidential missionary (NRM) paradigm," where the NRM was to develop "a unique strategy specifically tailored to a specific people group . . ." (Richard Bruce Carlton, "An Analysis of the Impact of the Non-Residential/ Strategy Coordinator's Role in Southern Baptist Missiology" [DTh diss., University of South Africa, 2006], 24, 35). Because the nonresidential missionary did not live among the people she hoped to reach, she was not to do the work of evangelizing and discipling people herself, but to "merely check that someone does" (David B. Barrett and James W. Reapsome, *Seven Hundred Plans to Evangelize the World: The Rise of a Global Evangelization Movement* [Birmingham, AL: New Hope, 1988], 36). This generally involved working with national partners.

34 John D. Massey, "Wrinkling Time in the Missionary Task: A Theological Review of Church Planting Movements Methodology," *Southwestern Journal of Theology* 55/1 (Fall 2012): 118.

- National believers may already speak the languages of the peoples we hope to reach, or at least related languages. This removes or lessens an enormous hurdle.
- National believers may come from cultures similar to the cultures of those we hope to reach and may have a more intuitive understanding of how to evangelize, disciple, and teach.

I've seen national believers minister across ethnic lines to unreached peoples with incredible effectiveness. I've also seen these endeavors fall flat. Here are a few disadvantages of centering a missions strategy around national believers:

- Though national believers don't need visas, strong ethnic prejudices may exist between national believers and their unreached countrymen. They sometimes face even greater relational obstacles in reaching the unreached than foreign missionaries.
- In many cases, national believers don't speak the languages of the unreached. In many impoverished cultures, where schools are rare and the value of study is less recognized, the discipline required to master new languages as adults may be very difficult for many to acquire.
- The cultural nearness between national believers and the unreached may allow national believers to imagine that they don't really have to accommodate the cultures of those to whom they are ministering. Often, when Christians just south of the Sahel band of Africa send missionaries to their Muslim compatriots in the north, they begin by building southern-style churches. These often feature crosses on top, chairs for attendees, preaching in French rather than Arabic, and southern-style music—even though *all* music is forbidden in Muslim worship. Such churches even allow for sensual dancing as they sing. The result of all this is predictable. Southern Christians in that city begin to attend the church at the missions outpost, while the church's Muslim neighbors refer to it contemptuously as "the church that plays drums."

Whenever entire peoples remain unreached, it's because significant barriers have stood in the way of the gospel. Whether national believers or foreign believers are the first to attempt to reach across those barriers, it's an enormous undertaking—indeed, a *cross-cultural* undertaking. God is pleased to use human means to propel the gospel across these barriers. Whether this happens through the ministry of expatriates or nationals, it's almost certainly going to take a lot of work.

Some national churches are already sending out qualified missionaries on their own. We should absolutely rejoice in this. But when we as foreigners attempt to mobilize or train missionaries from national churches, we must invest enough in the process to be sure that we're doing it well. My word of advice is this: be kind and charitable in your assumptions about national believers, but don't assume that working through them is necessarily going to lessen your workload. A mature and gifted national missionary will almost certainly be more effective than you. But if your help is needed in mobilizing and sending him, it will likely require full-time investment. Let me explain why.

Foreigners hoping to mobilize or partner with national believers face the same pragmatic hurdles they would face in planting churches among the unreached: *they must build relationships across enormous geographical, linguistic, and cultural divides.* When we go ourselves as church planters, we invest years in language and culture acquisition. Then we patiently teach, disciple, and observe leaders before we leave churches to stand on their own with their own indigenous leadership. If we invest this much care in raising up church leaders, should we not take a great deal of care in sending out *church planters*? Cross-cultural missions mobilization and partnering cannot be done well as a side ministry. Sometimes, national partners may need substantial discipleship. In all cases, we must know their language and culture well enough to build close relationships, and in these relationships—over time—we must grow to trust their character and gifting before sending them out. Paul knew that not all missionaries were of high character. That's why he writes to the Philippians that "I hope to send Timothy" because "I have no one like him, who will be genuinely concerned for your welfare. For they all seek their own interests, not those of Jesus Christ" (Phil. 2:19–21). Like Paul, we hope to send missionaries whose character we trust entirely.

Sadly, Western missions efforts often funnel resources, ministry responsibilities, and money to national partners without doing their due diligence.[35] Near where I work, a Muslim-background believer—whom I will call Khamis—receives over $1,000 per month from an American church for his work as an evangelist. This makes him one of the richest men in the region. What his supporting church in America doesn't know is that he avoids other Muslim-background believers, has a reputation as a thief, and rarely, if ever, shares his faith. Though I have no reason to believe that Khamis has sent false reports describing large numbers of converts, many men in this situation do. To repeat the observation of Aubrey Sequeira, noted in chapter 2, "when supporting partners in the West are impressed, that typically means the dollars will rush in. Unfortunately, Western churches seldom—if ever—learn that in many cases, the numbers are inflated, testimonies fabricated, and the 'gospel work' that they've been investing in is a mirage."[36]

Khamis's financial arrangement with the American church is convenient for both parties. He receives an easy income. The church is able to give money—the easiest of gifts—and to feel good about its support for his kingdom work in the Muslim world. But the church doesn't have to dirty its hands by getting involved or even wondering what effect its money actually has on gospel witness in Khamis's community.

---

35 See, for example, David Hunt's report of a *disciple-making movement* in Ethiopia (David F. Hunt, "A Revolution in Church Multiplication in East Africa: Transformational Leaders Develop a Self-Sustainable Model of Rapid Church Multiplication" [DMin diss., Bakke Graduate University, 2009], 129–30). Hunt notes that "it takes years for someone to learn to communicate in the heart language of another people." Thus, he recommends saving time by working with nationals, rather than learning the language to a high level of proficiency. Hunt hopes that despite a missionary's "significant language limitations," ministry may succeed when "the church planter with significant language limitations disciples the insider and the insider takes the message to the people . . ." But, to repeat an earlier note of caution, if a missionary has "significant language limitations," how will he know if he has discipled an "insider" successfully? How will he know whether the insider has understood Christ's message well enough to convey it to others?

36 Aubrey Sequeira, "A Plea for Gospel Sanity in Missions," *9Marks Journal* (December 2015).

While convenient, this arrangement is good for no one. It's an irresponsible and unprofessional approach to missions. We could never imagine, for example, a secular company investing money so unwisely. In the professional world, significant investments are made only after careful research—and afterward, the return on the investment is carefully monitored. It is not without reason that Jesus observed, "For the sons of this world are more shrewd in dealing with their own generation than the sons of light" (Luke 16:8).

Sadly, partnerships like Khamis's are common. National pastors who are good talkers often find multiple Western donors, each of whom—without knowing about the others—may fund the entire cost of the pastor's ministry.

Partnering with national believers is not wrong, but in the case of Khamis it was certainly unwise. Before partnering with Khamis, the church should have learned how patron-client relationships work in Khamis's culture. If it had, it would have structured the financial side of the partnership much differently—or would not have entered into a financial relationship at all. It should have taken time to learn about Khamis's character, which was no secret to the local missionary community. It should have had missionaries on the ground who spoke Khamis's language and could disciple him out of his greed and financial impropriety. Nonresidential missionary service may be necessary in extreme cases (e.g., if a country denies access to foreigners), but cases like Khamis's show why it is rarely ideal. There's too much opportunity for miscommunication, incorrect evaluation of character and/or ministry success, and even abuse. If Khamis's supporting church had partnered with him responsibly—and if he had been willing to stick around for the process; including being discipled through key character issues—he might have become a highly effective missionary.

Conclusion

As ambassadors of Christ committed to communicating his message well, missionaries must take time to make sure that his terms of peace are accepted and implemented. As we saw in chapter 1, doing our job well includes avoiding shortcuts by allocating adequate time, energy, and resources to the task.

In all other major endeavors in life—whether we're running for office, training for a marathon, or studying for a degree—we plan. We set aside time and resources. The sheer audacity of what we're hoping to do as Christ's ambassadors dwarfs any other goals. We want to disciple new believers and raise up new churches. We want to call sinners to live holy and blameless lives. Certainly, it's only through God's blessing that we can succeed! But in ministry, as in other parts of life, God is pleased to work through our patient investment of time and energy. So it isn't enough to simply hope that everything will turn out as we intend. We must make careful plans and set aside adequate time and resources for our task. We must be ready to patiently work until God grants success. The Lord has been so patient with us, and we also must patiently pastor new believers through their slowly changing beliefs, habits, and character. We must stick with them as they grow, teaching thoroughly "with all wisdom, that we may present everyone mature in Christ" (Col. 1:28).

9

Equipping and Sending

IN CHAPTER 8, we examined a broad ministry pathway for missionaries to follow. If that sketch is accurate, then while the amount of time it takes will vary from location to location, it will usually take several years—and maybe a couple of decades—for missionaries to complete their task professionally and well.

Leaving one's country for a few years is difficult. But leaving for a few decades? That takes a different level of resolve. Missionaries need uncommon staying power, especially in our day when wanderlust and the desire for novelty reign and where people switch jobs and locations every few years.

So how can we find and equip missionaries who will endure until mature churches are established? Because the sending process is complex, it may help to give an overview of the themes that we'll cover in this chapter. I will address the following questions:

- How can we help people to discern their "calling"? How can we identify those who are gifted to serve on the mission field?
- When we find gifted people to serve as missionaries, how can we send them well? How can we set them up to succeed? How should they choose between available fields and teams?
- Once missionaries arrive on the field, how can they cultivate the staying power to endure?

"Every arrow needs a bow." Sending churches, missions agencies, and supporters play a vital role in the missionary task. Like all Christians, missionaries depend on the wider church for wisdom and strength. This chapter is intended as much for missionary supporters as for missionaries themselves.

A. Finding Those with Grace to Go

Let's begin with perhaps the most pressing question: how do we find qualified candidates for the mission field in the first place? We must avoid simplistic and easy approaches. We don't just send everyone who is willing. Why? Because not everyone is gifted to go overseas, and no one benefits when we assume otherwise.

A recruitment pamphlet titled "Why YOU should go to the mission field" was deeply influential in encouraging a generation of missionaries to go in the 1980s and 1990s. It states,

> ... He commands you to go ... "Go ye into all the world and preach the Gospel to every creature." (Mark 16:15) That's right ... YOU ARE CALLED!
>
> In fact, if you don't go, you need a specific calling from God to stay home. Has God definitely told you not to "go" somewhere outside your country to preach the Gospel? If he hasn't, then you'd better start praying WHERE to go, instead of IF you should go—for again, you're already called![1]

Ideas like these are still around today. The pamphlet goes on to list "excuses" people give. It accuses those who don't go of halfheartedness and ever-so-subtly doubts their salvation: "You need to decide whether or not you are a disciple of Jesus—that is the question." But that's not the only question, nor—in context of the pamphlet—does it seem much like a question. It's an accusation, and the important questions are sidestepped.

---

[1] Keith Green, *Why YOU Should Go to the Mission Field* (Lindale, TX: Last Days Ministry, 1982).

We all have different gifts, and that's how the Spirit wanted it. As Paul writes, "Having gifts that differ according to the grace given to us, let us use them" (Rom. 12:6ff.). One implication of this: some people are well-suited for missions work, and some people are not. As in all other professions, that's okay. Paul again: "The eye cannot say to the hand, 'I have no need of you,' nor again the head to the feet, 'I have no need of you'" (1 Cor. 12:21).

We should steer people to serve God in ways that use their gifts for at least two reasons: because the people doing ministry matter, and because the people they are ministering to matter. Going to the mission field means upending one's life. Burnout and attrition are high, especially when we're talking about decades and not years. Because missionaries invest so deeply in their work, those who leave the field often struggle with a severe sense of loss. They're often weighed down by regret. And aside from personal losses, the importance of the ministry itself should motivate us to send the right people. Consider this plea from Indian pastor Harshit Singh:

Please don't send bad workers. If a person cannot be an elder in your church, then don't send them. . . . We don't want mavericks. We don't want entrepreneurs. We don't want go-getters. We don't want people who can make things happen. We want people who have love for the local church back [home] first, who have proved to be faithful teachers.[2]

Can you hear the frustration in Singh's voice? I can. It's likely born out of painful experiences with immature missionaries. That's why we need to find those who have the grace to go—and pass over those who don't.

But how? In chapter 1, I said that professionalism includes a "wise evaluation of practical circumstances as we make decisions." Here, we encounter a problem. Most Christians want to be wise and practical. At

2 Harshit Singh, "How Western Methods Have Affected Missions in India," 9Marks' First Five Years Conference, Columbus, OH, August 4, 2017. Accessed May 3, 2019, https://www.9marks.org/message/how-western-methods-have-affected-missions-in-india.

the same time, many Christians also feel that for major life and ministry decisions, God will guide them primarily through subjective, mystical impressions. They may even wonder whether thinking carefully through decisions could be unspiritual. Let me share a story as an illustration.

Mystical Callings and Practical Wisdom

Years ago, I watched as a missions team pondered whether they should split up and send a second team to a new area. As they discussed possible locations, weighing the pros and cons, a woman I'll call "Hannah" stood up and said, "I think we are depending too much on human reasoning. Why don't we pull out a map and pray over it and see which part of the map we feel led to?" What still surprises me today is that her suggestion seemed so profoundly right to everyone in the room. No one questioned it. It wasn't until later that the meaning of what she said struck me.

Did you catch what Hannah's suggestion assumes? That reasoning is "human" and must therefore be essentially different than being "led" by God.

One major theme of this book is that God doesn't despise so-called "human" ways of doing things. He created us to be human and works through us in our humanity. Might he also work in our human reasoning? Might he even use it to guide us? Paul indicates that we should relate to God, at least in part, through our reasoning: "I will pray with my spirit; but I will pray with my mind also" (1 Cor. 14:15). What astounded me is that Hannah's suggestion—which sounded so scriptural and right—essentially put reason aside and asked the Holy Spirit to "draw us" to a place on a map. It recalls the way neo-pagans put reason aside and ask the spirits to draw them to a letter on a Ouija board! Of course, she was counseling us to call on the true God, not pagan spirits. That's an important difference. All the same, we should hold reason in higher esteem. After all, an entire book of the Bible is dedicated to training us in recognizing it.

But as Hannah's comment suggests, pragmatic decision making—especially when it concerns "spiritual" decisions, such as choosing a ministry path—has gone out of style. To address this, I'd like to respond first by examining how God speaks to us, and then by considering how this ought to affect our approach to missions work, especially as we discern whether or not we're gifted to go to the mission field.

The Still Small Voice

Many evangelical traditions today teach that when God speaks, his voice is often dim and unclear. We're told "nudgings" from the Holy Spirit[3] will come into our minds in much the way that our own thoughts or imaginations do. We're told it may be very difficult to distinguish between God's voice and our own emotions, intuitions, and imaginations. We're told that in order to hear God's voice at all, we have to practice "listening prayer" by lowering "the ambient noise of [our] life" and sitting quietly until we hear his "still, small voice."[4,5,6] As one author puts it, "God's radio station is always on. . . . 24 hours a day, seven days a week. The trouble is, we are not dialing it in. Our radios aren't working."[7]

What do we do with this? Should we consider our emotions and intuitions as just one part of a wise decision-making process? Or should we expect that they may be God's own voice—provided that we tune in to the exact right spiritual radio channel and can differentiate his voice from the static?

The Scriptures paint a different picture. We never once see someone struggling to differentiate God's voice from their own emotions or intuitions when he offers direct guidance. Nor do people ever set aside times of "listening prayer," as we're encouraged to do today. When God

3   Jerry Trousdale and Glenn Sunshine, *The Kingdom Unleashed* (Murfreesboro, TN: DMM Library, 2015), ch. 18.
4   Seth Barnes, *The Art of Listening Prayer: Finding God's Voice amidst Life's Noise* (New York: Praxis, 2004), 19.
5   Bill Hybels, *Simplify: Ten Practices to Unclutter Your Soul* (Carol Stream, IL: Tyndale, 2014), 235.
6   Barnes, *Art of Listening Prayer*, 22.
7   Brad Jersak, *Can You Hear Me? Tuning In to the God Who Speaks* (Abbottsford, BC: Fresh Wind, 2012).

speaks, it's usually unexpected, it's always clear that he is *speaking*, and it's always clear what he is saying. Even Elijah's "still small voice" was audible (1 Kings 19:11–13, KJV). And while the Spirit does speak to us, Scripture never records indistinct "nudgings" in which the Spirit tells us—through vague, inward impressions—what to say or do. Instead, Scripture speaks of the Spirit guiding us "into all the truth" (John 16:13) in our beliefs about God. The Spirit speaks primarily to "bring to your remembrance all that [Jesus has] said to you" (John 14:26), not to guide us in our ministry decisions. When the Spirit does give direct ministry guidance—for example, when he sends Philip down the Gaza road—he doesn't do so through indistinct "nudgings" or vague impressions. The actual words the Spirit spoke to Philip are recorded (Acts 8:26, 29). I agree with M. B. Smith, who wrote, "No example can be found anywhere in Scripture . . . where someone regarded an inner impression as the *direct* voice of God, an *infallible* sign from God or the sole indication of His will."[8]

If God wants to command us to make specific choices in our lives—and if the choices he wants us to make are not already clear from Scripture—he has the means to be extremely clear about it. God is not like "the mediums and the necromancers who chirp and mutter" (Isa. 8:19).

If God wants to command us to make specific choices in our lives—and if the choices he wants us to make are not already clear from Scripture—he has the means to be extremely clear about it. God is not like "the mediums and the necromancers who chirp and mutter" (Isa. 8:19).

But when we don't hear God's clear voice, we should remember that most decisions made in Scripture are made without direct, specific

8   M. Blaine Smith, *The Yes Anxiety: Taming the Fear of Commitment in Relationships, Career, Spiritual Life, Daily Decisions* (Damascus, MD: SilverCrest, 2011), ch. 8, emphasis original.

input from God. Is God still guiding us in these situations? Yes, but he's doing it *indirectly* through how he shapes circumstances in the world around us and thoughts and desires within us. He intends us to evaluate those factors and make wise decisions: "The wisdom of the wise is to discern his way" (Prov. 14:8). Because God hasn't actually "spoken," we may not be entirely certain what he wants, in the same way that we can't be entirely certain of what other people intend simply by observing their actions. But we can use the best wisdom we have to discern what seems likely to serve his purposes, and God will provide added clarity if he thinks we need it.

We see Paul make decisions like this throughout the book of Acts. He takes Timothy on board as a ministry partner, in part because it's wise to choose coworkers who have good reputations (Acts 16:1–2). When Paul is stoned in Lystra, he decides—quite wisely!—to leave. He wisely leaves Philippi after a riot starts and he is beaten. When he's well received in Ephesus, he stays for three years—until problems arise. Scripture gives us no reason to believe Paul heard an audible voice telling him what to do when he made these decisions. Instead, he demonstrates the same pragmatism that Jesus taught to his apostles years earlier: "When they persecute you in one town, flee to the next, for truly, I say to you, you will not have gone through all the towns of Israel before the Son of Man comes" (Matt. 10:23).

I feel the need to clarify: I'm *not* saying that wise decision making ignores feelings entirely. Paul counsels those who feel a strong desire to marry that they should marry (1 Cor. 7:7–9). He takes Timothy on as part of his missions team, in part because he "wanted Timothy to accompany him" (Acts 16:2–3). He tells the Corinthians, "Each one must give as he has decided in his heart, not reluctantly or under compulsion, for God loves a cheerful giver" (2 Cor. 9:7). God created us with desires, and the fact that a certain decision "feels right" is generally one argument in favor of making that decision, especially if what we want to do is good or charitable (Ps. 37:4).

But of course that's not the whole story. Sometimes, decisions that "feel right" can be foolish or even sinful. And even when they're not, practical considerations often stop us from doing what we want. Paul leaves many cities he wants to minister in when it becomes practically impossible to stay there due to the crowds' hostility. Put simply, what we feel about a decision is only one facet of decision making, and we must weigh all facets wisely.

This can be a difficult process. We must wrestle through ministry decisions—even the most significant decisions, such as whether to go to the mission field—using good, old-fashioned common sense. Maybe no option feels completely right, and we simply have to choose whichever seems best. The lack of certainty can be disorienting, but we need not worry. Even when God doesn't tell us exactly what to do, he continues to guide us like a shepherd. Most of the time, sheep aren't aware when their shepherd guides them. From their point of view, things just happen. They *can't* keep walking toward the cliff because there's a fence. But they don't realize that the shepherd put the fence there and used it to guide them away from terrible danger. In the same way, God protects us from taking dangerous paths even when we're not aware. So though we may not always have "peace" about which decision is best, we can always be at peace that God is watching over us and will get us where he wants us to go:

> The lot is cast into the lap,
> but its every decision is from the LORD. (Prov. 16:33)

The "Calling" Experience

We've laid some groundwork for how we can honor God as we make decisions. Now let's specifically explore how this relates to the missionary "calling." Many people imagine that if God wants them to go as a missionary, he will confirm it through either a strong, mystical sense of calling or an emotional experience. For example, he might give them a deep sense of peace about going overseas as they pray. Similarly, the absence of such an experience may mean that God has not in fact called them. But in other parts of life, we understand that emotions and intuitions are only one facet of our decision making. They're not the voice of God. So if a young couple tells their pastor that they're in love and feel "called" to marry each other, the pastor will rightly see their enthusiasm as an encouraging sign. Nevertheless, he'll ask hard questions in premarital counseling to make sure they're ready for the changes and practicalities of marriage. He will want to know that their sense of "calling" isn't simply infatuation but reflects a deeper commitment in which both parties understand what they're committing to and—after serious introspection—joyfully accept.

It is an encouraging sign when someone expresses a desire to serve in missions. But missionary candidates' sense of calling should be evaluated more deeply. Most major missions organizations make some effort to slow down unqualified candidates. But even then, the primary focus is on weeding out those most likely to experience emotional or spiritual collapse—not on finding and refining those most gifted for life on the field. Beyond basic assessments of psychological and spiritual stability, a personal sense of "calling" is usually sufficient to get to the field. Multiple stories come to mind:

- When I met Mark's family, they were struggling heavily with their transition from the United States to a large African city. Nevertheless, they felt called to move out into a war-torn area deep in the bush. This put enormous stress on their family and caused conflict between them and their ministry team. They returned a few years later to their country of origin.
- Jennifer was a single woman in her early thirties. She had a strong desire to be married, but she didn't feel she could keep "waiting forever for Mr. Right." Instead, she followed her sense of calling to a remote mission field that had no single men. Jennifer struggled with loneliness and depression for years on the field before eventually returning home.
- Brian felt called to serve in North Korea, even though he was told that it was nearly impossible for American citizens to get visas. He spent four years in South Korea learning Korean before realizing that his dream of getting into North Korea was impossible. He returned home discouraged.

What might be a better way for us to make decisions?

Sober Judgment

The Scriptures don't teach us to rely entirely on a subjective sense of calling to determine our ministry direction. Instead, we're told to use sober judgment to determine where we can best serve the church. Paul writes to the Romans,

> I say to everyone among you not to think of himself more highly than he ought to think, but to think with *sober judgment*. . . . In one body we have many members, and the members do not all have the same function. . . . Having gifts that differ according to the grace given to us, let us use them. (Rom. 12:3–6)

As is his pattern, Paul uses the term *grace given* to describe what we usually call "spiritual gifts."[9] God's grace not only saves us from our sin; it also empowers each of us to serve others in different ways. Paul wants us to soberly assess how God's grace enables us to serve, so he gives pointers as to how we might assess our giftedness, and they seem to describe a remarkably commonsense decision-making process.

First, in Paul's view, the gifts aren't given for our personal benefit, nor are they given to make us feel significant. They're given so that we can serve the whole church. The use of tongues, for example, is ineffective for those hearing "unless someone interprets, so that the church may be built up" (1 Cor. 14:5). Similarly, Paul writes that

> Grace was given to each one of us according to the measure of Christ's gift. . . . [God] gave the apostles, the prophets, the evangelists, the shepherds and teachers, to equip the saints for the work of ministry, for building up the body of Christ. (Eph. 4:7, 11–12)

---

9   For example, Paul describes the gifts as grace given to us in Rom. 12:6–8; 15:15–16; 1 Cor. 3:10; Eph. 3:1–2, 7–8; 4:7–11.

Notice that in this passage, Paul doesn't say that *the gifts* of apostleship, prophecy, evangelism, shepherding, and teaching are given to us. Rather, the gifts are *people*: apostles, prophets, evangelists, shepherds, and teachers. They're given to the larger body so that they may expend themselves in its service.[10] So the common question "What am I passionate about?" has a limited role in determining our calling. Absolutely, willingness to serve is often a part of the grace God gives us (Rom. 12:3–5; 2 Cor. 8:1–2). But this willingness is focused on what will benefit the church, not on how we might fulfill our own dreams or passions. "What am I passionate about?" is a fine question to ask, but its value is limited. "How can I best serve the church?" is better. This may involve doing things we don't feel particularly called to and aren't very excited about or even very good at. But we do them simply because they must be done. Serving "the least of these" (Matt. 25:40, 45) is rarely exciting, but all believers are called to do it. We must keep this in mind as we seek to discern how God has gifted us. Like soldiers in a war effort, we serve a cause greater than ourselves, and we must be willing to lay down our personal preferences and goals in order to serve the larger call of Christ.[11]

Second, according to Paul, God has given us the grace to do things we actually have the ability to do. He writes, "According to the grace of God given to me, like a skilled master builder I laid a foundation" (1 Cor. 3:10). This skill to build well was a fundamental part of the grace given to Paul. Where we lack the ability to minister skillfully, to use Paul's word, we can generally assume that God has not given us grace to minister in that particular area. As we saw in chapter 6, when Henry

10 In fact, the Psalm that Paul quotes in this passage ("When he ascended on high he led a host of captives and gave gifts to men" [Ps. 68:18]) speaks of God returning victorious in battle and giving conquered slaves to his people. These slaves, in Paul's mind, are the "apostles, the prophets, the evangelists, the shepherds and teachers . . ." who serve the church.

11 A particularly vivid example of how this might happen occasionally occurs in missionaries' marriages. If the husband feels called to one field and the wife feels called to another, one (or both) of the two must lay down their individual sense of "calling" to pursue Christ's larger calling to them to live in harmony together.

214 PART TWO: CORRECTING OUR COURSE

Guinness applied to China Inland Mission, Hudson Taylor reluctantly turned him down, explaining that with a wife and three children, there was "little likelihood of his being able to learn the language sufficiently well as to be as useful in China as he was at home."[12] Notice the pragmatic nature of Taylor's decision: if Guinness couldn't learn Chinese, then he hadn't been given grace to go to China. On the other hand, if you have the opportunity and ability to minister well overseas, you might be gifted to go.

Third, God has only given us grace to do things that we have the spiritual and emotional capacity to do joyfully. Paul writes, "Having gifts that differ according to the grace given to us, let us use them." But then he keeps going: "The one who contributes, in generosity . . . the one who does acts of mercy, with cheerfulness" (Rom. 12:6, 8). Serving God will be painful at times, but where he has gifted us to serve him, there will be ways to rejoice even in the difficulty. For example, Paul concludes that it's because of "the grace of God that has been given" to the Macedonians that "in a severe test of affliction, their abundance of joy and their extreme poverty have overflowed in a wealth of generosity on their part" (2 Cor. 8:1–2). God may lead us, like the Macedonians, to give of ourselves in ways that involve suffering. But when he does, he will give us the grace to rejoice in our suffering. Does that mean that if you can't imagine yourself being joyfully able to endure the mission field, you shouldn't go? Well, not exactly. You may just be at the start of the process. As you grow to learn more about the mission field—to the point that moving overseas doesn't just seem terrifying—and as God grows his love for the lost world in you, you may feel a growing joy and desire when you think about going overseas. You may start to suspect that you would be willing to endure the hardships involved. If so, God may be giving you the grace to go.

Importantly, this grace to endure suffering well isn't given to us for all types of suffering. For example, with regard to the question of

---

12 Alvyn Austin, *China's Millions: The China Inland Mission and Late Qing Society, 1832–1905* (Grand Rapids, MI: Eerdmans, 2007), 96.

whether or not we should marry, Paul writes, "Each has his own gift from God. . . . To the unmarried and the widows, I say that it is good for them to remain single, as I am. But if they cannot exercise self-control, they should marry. For it is better to marry than to burn with passion" (1 Cor. 7:7–9). For the ungifted single, loneliness and desire for marriage cause enough distraction that he's significantly challenged in his ability to "[look] to Jesus" and the joy set before him (Heb. 12:1–2). This may even lead him into sin. So Paul concludes that if singleness causes us to "burn" with desire or loneliness, then we're not gifted as singles and should try to marry. Pretending otherwise will only lead us into danger.

Similarly, if you lack the emotional, physical, or spiritual stamina necessary for life on the mission field, then you haven't yet been given grace to be a missionary. Pretending otherwise is dangerous. It doesn't help anyone when a missionary collapses on the field. I've seen this happen, and I can tell you that it only makes other missionaries' jobs more difficult. They must now help a floundering teammate in addition to pursuing their own ministry responsibilities. It's better for everyone if we honor the limits God has placed on us. If God hasn't given you grace to go to the field, there will be other places where you can serve him.

Accurate Expectations

In order to assess our giftedness for missions, we need to have a realistic idea of what we're signing up for. That's why I've emphasized the long-term nature of the work. Missionaries who imagine that little will be required of them are going to feel like they've been tricked. They can hardly be blamed if they later reconsider their choice.

Short-term and medium-term mission trips can help young people learn enough about the field to know whether they have the grace to serve overseas as long-termers. As you can probably guess, I don't think short-term missionaries are going to play a key role in helping us disciple the nations. More than once, Adoniram Judson complained of missionaries who came to the field committing for "only" a few years, that

216 PART TWO: CORRECTING OUR COURSE

As usual, they could not be of much real use until they became fluent in the language; and that would be a matter of years.[13]

I have seen the beginning, middle, and end of several limited term missionaries. They are all good for nothing. . . . If the limited term system . . . gains the ascendancy, it will be a death blow to missions, and retard the conversion of the world a hundred years.[14]

Certainly, short-term mission trips will never be a replacement for long-term missionaries. But perhaps we don't need to be as despairing of their usefulness as Judson was. Short-termers—when they bring needed skills or man-power—can help long-term missionaries. More importantly, short-term trips can be an essential ingredient in helping people decide whether or not to serve long-term. I'm on the mission field today, in part, because of a six-month trip I took years ago. Tucker McPherson writes,

These short-term trips really are contemporary versions of an ancient Christian practice called pilgrimage. . . . A pilgrim goes on a journey to meet God in a faraway place, hoping to return a different person from the one who left. . . . Pilgrims had no illusions that they were going to "change the world" by their pilgrimage, but they surely did hope that being exposed to the world . . . would change them. They were much more than tourists who travel simply for the fun of it. . . . Pilgrims travel for transformation. And that's a very good thing.[15]

This perspective is both generous and helpful. Few people find themselves ready to commit to the mission field without experiencing

13 Courtney Anderson, *To the Golden Shore: The Life of Adoniram Judson* (King of Prussia, PA: Judson Press, 1987), 409.

14 Judson, quoted in Francis Wayland, *A Memoir of the Life and Labors of the Rev. Adoniram Judson* (Boston, MA: Phillips, Sampson, 1853), 62.

15 Tucker McPherson, "Go as a Pilgrim, Not a Hero," in *Go, but Go Wisely: Finding Your Way as You Go on Mission*, ed. Matt Brown (Colorado Springs: Global Mapping International, 2015), ch. 3.

it, just as few people find themselves ready to get married after only a few dates. As in other careers, a little exposure to life on the field may help the pilgrim to assess whether she's gifted to serve as a long-term missionary. If she finds that she is, her short-term trip may ultimately have a profound long-term impact in missions.

Factors to Consider

Let me be more concrete. Consider these indicators that might direct your decision:

- Missionaries should expect that their physical health will allow them to stay overseas.
- Missionaries who are married should have strong marriages, and their children should be doing well. Both spouses should be strongly committed to going overseas. If one spouse is considerably more committed to the mission field than the other, problems lie ahead.
- Singles who desire to be married should avoid mission field placements where their options for marriage partners are severely limited.
- People who struggle with depression or severe emotional downturns should seek counsel before going to the field.
- Missionaries should have the capacity to learn a new language. If they don't, either due to simple inability or life circumstances, then they should only consider roles that aren't directly tied to teaching or sharing the Word.
- Missionaries who hope to play a teaching or pastoring role must know the Scriptures well. Those with a limited knowledge of Scripture should pursue training before going to the field if they hope to disciple or teach.
- Missionaries should be able to hold a job in their home countries. Some actual work experience is usually the best way to determine this.
- People who struggle with besetting sins or addictions should have them under control to the degree that neither they—nor those

who know them well—envision their struggles undermining the health of their families or ministries.

- Missionaries should have strong relationships with their church at home, and their church leaders should recommend them for missionary service.

Keeping factors like these in mind, we can soberly evaluate how our gifts coincide with various kingdom opportunities. Of course, we must pray for wisdom. But we also must eventually decide, trusting that if we've overlooked something, God will redirect us.

What if you don't meet many of the recommendations above? Does that mean you're a less-than Christian? A defective believer? No. It just means you probably shouldn't go into mission work—at least not yet, even if you feel a strong calling. The reverse is also true. If by God's grace, you do meet many of the recommendations above, then I'd encourage you to prayerfully consider a ministry in missions—even if you don't presently feel called.

There's a sense in which I've focused heavily on all these practical concerns in order to deter people from the field. But there's another side of the coin. Missionaries don't need to be superhuman. They don't need to be flawless. They just need to know the Scriptures well enough to teach others. They need to be culturally flexible and moderately healthy. They need to have strong families or to be stable in their singleness. Not every missionary has experienced a specific and clear "calling." You might miss an incredible opportunity if this stops you from considering the mission field. A lifetime of rich, indescribable blessing could lie ahead, and the Lord may use you to bring many people to himself!

Family Resiliency

Earlier, I suggested that missionaries should have healthy families. It's worth exploring this further.

Missionary families must be strong families. Now I want to be clear: "strong" doesn't mean perfect. It doesn't mean without stress or sadness or difficulty. It *does* mean that unusually weighty tensions, sin patterns, and addictions should be overcome before a family goes to the mission field.

Overseas ministry involves a great deal of sacrifice. If both partners aren't on board when sacrifice and suffering comes, the ministry simply won't endure. A husband who pushes a wife—or a wife who pushes a husband—to serve in ways that he or she isn't ready for risks failure on the field and damage to the marriage. Common difficulties include:

- Less family time together.
- Increased irritability due to the stress of overseas living.
- Less privacy, and fewer places to go on dates or spend time alone.
- Distance from friends, family, and church structures that provided stability back home.
- A sense of inferiority or competition if one spouse is more adept than the other in ministry or in the language and culture.
- Children struggling to find a sense of home amid constant change.
- Lack of stability in children's extended social circles, as other families come on and off the field and children are far from their cousins, aunts, uncles, and grandparents.
- Children being gawked at, laughed at, and prodded for reasons they don't understand.
- Children witnessing disturbing acts of violence.
- Children or family members being victims of violence.[16]

---

16 When I list violence against children and family members as a risk, I am simply acknowledging that many of the countries to which missionaries go are not as safe as their home countries. While we cannot avoid this, we should only bring children to mission fields where we have some reasonable expectation of providing for their basic physical safety. Though we must not love our children more than we love God, God himself says of child sacrifice that "I did not command or decree [it], nor did it come into my mind" (Jer. 19:5). This means some mission fields may be too violent for families with children. Singles—or couples without children—can serve on these fields instead. Tragedy results when we emphasize "the saving of souls at the expense of children" (*Amended Final Report for the Investigatory Review of Child Abuse at New Tribes Fanda Missionary School* [Lynchburg, VA: Godly Response to Abuse in a Christian Environment, 2010], 2). Indeed, such emphases have resulted in scandals that threatened to undermine the "saving of souls," and did great damage to children, whom Jesus loves.

- Children being sexually harassed or witnessing sexual situations.[17]
- Doubts surfacing about whether God wants the family to stay on the field, as they experience difficulties while seeing little or no fruit for years on end.

Of course, missionary families may avoid many of the difficulties mentioned above, and even if we stay at home, there's no guarantee that such things won't happen. Thankfully, God promises to work all things—even terrible things—together for good in the lives of his children (Rom. 8:28). But that doesn't mean we can take these sufferings lightly. A family shouldn't put itself in the way of such suffering if both parents aren't in agreement on accepting the risk.

If ministry is truly a priority for the whole family—if it is one of the things the family is fundamentally "about"—then family members can appreciate each other's sacrifice and commitment to ministry even when it affects them in ways that are hard. Spouses, in particular, must learn to have emotionally resilient marriages. They must be able to retain trust and positivity toward each other even during spells when they must spend time apart and are unable to communicate about growing irritations.

Of course, married missionaries must not love ministry more than their spouses or children. In a strange paradox, the success of our ministries may depend on loving our families first. Why? Because if a neglected spouse or child goes off the rails, you *will* end up back home—probably sooner than you think! What's more, healthy families validate our message. This is true no matter the culture. That's why we must love our families enough to be willing to joyfully leave our ministry forever if our spouse or children need us to.

But strong families will also recognize the unique call of Christ on each other's lives. They'll encourage each other to pursue ministry

17   As in the previous footnote, I am simply acknowledging that in some fields, the sexual harassment of our children is more likely than it would be at home. I am *not* suggesting that we should resign ourselves to letting our children be attacked in sexual ways. We should only bring children to mission fields where there is some reasonable expectation that we can provide for their basic physical safety. Fields where this is not the case are more appropriate for families without children, or for singles.

even if it means having fewer opportunities to be together. Such families don't lack love and support. Rather, because they share a united motivation and focus, each is able to admire and appreciate the other as they pursue a common goal.

This means the decision to serve cross-culturally isn't merely the parents' calling, inflicted on the children. It's a calling the parents have discerned, *and* one the children are *privileged to participate in*, even as they recognize the difficulties. Parents who don't fully believe this will constantly try to make up to their children for the difficulty of cross-cultural life, and the children—realizing that their parents feel guilty—may feel hard done by. But children whose parents believe in the nobility of their calling—that it's a privilege despite the suffering—have a way to believe that their sufferings are worthwhile.

Preparing Singles

It's important to address singles as well. Singles can experience intense loneliness on the field. Generally speaking, single women outnumber single men heavily enough that they face significant additional hurdles in finding a spouse. Thus, singles—and especially single women—must be encouraged to honestly come to terms with the risks that they take when they go overseas. Of course, staying home offers no guarantee of finding an acceptable spouse either. But will they be able to accept a lifetime of singleness if they never marry because of their decision to go to the field?

Let's be clear what's at stake here. This isn't simply an issue of personal comfort. Paul advises us that singleness is a gifting given to some, but not to others. For many, the experience of singleness is more than a hardship; it can lead to despair and brings increased temptation to sin:

> . . . each has his own gift from God, one of one kind and one of another.
>
> To the unmarried and the widows I say that it is good for them to remain single, as I am. But if they cannot exercise self-control, they should marry. For it is better to marry than to burn with passion. (1 Cor. 7:7–9)

Despite this advice, singles are often led to believe that hesitating to go to the mission field until they marry might be unspiritual:

> God does not want you to look for a husband or wife, he wants you to be married to **Him**, and trust Him for any mate he may bring into your life. I know of many single Christians serving Jesus overseas who are trusting Him for everything. And some of the most beautiful stories of God's grace I've ever heard are told by couples who went to the mission field single, and then God led them to marry another whose heart was also fully devoted to serving Him there. Remember, *"Your Father knows what you need before you ask Him."* *(Matt. 6:8)* Trust Him![18]

This advice seems pious and self-sacrificial, but ultimately it is self-defeating. It contradicts Scripture's clear advice that those who aren't gifted as singles should do what they can to marry. Because many single missionary candidates are young and may not fully understand the implications of their decision, sending churches and mission boards should probe more deeply when singles aim for fields in which marital choices are sparse. In some cases, these choices may be well thought out. However, we must make sure singles know that choosing to "find more satisfaction in Jesus" isn't always wise. Indeed, part of finding satisfaction in Jesus is accepting the limitations he places on us. Singles must come to terms with the fact that even before the fall, there were types of loneliness that God didn't intend to fulfill for Adam. If we don't encourage singles to evaluate how this loneliness will affect their spiritual lives, they may go to the field embracing their singleness in ways that are *unspiritual* and unwise. Singles who do so may be applauded by their churches for their courage and commitment, but many will come off the field in their early- or mid-thirties. This trend could be largely avoided if singles knew they would have the full support of their churches—and wouldn't be seen as halfhearted or deficient

---

18   Green, *Why YOU Should Go to the Mission Field* (emphasis original).

Christians—if they delayed going to the field until marriage, or sought placements that gave them a better chance of meeting other singles, or even if they chose a different direction altogether.

Those who are gifted to serve as singles overseas can have powerful ministries and joyful lives. In fact, part of the reason Paul hopes those who are gifted as singles won't marry is that he thinks married people will have harder lives (1 Cor. 7:28). Importantly, a single person's experience of singleness can change. Many singles who struggle with their position can grow in their ability to joyfully sustain a single lifestyle. This may involve training themselves through various disciplines. In the same way, people who are naturally gifted runners still need to train before they can run marathons, and naturally gifted musicians still need to practice an instrument before they can master it.

B. Sending Well

After we've identified missionary candidates, how do we send them well? How do we set them up to succeed? Just as sober judgment helps us to choose missionaries wisely, so it can help us to launch them well.

Choosing a Field Placement

Missionary candidates tend to choose *where* they serve in the same way they choose *why* they serve, leaning heavily on feelings of calling. As discussed earlier, a desire to go to a particular area is a good sign, but it shouldn't outweigh practical concerns unless there's a definitive reason.

Usually, missionary candidates' sense of calling comes through emotional experiences. People feel called to places they've visited. They also tend to want to go to places they've heard about on the news, especially when news coverage has been particularly dark. As I've done recruiting talks throughout the years, I've noticed that missionary candidates often feel a strong calling to "closed" countries and countries that are regularly throttled by war, persecution of Christians, genocide, or terrorism.

But if we let our feelings guide our decisions about where we go, how will we reach those who are hard to visit and receive little media coverage? The country I currently work in rarely hits the news, and few people feel called here because few people know it exists! While the compassion that draws us to the darkest parts of the world may seem admirable, it might not always be very helpful. Jesus offers more pragmatic ministry advice to his apostles:

> When they persecute you in one town, flee to the next, for truly, I say to you, you will not have gone through all the towns of Israel before the Son of Man comes. (Matt. 10:23)

As we have seen, Paul follows this exact pattern on several occasions, fleeing when violence erupts (Acts 14:19–20; 16:39–40; 17:9–10; 20:1). We can only minister where it's *possible* to minister.

I remember recruiting missionaries to work in a nation that grants missionary visas to Christians so that they can work with large, unengaged Muslim people groups. These candidates didn't want to work in this country precisely *because* it was legal to do so; they didn't feel these particular people groups were "hostile enough" to merit their attention!

I'm not advocating that we simply turn away from mission fields that are hard to access. But I was expelled from my first country of service, so I'm well aware that such obstacles can stop us from accomplishing what we hope. The lack of apparent obstacles should be an argument *in favor* of serving there. Why do we have trouble seeing this, despite Jesus's own instructions? I wonder if our own desires to feel significant might be driving our decisions more than they should.

A Compatible Team

In any ministry or profession, we should carefully consider our potential coworkers. A team must share a common vision in order to work well together. They need to agree on foundational issues of ministry approach, and where they disagree, they need to know how to work through their differences. Because missionaries depend on each other so heavily—for fellowship, for logistical support, for help—conflicting ideas *will* boil over. Simply ignoring them isn't an option—at least not for long.

Teams with fundamental differences on theology or ministry won't hold together. Paul and Barnabas provide an example of how differences in ideas can split teams. Paul thought John Mark was too unreliable because he had deserted them. Barnabas believed John Mark deserved a second chance. Luke doesn't tell us whether Paul or Barnabas was right. But we know that "there arose a sharp disagreement, so that they separated from each other. Barnabas took Mark with him and sailed away to Cyprus, but Paul chose Silas and departed" (Acts 15:39–40).

And thus ended Christianity's first missionary team! Splitting up isn't necessarily sinful—sometimes, it's the best way to handle irresolvable disagreements. But it never occurs without loss. In order to avoid such splits, missionaries should consider the following issues when choosing missions teams:

- How are decisions made? Who (if anyone) has final say?
- How will the team handle conflict?
- On multicultural teams, are significant cultural differences present within the team? How will they be handled?
- What's the team's philosophy of ministry?
- What theological issues are important to the team? What position does the team take on theological issues that are important to the missionary candidate?
- Who wields authority—and how? If the team has leaders, how far-reaching is their authority? Does their authority stretch into areas that are not their business?

A missionary who desires to take a professional approach to ministry—like the one I've described—must find a ministry team that supports him. It will be hard for him to devote himself to language and culture acquisition if the team leaders expect him to be heavily involved in business or humanitarian projects. Similarly, it won't be useful for him to disciple new believers to maturity before appointing them as elders if teammates want to overrule him and appoint them earlier.

As in any career or ministry, a good team is worth sacrificing for. In my first country of service, nearly every man sent by my organization had been appointed as a team leader, and each felt "called" to a different city. In practice, this meant that most team leaders were on a trajectory to serve without any team members. And because each one felt called to lead rather than follow, we couldn't work together. All this was well-intentioned, but it doesn't reflect a serious, professional approach to the task. Professionals do what they must to get the job done. They're willing to sacrifice personal position and projects to pursue corporate goals. Similarly, our *corporate calling* as Christians—to live together in love—and the church's *corporate calling* to evangelize the nations should outweigh our personal dreams of leadership or serving in this or that particular location. Surely it matters more for missionary teams to be effective in bringing people to faith than it does for me to accomplish various ministry goals. When we describe our dreams as "callings," we run the risk of confusing our dreams with God's sovereign will, clutching on to them more tightly than we ought.

C. Sustaining Life on the Field

Once we have identified and sent gifted missionaries, how do we sustain them amid difficulties on the field? It's vital for missionaries to maintain healthy rhythms of rest and family time alongside their ministry. They must avoid unhealthy, obsessive ministry patterns. But provided they are doing so, we should encourage them to think more about what's required to succeed than about what is and isn't sustainable. This may require them to take difficult stands. Let me share a story to explain.

In my early years of language learning, my fellow missionaries often reminded me to take a Sabbath. I was keeping a weekly Sabbath and getting the rest I needed, but I was grateful for their concern. Here's what's interesting, though, and a bit telling: *none of them ever asked whether I was making adequate progress in learning Arabic.* They rightly wanted to shield me from burnout, but seemed not to care at all to protect me from ineffectiveness. Who would have worried if I established a sustainable pace of life, even if that "sustainability" made it impossible for me to learn enough Arabic to minister well? If we want to succeed, then *sustainability* and *feasibility* must go hand-in-hand.

Again, people get this in the professional world. We can't tell our managers that our work schedule is unsustainable and go home early. If we do, we'll quickly be told we need to figure out whether our current job is a good fit for us. And what do you know? In most cases, unless our work situations are deeply unhealthy, we find ways to get the job done.

On the mission field, however, coworkers and supervisors seem to support and even encourage patterns of work that won't get the job done. After giving up so much, they imagine we need a break. But a break isn't what we need. What we need is to minister effectively. To be sure, we *have* given up a great deal. That's precisely why we should work hard and endure difficulties. We don't want to squander our investment. We didn't move to the field to get a break. If the hardship is worth it, then we will learn to sustain more than we imagine we can.

Missionary Suffering

Paul provides an excellent example of how we can joyfully endure suffering when the goal is worth it. Just look at what he went through:

> . . . far greater labors, far more imprisonments, with countless beatings, and often near death. Five times I received at the hands of the Jews the forty lashes less one. Three times I was beaten with rods. Once I was stoned. Three times I was shipwrecked; a night and a day I was adrift at sea; on frequent journeys, in danger from rivers, danger from robbers, danger from my own people, danger from Gentiles, danger in the city, danger in the wilderness, danger at sea, danger from false brothers; in toil and hardship, through many a sleepless night, in hunger and thirst, often without food, in cold and exposure. (2 Cor. 11:23–27)

Such suffering was an unavoidable part of Paul's calling as a missionary. The weakness and suffering he and his ministry team endured helped to demonstrate Christ's all-surpassing power:

We have this treasure in jars of clay, to show that the surpassing power belongs to God and not to us. We are afflicted in every way, but not crushed; perplexed, but not driven to despair; persecuted, but not forsaken; struck down, but not destroyed; always carrying in the body the death of Jesus, so that the life of Jesus may also be manifested in our bodies. (2 Cor. 4:7–10)

I don't mean to romanticize Paul's suffering. Suffering should never be romanticized or pursued for its own sake. But it is rarely avoidable, and even amid intense suffering, we can maintain courage. As Paul put it, "This light momentary affliction is preparing for us an eternal weight of glory beyond all comparison" (2 Cor. 4:17). Rather than focusing on his sufferings or asking whether they were sustainable, Paul fixes his gaze on something far more significant: an eternal weight of glory beyond all comparison.

We must pay careful attention here. This incomparable glory is not some treasure in heaven that Paul will experience only in the afterlife. This incomparable glory is the ministry of the Holy Spirit in the hearts of the Corinthians. We know this because of what Paul said when he started talking about it a chapter earlier:

You are a letter from Christ . . . written not with ink but with the Spirit of the living God, not on tablets of stone but on tablets of human hearts. . . .

Now if the ministry of death, carved in letters on stone, came with such glory that the Israelites could not gaze at Moses' face because of its glory . . . *will not the ministry of the Spirit have even more glory?* . . . For if there was glory in the ministry of condemnation, *the ministry of righteousness must far exceed it in glory.* (2 Cor. 3:3, 7–9)

Simply put, the glory of the Spirit's work in the Corinthians outweighs Paul's suffering. So he continues:

For we who live are always being given over to death for Jesus' sake, so that the life of Jesus also may be manifested in our mortal flesh. . . . *It*

is all for your sake, so that as grace extends to more and more people
it may increase thanksgiving, to the glory of God. (2 Cor. 4:11, 15)

It's all for your sake, Paul says. That's why he gladly suffers. The people
in whom God is at work—*that's* what Paul sees as his reward. It is
people whom Paul describes elsewhere as "my joy and crown" (Phil.
4:1). And then again to the Thessalonians: "For what is our hope or
joy or crown of boasting before our Lord Jesus at his coming? Is it not
you?" (1 Thess. 2:19).

Because Paul's reward and hopes for the future are tied up in the
health of the churches, he gladly suffers for their sake:

I will most gladly spend and be spent for your souls. (2 Cor. 12:15)

Even if I am to be poured out as a drink offering upon the sacrificial
offering of your faith, I am glad. (Phil. 2:17)

I rejoice in my sufferings for your sake, and in my flesh I am filling
up what is lacking in Christ's afflictions for the sake of his body, that
is, the church. (Col. 1:24)

Paul suffers for his churches as gladly as if they were his own children.
And that's how he sees them:

I will not be a burden, for I seek not what is yours but you. For children are not obligated to save up for their parents, but parents for
their children. (2 Cor. 12:14)

. . . like a father with his children, we exhorted each one of you and
encouraged you. (1 Thess. 2:11–12)

Like members of a family or members of a body, Paul's destiny and
theirs are truly intertwined: "If one member suffers, all suffer together;
if one member is honored, all rejoice together" (1 Cor. 12:26).

Paul cares for these churches as if they were his children. On their behalf he joyfully sustains all that his human frame can handle. Such an attitude will sustain us—as it sustained him—through great suffering. May God give us grace to grow a similar love for his people.

Conclusion

Missionaries need to be prepared before they head to the field. They need to be able to offer confident answers to difficult questions: *What will it take to succeed? Do I have the necessary resources and skills? Can I handle the difficulties?* Such questions often feel uncomfortable, even unspiritual. They seem too human, too coldly pragmatic, too professional. But prudence is a virtue, and the Holy Spirit guides his people through their exercise of human wisdom.

People in the secular world ask these questions because they understand that when money is on the line, outcomes matter. Jesus acknowledges their wisdom with the things of the world: "For the sons of this world are more shrewd in dealing with their own generation than the sons of light" (Luke 16:8).

Missionaries have far more on the line than money, in terms of both what they invest and the gains they hope to see. Troubled days on the field will shake them, just as troubled markets shake investors. And missionaries, like investors, must carefully assess whether they have the resources to stay in the game until their investment pays off.

This doesn't mean something has gone wrong whenever a missionary leaves the field. We do our best to evaluate ourselves, but we won't always know what we can endure. God gives grace to go, but we remain dependent on him daily for the grace to stay. We should never harbor dark suspicions about those who leave. As Paul says, "Who are you to pass judgment on the servant of another? It is before his own master that he stands or falls. And he will be upheld, for the Lord is able to make him stand" (Rom. 14:4).

Nonetheless, attrition results in real loss, so we seek to avoid it. That's why we ought to consider our decision carefully. We need to know what we can endure so that we can more readily find a ministry situation in which we have a high chance of success.

And this possibility—the hope of success—should weigh heavily in our thinking. Wise decision making prepares us to take advantage of the tremendous opportunities that await. Indeed, suffering lies ahead. But so do great blessings! I've had many low points on the field, but my life hasn't been characterized by suffering and a sense of sacrifice but by satisfaction and joy. It is truly a privilege to serve the Lord like this. I wouldn't trade it for anything.

It is sobering to think that, not too many years ago, I nearly turned away from the field simply because my inner sense of "calling" wasn't strong enough. I'm thankful for those who persuaded me otherwise.

So, let us wisely evaluate our opportunity—neither rushing to the field nor turning away from it prematurely due to an unnecessary focus on mystical, inward guidance. Those with the grace to go will find that great joy awaits them. The difficulties they face will be sustainable in light of the reward they hope for: Christ's incomparable glory coming to life in new brothers and sisters. It is these people who are our joy, our reward, and our crown.

10

Work and the Holy Spirit

IT HAS BEEN A RECURRING theme of this book: the Holy Spirit uses mundane stuff like human communication, human planning, and human labor. This is true on the mission field, and it's true off the mission field. We are all dependent on God's blessing to succeed: "Unless the Lord builds the house, those who build it labor in vain" (Ps. 127:1). But . . . the Lord is unlikely to build the house apart from our labor. So there's no tension between doing our work well and depending fully on the Holy Spirit. Our work doesn't crowd out the Spirit. It offers a space for him to move. He's at work as we raise money, go to our place of mission, study languages, learn about new cultures, build friendships, and proclaim Christ.

We see this pattern throughout Scripture. When Nehemiah's enemies seek to attack him, he "prayed to . . . God and set a guard as protection against them" (Neh. 4:9). He's dependent on God, but he still has to take action. Or look at Esther. She asks Israel to fast and pray for deliverance (Est. 4:16). But she must use her royal influence—and put her own life on the line—before deliverance comes. Prayer doesn't replace our actions; it enlivens them. For example, it's more useful to ask God to bless our language study than to ask him for the gift of tongues.[1] Why?

---

1 As we saw earlier, Hudson Taylor rebuked C. T. Studd and his companions for hoping for the gift of tongues, declaring, "If I could put the Chinese language into your brains by one wave of the hand I would not do it" (Alvyn Austin, *China's Millions: The China Inland Mission and Late Qing Society, 1832–1905* [Grand Rapids, MI: Eerdmans, 2007], 222).

Because prayer isn't a magical escape from the difficulties of human life or of ministry. Instead, it empowers us to succeed amid the difficulties.

We must be wary of missions approaches that depend on God to bypass our human efforts in flashy, supernatural ways, or that ask us to bypass our human frailty through unusual heroism. God is at work in both our human efforts and our human frailty. In this chapter, I want to suggest a few areas in which God is at work in the ordinariness of our work and spirituality.

The Everyday and the Supernatural

Some popular missions literature suggests that God has recently begun to communicate more often through dreams, visions, and healings:

> In some places, a team has gone prayerwalking around an area, asking God to send dreams and visions there, and not long thereafter a person has had a dream about [Jesus] and becomes the key to reaching the entire community.[2]

> Depending on the region, a minimum of 50 percent (in the most extreme and violent Muslim areas) and a maximum of 70 percent of all new churches planted among Muslims happened in part because of signs and wonders (typically miracles of healing and deliverance). Sometimes the divine interventions have unexpectedly happened the first day that pioneer teams entered a community.[3]

> All of the Church Planting Movements I've seen in China are full of healings, miracles, and even resurrections.[4]

I can't speak to these claims because I have no way to investigate them. I can say that in the countries I've had the privilege to minister

---

2   James Nyman, *Stubborn Perseverance: How to Launch Multiplying Movements of Disciples and Churches among Muslims and Others* (Mount Vernon, WA: Missions Network, 2017), 35.

3   Jerry Trousdale, *Miraculous Movements: How Hundreds of Thousands of Muslims Are Falling in Love with Jesus* (Nashville: Thomas Nelson, 2012), 135.

4   David Garrison, *Church Planting Movements: How God Is Redeeming a Lost World* (Bangalore, India: WIGTake Resources, 2007), 233.

in, such events *did* seem to happen. But they weren't common, and some reported miracles turned out to be questionable at best. Of course, little is gained by pitting my claims against the others. Instead, let's see what the Scriptures say.

Surprisingly, while miracles happen throughout the book of Acts, they're not nearly as common as we might think. Only the apostles and two of the seven deacons are recorded as having miraculous gifts.[5] Luke makes this point explicitly:

> . . . awe came upon every soul, and many wonders and signs were being done *through the apostles*. (Acts 2:43)

> Now many signs and wonders were regularly done among the people *by the hands of the apostles*. (Acts 5:12)

It is Peter whose shadow heals—not the shadow of rank-and-file believers (Acts 5:15). It is Paul's handkerchiefs that get carried to the sick (19:11–12)—not yours and mine (thankfully!).

Furthermore, even when supernatural events happen in Acts, capable teachers must be ready to follow up. A man is healed in the temple (Acts 3:7), but it is through the sermon that follows that thousands are saved. An angel appears to Cornelius, but his only instruction to Cornelius is to find Peter, who explains the gospel to him. Though God is perfectly capable of speaking directly, he seems to prefer to work through human agents, despite their limited capacities.

We welcome God's supernatural interventions when they happen. But we must remember that in the Scriptures, even when God works supernaturally, he still uses ordinary, human follow-up to bring people to Christ. So rather than expecting God to work primarily in eye-catching,

---

5   Additionally, Paul's vision is miraculously healed when the prophet Ananias prays for him (Acts 9:17–18), but there is no indication that Ananias regularly performed miracles. Rather, Paul has been blinded as a supernatural judgment and has been told that his blindness will be healed as a part of God's forgiveness. Ananias happens to be the person chosen to bring this larger story to a close. Luke does not indicate whether or not Ananias had a healing ministry beyond this incident.

supernatural ways, we should cultivate ministry strategies that expect God to work primarily through our normal world of relationships and abilities. It is *this* expectation that often requires greater faith.

For example, praying for "divine appointments" while walking through crowded markets isn't an adequate ministry *strategy*—though we lose nothing, I suppose, by asking—unless this is a normal way to make acquaintances in the place where you are ministering. Our strategies should be grounded in the everyday, human realities of life. The apostle Paul does miracles in some cities and not in others, but whether or not miracles occur, his *strategy* is the same: he goes to the synagogue and teaches. This ministry strategy makes complete sense in Paul's cultural context. People regularly talked about God in the synagogue, so his strategy relies on God to work within normal patterns of life.

Extraordinary Prayer

In chapter 3, we saw that some have grown increasingly wary of how missionaries influence the people to whom they minister. They fear that missionaries' "cultural and religious experience can negatively influence their disciple making,"[6] which leads many to conclude that "the church planter, as a foreigner in the culture, must remain in the background and minimize cultural transmission."[7]

As a result, new patterns have emerged. Instead of expecting the Spirit to work through direct relationships or direct teaching, missionaries are now being told to stay in the background. They're told to depend on the Spirit to work through them in unseen realms as they pray. These prayers, it's assumed, should go beyond easily accessible, "ordinary" prayers. Those are insufficient. Instead, missionaries are told to give themselves to longer and more intense prayer sessions, often idealized as "extraordinary prayer."[8] The old pattern of God working

---

6   David Watson and Paul Watson, *Contagious Disciple Making: Leading Others on a Journey of Discovery* (Nashville: Thomas Nelson, 2014), 35.

7   Younoussa Djao, "Church Planting Movements: A Golden Key to Missions in Africa," *CPM Journal* (January–March 2006), 86.

8   Garrison, *Church Planting Movements*, 172.

through us in ordinary ways and answering ordinary prayers has been replaced by heroic wrestling—by towering, otherworldly struggles.

I don't mean to undermine prayer. It is vital, essential work. But there's a danger here if we imagine that our prayers are more effective if we pray in heroic ways. This is, in fact, what missionaries are often taught. Consider two examples:

> In a meeting of the top one hundred disciple-makers in our ministry, we looked for common elements among these high-producing leaders. . . . These leaders spent an average of three hours per day in personal prayer. They spent another three hours in prayer with their teams every day.[9]

> **Extraordinary prayer** . . . permeates Church Planting Movements. Whether it's Koreans rising at four in the morning for a two-hour prayer time, or Spanish gypsies *"going to the mountain,"* as they call their all-night prayer vigils, Church Planting Movements are steeped in prayer.[10]

God may give special gifts of intercession, so I'm not about to criticize those who pray for six hours a day. Who am I to "pass judgment on the servant of another" (Rom. 14:4)? But there's something dangerous about suggesting that only these types of men are likely to succeed. Jesus tell us, "And when you pray, do not heap up empty phrases as the Gentiles do, for they think that they will be heard for their many words. Do not be like them, for your Father knows what you need before you ask him" (Matt. 6:7–8). If we forget this, then we will discourage those who don't have special gifts of intercession. We will make the practical ways in which God has gifted them seem less spiritual.

Perhaps our tendency to do so reflects a secret fear among many Christians that our less extravagant prayer lives aren't enough.[11] Most

---

9   Watson and Watson, *Contagious Disciple Making,* 79.

10   Garrison, *Church Planting Movements,* 172–73, emphasis original.

11   See Philip Yancey, *Prayer: Does It Make Any Difference?* (Grand Rapids, MI: Zondervan, 2010), 14. Yancey writes of finding that many Christians he interviewed about prayer

Christians already live with a gnawing sense of guilt that their prayers aren't what they should be: *I should be praying more. I should be praying longer. I should be praying harder and with more faith.* We even call gifted pray-ers "prayer warriors." This suggests that we think prayer succeeds through our struggling—perhaps even through heroic struggling.[12] But Jesus is not interested in our hyper-spirituality. He wants us to come with humble faith, and that is why he almost always describes prayer in family terms—as helpless children coming to their loving Father.

This false conception about the need for heroic prayer can take deep root in missionaries. After all, we tend to be go-getters. We tend to be naturally intense. *If we don't pray enough, then we won't see a break-through,* we tell ourselves. Readers who are in ministry can test how easy it is to fall into this type of thinking: try saying at your next ministry team meeting, "We need to spend more time in prayer." Everyone will quickly agree! Now try suggesting we need to spend *less* time in prayer. Quiet shock will descend over the room. But Jesus paints a different picture. He tells us we won't be heard for our many words. So there *are* times to pray less.

Prayer is most certainly extraordinary, but not at all because *we pray* in extraordinary ways. Prayer is extraordinary because God answers us so generously when he need not answer us at all.

Ironically, in making much of our need for extravagant prayer, we can end up making less of God's generosity. "Prayer," Oswald Chambers writes, "is the greater work."[13] But that's not quite right. Prayer is *not* the greater work. Prayer is our coming to God needy and helpless. It

---

"experienced prayer more as a burden than as a pleasure. They regarded it as important, even paramount, and felt guilty about their failure, blaming themselves."

12   On two occasions, the New Testament does describe people "striving" or "struggling" in prayer (Rom. 15:30; Col. 4:12–13). This may reflect the fact that prayer clearly involves us in a struggle between God's kingdom and the powers of this world. Additionally, it sometimes is a struggle for us to pray; our minds wander, and we are tempted by laziness. But neither of these passages implies that our prayers must reach a certain level of emotional intensity in order to be accepted by God.

13   Oswald Chambers, "The Key of the Greater Work," in *Contemporaries Meet the Classics on Prayer*, ed. Henri J. M. Nouwen and Crawford Leonard Allen (Grand Rapids, MI: Discovery, 2012), 2012.

is God's *responses* to our prayers, and not the prayers themselves, that are the greater work. Our prayers, like most of the things we do, are hopefully sincere but are laughably lacking without God's help. "Jesus has justified our prayers,"[14] and it's only because we pray in his name that our prayers are acceptable. We aren't prayer "warriors." We're helpless children calling to a Father who loves us.

We aren't prayer "warriors." We're helpless
children calling to a Father who loves us.

We don't need to pray for a certain number of hours per day.[15] Jesus's logic can feel too good to be true: "Or which one of you, if his son asks him for bread, will give him a stone. . . . how much more will your Father who is in heaven give good things to those who ask him!" (Matt.

---

14 Graeme Goldsworthy, *Prayer and the Knowledge of God: What the Whole Bible Teaches* (Downers Grove, IL: InterVarsity Press, 2004), 50.

15 A common objection here is that when Jesus finds Peter and his friends "sleeping for sorrow" (Luke 22:45) in Gethsemane, he rebukes Peter, saying, "So, could you not watch with me one hour? Watch and pray that you may not enter into temptation. The spirit indeed is willing, but the flesh is weak" (Matt. 26:40–41). Is Jesus implying that Peter must pray for at least one hour before God will accept his prayer? Here, two observations will be helpful.

First, if we take Jesus's words literally, he actually rebukes Peter for two things. Peter has fallen asleep rather than praying for strength to face temptation. Additionally—and separately—Peter has fallen asleep when he should have been keeping watch. Jesus is in danger and has assigned Peter and his friends to keep watch for his enemies while he prays and gathers strength for what he is about to endure. It is in regard to their failure to keep watch—not their prayerlessness—that Jesus mentions how long they should have stayed awake.

Second, it is true that Jesus prayed for three hours in Gethsemane. Beneath the weight of overwhelming sorrow, he did not find instant relief. Though the passage does not say so, it is possible that the disciples should have followed his example, taking considerable time in prayer to work through their own sorrows in the same way. But if this is the case, we cannot assume that a certain amount of time in prayer was needed in order for God to answer. Rather, the disciples may have needed to take considerable time in prayer for their own sakes—when grief and fear are great, we cannot always work through them in prayer all at once.

7:9, 11). And which of us, if our child asked for breakfast, would refuse her because she hadn't spent enough hours pleading? What general would refuse to send in air support simply because his troops hadn't yet pleaded long enough?

I'm not saying we should be lazy in prayer. There *are* requests a child shouldn't simply call out over her shoulder as she's running out the door. But it may be that we don't need to do any more than express to God, respectfully and seriously, what we hope for. Sometimes, when we're distressed or have a lot on our minds, this may take a long time—Jesus prays for three hours in agony at Gethsemane. But *the amount of time* we pray isn't the main point. Paul tells the Thessalonians to "pray without ceasing" (1 Thess. 5:17), but this doesn't mean we should pray twenty-four hours a day. In the same way, when Paul tells the Thessalonians he gives thanks for them without ceasing (1 Thess. 2:13),[16] he doesn't mean he is thanking God for them every waking moment. When he tells us to pray without ceasing, he's not telling us to pray without *pausing*. He's telling us not to cease making prayer a part of our lives.

So the amount of prayer doesn't seem overly important. What about the intensity of prayer? Must we pray with unusual intensity? Let's recall Jesus's logic again: which of us, if our children asked for breakfast, would make them plead with unusual passion before giving it to them? It was the prophets of Baal, not Elijah, who leapt and shouted and gashed themselves on Mount Carmel (1 Kings 18:26–38). Deep inside, they hoped the fervor and commotion of their prayers could make up for Baal's lifelessness. But Elijah was under no such constraint, because his God was a Father, not an idol.[17] Some have argued that we

---

16   The same Greek word, *adialeiptōs*, is used on both occasions to indicate an activity that has not ceased.

17   A possible objection is that James later tells us,

> Elijah was a man with a nature like ours, and he *prayed fervently* that it might not rain, and for three years and six months it did not rain on the earth. Then he prayed again, and heaven gave rain. (James 5:17–18)

Does James mean that God granted Elijah's request, in part, because he prayed hard enough? I do not think we can interpret Elijah's "fervency" simply as powerful emotion.

must struggle with God in prayer because Jacob wrestles with God. But Jacob didn't think he was praying during the wrestling match—in fact, he's surprised to find that it's the Lord he is wrestling with (Gen. 32:30). Furthermore, the Scriptures never indicate that Jacob's wrestling match is a model for prayer. The only other place in Scripture in which Jacob's wrestling match is mentioned is when Hosea criticizes Jacob for striving with both God and man (Hos. 12:3). Strong emotions certainly have a place in prayer. We should bring them to God when we feel them. But we don't need to manufacture emotional intensity when it isn't there.[18] We can still make sincere requests.

Okay, what about expectation? Sometimes we feel that God is disappointed when we wonder whether or not he will grant our prayers. Surely we need to pray with extraordinary expectations, right? Actually, since he's God and we're not, we *should* often wonder whether he's going to do what we ask of him. He has the right to say no! Jesus doesn't do many miracles in his hometown because of the people's unbelief (Matt. 13:53–58). This isn't because the people wonder if he will heal them. The apostles often doubt whether Jesus will work miracles, and he does them anyway. No, the problem in Matthew 13 is that *the people don't believe in Jesus at all.* They reject him outright! God has compassion when we're unsure of what he will do. We don't have to fully expect he will say "yes" for him to be pleased with our prayers.

The Greek literally reads that Elijah "prayed with prayer"; translators have seen the repetition as an intensifier, rendering it "prayed fervently" (ESV) or "prayed earnestly" (NIV). But if the repetition is to signal intensity, it is not at all clear that it signals emotional intensity (rather than sincerity or perseverance). In fact, just before he "prayed again, and heaven gave rain," we find Elijah's calm confidence starkly contrasted with the emotional frenzy that the prophets of Baal have worked themselves into, as they attempt to convince their god to respond (1 Kings 18:25–28).

18   The parable of the persistent widow is also commonly understood as a teaching that we may need to struggle with God before our prayers will be heard. In fact, in Luke 18, Jesus has just been talking about his return (Luke 17:22–37). He tells the parable of the widow so that as the disciples wait for his return, they will "not lose heart" (Luke 18:1). This statement, and his closing question ("Nevertheless, when the Son of Man comes, will he find faith on the earth?" [v. 8]), indicate that he is not asking us to struggle with God in prayer but to be persistent in prayer. He wants to make sure that when God seems to be taking his time, we do not give up on prayer and assume he has forgotten us.

We simply have to have faith in him. Even a tiny amount of faith will do. A mustard seed can grow into a mustard tree; a mustard seed can move mountains (Matt. 13:31, 32; 17:20). Hudson Taylor reminded us that "It is not great faith you need . . . but faith in a great God."[19] David writes of God's mercy when his faith had failed:

> I had said in my alarm,
>   "I am cut off from your sight."
> But you heard the voice of my pleas for mercy
>   when I cried to you for help. (Ps. 31:22)

Prayer works because God is great, not because we are. God loves us and wants us to be secure in the fact that he is pleased with our prayers, as weak and human as they are, in the same way that we are pleased with our children's first poor stammerings as they attempt to speak with us. As weak and distracted as we can be, as downright *ordinary* as we are, our extraordinary God is overjoyed to answer us anyway.

We shouldn't imagine that we'll succeed on the mission field—or in any ministry—without praying. But provided that we pray respectfully and seriously and don't give up, then we need not worry about the rest. The length of time we pray, the intensity with which we pray, the certainty we have as we pray—none of that is very important. We live ordinary lives. We do ordinary work. We pray ordinary prayers. And through it all, we ask our extraordinary God to be at work. Let's entrust our prayers into his loving hands and then get back to the small but necessary tasks he has given us.

Fasting

During my first year on the field, my team set aside forty days to fast and pray for spiritual "breakthrough" in our neighborhood. We made a schedule so that during these forty days, someone was always fasting,

---

19 Howard Taylor and Geraldine Taylor (Mrs. Howard Taylor), *Hudson Taylor and the China Inland Mission: The Growth of a Work of God* (Philadelphia: Morgan & Scott, 1919), 428–29.

and someone was always praying. We often prayed and fasted together, and some team members used these prayer times to bind demonic powers that they believed held our neighborhood in darkness. At the end of the forty days, spiritual breakthrough hadn't occurred. We wondered why. A senior leader stood up and suggested we hadn't fasted enough. "We must fast another forty days," he declared.

This reflects a common approach to fasting. It's widely assumed that fasting adds to the efficacy of our prayers, especially when we seek to bring large groups of people to Christ. As one missionary writes, "The goal of fasting is to pray more effectively."[20] And another: "all discussion about Disciple Making Movements begin[s] with prayer and fasting. . . . Behind any success in planting churches and making disciples there is a lot of prayer and a lot of fasting, a lot of bending knees, a lot of crying and weeping before God."[21]

Before examining what the Scriptures actually teach about fasting, I'd like to suggest that our team's lack of breakthrough may have been due to the fact that, at this point, *none of us spoke Arabic well enough to share the gospel in easily understandable ways.* In fact, our intense emphasis on prayer and fasting had interfered with our ability to learn Arabic. Prayer is our single most important task as missionaries. It invites God's almighty power into our frail efforts. But it should empower our work, not replace it.

Just as we should be wary of imagining that praying longer or more intensely adds power to our prayers, so we should be wary of seeing fasting as the "atomic bomb" of prayer.[22] Why would we imagine that our loving Father is *less* likely to grant our requests if we don't deprive ourselves while asking him for help?

I have no desire to criticize those who pray with "fasting . . . [or] bending knees . . . [or] crying and weeping before God." The Scriptures

20 Nyman, *Stubborn Perseverance*, 274.

21 Younoussa Djao, "Engage! Africa Video Series," quoted in Jerry Trousdale and Glenn Sunshine, *The Kingdom Unleashed* (Murfreesboro, TN: DMM Library, 2015), ch. 9.

22 Bill Bright, "7 Basic Steps to Successful Fasting and Prayer," accessed December 2, 2019, https://www.cru.org/us/en/train-and-grow/spiritual-growth/fasting/7-steps-to-fasting.html.

give us freedom to engage in such practices as our hearts move us. It is this freedom that I hope to preserve. You are free to fast as you please—but equally, others are free not to! There is no suggestion in the Scriptures that fasting makes our prayers more powerful or that it is necessary for success in ministry. In the Scriptures, people don't fast in order to pray more effectively. They generally don't fast when praying for important requests. Instead, people fast almost exclusively in times of distress, particularly when they realize God is about to judge their sin. Fasting is a unique way of humbling oneself to request God's mercy. It's often mentioned alongside wearing sackcloth (1 Kings 21:27; Neh. 9:1; Ps. 35:13; Isa. 58:4; Dan. 9:3; Jonah 3:5). The connection of fasting with mourning—especially mourning over sin—is all over the Old Testament. Israel fasts when God judges the people's idolatry by allowing the Philistines to conquer them (1 Sam. 7:6). David fasts when his illegitimate son, newly born, is about to die (2 Sam. 12:16). Ahab fasts after Elijah prophesies that his family will be judged for his murder of Naboth (1 Kings 21:27). Ezra proclaims a fast when the exiles return to their land after they have sinned (Ezra 8:21–23). He does so again when they sin by marrying foreign wives (Ezra 9:5). The Ninevites fast when Jonah prophesies that God will destroy their city (Jonah 3:5). Daniel fasts to pray for mercy near the end of the exile and to mourn for Israel's sin (Dan. 9:3, 5–15; 10:2–3). Nehemiah appears to be seeking mercy in his fast (Neh. 1:4), as do the Jews in Esther's day (Est. 4:16)—in both cases, it would have been impossible for law-observing Jews who were familiar with the prophets not to see their misfortunes in exile as a direct result of their nation's sins. This is even clearer in Nehemiah's second fast, when the people confess their sins and the sins of their forefathers (Neh. 9:1–2). In Isaiah 58, God rejects Israel's fasting because they fasted without repenting of their wickedness:

> Behold, you fast only to quarrel and to fight
>   and to hit with a wicked fist.
> Fasting like yours this day
>   will not make your voice to be heard on high. (Isa. 58:4)

Joel threatens judgment and then tells Israel to repent with "fasting, with weeping, and with mourning" (Joel 2:12). God indicates that when he forgives Israel, regular fasts should be replaced with feasting (Zech. 8:14–19). Why? Because once judgment is over, fasting will no longer be appropriate.

This connection is echoed in the New Testament. Jesus himself connects fasting and mourning explicitly in Matthew 9:14–17. Similarly, Saul fasts for three days after the risen Christ confronts him on the road to Damascus (Acts 9:9). While we know little about the purpose of Anna's fasting, it may have been tied to her "waiting for the redemption of Jerusalem" (Luke 2:38) since Jerusalem saw itself as under God's judgment due to Rome's continued occupation. Other instances of fasting exist in Scripture, but they are sparse, and we should be wary of reading too much into them.[23]

---

23 For example, Jesus fasts for forty days in the wilderness beyond the Jordan (Matt. 4:1–11). Jesus clearly intends to recapitulate Israel's forty years in the wilderness, since he goes to the same desert and answers all the devil's temptations with quotes from Deuteronomy, the collection of lessons that the children of Israel learned while wandering there. Jesus's purpose in repeating Israel's sojourn in the wilderness—and succeeding where Israel had failed—is not fully clear. He may be fasting, in part, to repent on Israel's behalf for its failures (as, for example, Daniel does in Dan. 9:3–19). But regardless of why, exactly, Jesus repeats Israel's journey in the desert, the fact that he clearly intends to do so makes it hard to imagine that his fast sets a pattern for our ministries. We are not Israel's Messiah and do not need to fast for forty days in order to succeed where Israel failed.

Elsewhere, Saul (Paul) and Barnabas decided to begin ministry together while "they were worshiping the Lord and fasting" (Acts 13:2). And Paul and Barnabas "appointed elders . . . with prayer and fasting they committed them to the Lord" (Acts 14:23). These passages have been used to argue that we should fast when seeking guidance or when beginning a new ministry. See, e.g., Lynne M. Baab, *Fasting: Spiritual Freedom beyond Our Appetites* (Downers Grove, IL: InterVarsity Press, 2009), 53, 78. See also Elmer L. Towns, *Fasting for Spiritual Breakthrough* (Bloomington, MN: Baker, 1996), ch. 7. But these conclusions are problematic. Against these two passages, we must remember that in every other situation in the book of Acts where guidance is given, fasting is not mentioned (Acts 1:26; 8:26; 10:9–16; 16:6–10; 18:9; 23:11), and there are numerous cases in the Luke/Acts narrative of important ministries beginning where fasting is not mentioned (Luke 6:12–14; Acts 1:15–26; 6:1–7; 16:1–3). Of course, we have freedom to fast if we please. Again, it is freedom that I hope to preserve—you may fast in these situations if you like, but the Scriptures don't seem to require it of you or of others. They never imply that fasting is a "better" way to handle these situations.

Fasting and Spiritual Warfare

It may be important to specifically address the idea—common among missionaries—that we should fast to strengthen our prayers as we engage in *spiritual warfare*.[24,25,26] As one popular missions book tells us, "Spiritual warfare is real. Prayer and fasting are major weapons in that warfare. Learn to use them."[27]

According to this common teaching, fasting has powerful effects on the war between God's kingdom—especially his angels—and demonic powers as they struggle to influence history and the fate of human souls. Would our generous Father be unwilling to help us in these struggles until we had inflicted a certain amount of hunger on ourselves?

Missionaries appeal to two scriptural passages to make this argument. First, Matthew's and Mark's Gospels contain a story in which Jesus's disciples are unable to cast out a demon. In older English translations, after Jesus eventually exorcises the demon, he explains to the disciples that they failed to cast it out because "this kind can come forth by nothing, but by prayer and fasting" (Mark 9:29 KJV; cf. Matt. 17:21 KJV). The final two words of Jesus's sentence—"and fasting"—do not appear in most modern English translations of Mark's Gospel (see ESV, NIV, NASB). The entire verse is excluded from Matthew's Gospel in these translations because it is missing from most ancient texts. In other words, these verses probably were not part of the Gospels' original text. Additionally, it is unlikely that Jesus would suggest that the disciples need to fast more. He had just told the Pharisees, not too many chapters before, that it was *inappropriate* for the disciples to fast while he was still with them (Matt. 9:14–17; Mark 2:18–22). So even

---

24   J. O. Sanders, "Effective Prayer," in *World Prayer: Powerful Insights from Four of the World's Great Men of Prayer* (Littleton, CO: OMF Books, 1999), 27.

25   David Allen Jacques, *Weapons Training for Spiritual Warfare and Frontline Ministry: A Guide to Winning Battles in the Spirit Realm* (Bloomington, IN: WestBow Press, 2014), 158.

26   John Eckhardt, *Fasting for Breakthrough and Deliverance* (Lake Mary, FL: Charisma, 2016), 1–2.

27   Trousdale and Sunshine, *Kingdom Unleashed*, ch. 9.

if the text in question is original to the Gospels, we still need another way to read it.[28]

Second, we have the story of Daniel's prayer. He fasts until—after some delay—an angel answers him. The angel is delayed by the "prince of the kingdom of Persia" (Dan. 10:13) for twenty-one days and anticipates the coming of the "prince of Greece" (Dan. 10:20). It is commonly assumed that these "princes" are demonic powers with which the angel must contend. It is also assumed that Daniel's fasting helps the angel to succeed in his warfare against these demonic forces. A few examples of this:

[In] Daniel, the Bible tells us that there are powerful spiritual beings ('princes') who have charge over human kingdoms and who oppose God's work.[29]

It was Daniel's continual wrestling on earth while the battle raged in the heavenlies, which finalized the victory.[30]

In fact, the "prince of the kingdom of Persia" (v. 13) with whom the angel struggles and the "prince of Greece" who "will come" later (v. 20)

28 For many reasons, it makes little sense here to imagine that Jesus wants the disciples to fast more. First, as mentioned above, he has commended them for not fasting during his ministry (Matt. 9:14–17; Mark 2:18–22). Second, Jesus has already given them power over demons (Matt. 10:1). It is possible that the demon they meet in this instance is a special type that the disciples were not given power over, but since Jesus gave the disciples "power and authority over all demons" (Luke 9:1), this is unlikely. Additionally, no one in the passage (even Jesus) reacts to the demon by praying and fasting, but the demon is cast out. While Jesus's previous fasting may have overpowered the demon, we should not forget that the disciples were John's disciples before meeting Jesus, and so they would have fasted previously as well (Mark 2:18). One possible way of reading this text—if authentic—is to note that what *does* convince Jesus to cast the demon out is the humble cry of the boy's father, "Lord, have mercy" (Matt. 17:15), and, "I believe; help my unbelief!" (Mark 9:24). This is certainly a prayer for mercy, and perhaps its humility reminds Jesus of the humble spirit which fasting embodies. Thus, he may have regarded the criteria of "prayer and fasting" as having been effectively met. After all, it is the spirit in which we fast and not the bare action itself that primarily matters to God (Isaiah 58; Luke 18:9–14). This is not a bulletproof reading of the passage, but it is less problematic than suggesting that Jesus is lecturing the disciples for not fasting enough.

29 Trousdale and Sunshine, *Kingdom Unleashed*, ch. 9.

30 Sanders, "Effective Prayer," 27.

can be understood only in light of Daniel's earlier vision, in which he's told that "the ram that you saw with the two horns, these are the kings of Media and Persia. And the goat is the king of Greece" (Dan. 8:20–21). These aren't simply demonic powers; they represent the kingdoms that will rule over Israel after Babylon falls.[31]

Now, it's possible that the wars by which the Medo-Persians and then the Greeks came to rule over Israel in the coming centuries were simply an outworking of angelic territorial wars that took place in Daniel's time. But we can only conclude this by reading our assumptions into the text. More likely, Daniel's visions, like much apocalyptic literature, simply employ heavenly imagery to portray earthly events.[32] Even if the succession of Babylon by the Medo-Persians and the Greeks was determined by an angelic struggle, there are reasons to think Daniel's fasting probably didn't influence the struggle:

- He didn't know any struggle was taking place. At the very least, we can assume he wasn't consciously engaging in spiritual warfare.
- The angel says that Michael helped him, not Daniel's fasting (Dan. 10:13).
- Daniel's fasting, like most Old Testament fasting, seems to be intended not to engage in spiritual warfare but to mourn and repent for his people's sin as they still lived in judgment and exile (Dan. 9:3–5; 10:2).
- The news brought to Daniel by the angel—that the Medo-Persians and later the Greeks would rule over Israel—wasn't the answer Daniel would have wanted. If his fast was a struggle with demonic powers, then he proved unsuccessful.

Simply put, the Scriptures do not indicate that we must fast in order for God to help us in spiritual battles. God is a generous Father. He grants our requests because he loves us, not because we pray intensely or with fasting.

---

31 N. T. Wright, *The New Testament and the People of God*, vol. 1 of Christian Origins and the Question of God (London: Society for Promoting Christian Knowledge, 1992), 290.

32 Wright, *New Testament and the People of God*, 290.

A Scriptural View of Spiritual Warfare

How then do the Scriptures indicate that we should take part in spiritual warfare? Paul writes to the Corinthians,

> . . . though we walk in the flesh, we are not waging war according to the flesh. For the weapons of our warfare are not of the flesh but have divine power to destroy strongholds. We destroy arguments and every lofty opinion raised against the knowledge of God, and take every thought captive to obey Christ, being ready to punish every disobedience, when your obedience is complete. (2 Cor. 10:3–6)

This is one of the clearest references to spiritual warfare in the Scriptures. Let's examine it more carefully. First, we should note that the "strongholds" Paul has power to destroy are not demons or demonic armies. Rather, they are "arguments," "opinions," and "thoughts." They are *ideas*.

This is consistent with depictions of spiritual warfare we find elsewhere. The sword of the Spirit "is the word of God" (Eph. 6:17). We use God's Word as a weapon in our warfare because we're contending with deceptive ideas. Most of the other pieces of the armor of God, as Paul describes it in Ephesians, also have to do with correct ideas or teachings: the belt of truth, the feet shod with the gospel, and the shield of faith (Eph. 6:14–17). Paul tells us to "put on the whole armor of God, that you may be able to stand against the *schemes* of the devil" (Eph. 6:11). The devil's schemes seek to deceive us, to entrap us with false ideas.

Spiritual warfare involves both praying and battling deceptive ideas by teaching the truth. God provides the power when we pray, and our teaching provides a means for that power to flow. When Paul sees that a "false gospel" has taken hold in the Corinthian church, he plans to wage spiritual warfare, in part, by coming to Corinth to correct false teaching (2 Cor. 10:1–6; 13:1–10).

Our role in spiritual warfare isn't grandiose. We don't overpower demons by fasting. We pray humble, human prayers. It is God who gives extraordinary answers. We communicate through humble, human words. It is God's power that moves in our words and dislodges demonic ideas that hold people captive.

Conclusion

We don't need to try to be more than we are. We're completely dependent on God. Our ministry strategies should center around humble, human work. As we humbly ask him to bless us, God will empower our work to succeed. He'll work through our ordinary efforts to do more than we could have asked or imagined. An old hymn says:

> We need not bid—for cloistered cell—
> Our neighbor and our work farewell,
> Nor strive to find ourselves too high
> For sinful man beneath the sky.
> The trivial round, the common task,
> Will furnish all we ought to ask;
> Room to deny ourselves, a road
> To bring us daily nearer God.[33]

---

33 John Keble, *The Christian Year* (London: Oxford, 1829), 3–4.

Conclusion

Words from William Carey

I WILL CONCLUDE as the Protestant missionary enterprise began—with words from William Carey. Carey inaugurated the first missionary society meeting in 1792 with two famous exhortations, "Expect great things from God; attempt great things for God!"[1] Carey's twin exhortations cannot be separated. God has chosen to demonstrate his greatness in our frail attempts to serve him. As preposterous as it may seem, he has appointed mere humans to be "skilled master builder[s]" of his glorious church (1 Cor. 3:10). Our ordinariness accentuates his glory, and we bear "this treasure in jars of clay, to show that the surpassing power belongs to God and not to us" (2 Cor. 4:7).

Indeed, it is only as God's "surpassing power" is released in our unremarkable, clay-jar, human lives that mission fields are won. Though our role is decidedly unimpressive, we dare not despise it as unimportant. Our role is *critically* important, and we must do all we can to discharge our responsibilities professionally and well. We saw in chapter 1 that this means focusing on things as mundane as:

- investing in adequate theological education;
- acquiring technical skills—including mastery of the language and culture we minister in—to clearly proclaim the gospel of Jesus among peoples who have never heard;

1 William Carey, quoted in William Edward Winks, *Lives of Illustrious Shoemakers* (London: Ballantyne, 1883), 165.

- avoiding shortcuts by allocating adequate time, energy, and resources to the task;
- and evaluating practical circumstances as we make decisions.

Though our role is decidedly unimpressive,
we dare not despise it as unimportant.

In chapters 2 and 3, we saw what happens when these responsibilities are neglected. We examined popular missions strategies and how their fascination with speed and numbers can lead to slapdash work and undermine the health of the churches we hope to leave behind us.

In chapter 4, we saw that rather than pursuing get-rich-quick strategies, we must see ourselves as Christ's ambassadors. Our primary task is to communicate his message in all its fullness and nuance. To that end, as we saw in chapter 5, we must learn to communicate his message clearly, credibly, and boldly. Chapters 6 and 7 showed that we'll have to engage in in-depth study of the Word—and often some type of theological education—before we know Christ's message well enough to communicate it well. We'll also have to invest long years in stretching our intellects to master the languages and cultures in which we must communicate.

In chapter 8, we explored what it means to allocate adequate time and resources to the missionary task. We don't stop evangelizing, shepherding new believers, and training leaders until we see that churches are mature enough to stand on their own. We devote long years of our lives—quite likely, a couple of decades—before we are finished.

Are we ready for the task? How can we know if we are called? Chapter 9 explored the role of practical wisdom as God guides our decisions about whether to go to the field. Chapter 10 cautioned against the appeal of flashy, hyper-spiritual approaches, reminding us that God's power is released in the humble, everyday patterns of human life.

So we press on. Why has God chosen to work in such a painful, cumbersome way? He doesn't need our labors. We bring little to the table. We're weak. We mature slowly. We're dimwitted, awkward communicators. The best of our work is unimpressive. Indeed, we could easily imagine a world in which God had chosen to sideline us in order to do the work himself. He could have chosen to work primarily through signs and dreams and visions. He could have sent his Holy Spirit or his angels to explain Scripture directly to new believers. He could have promoted new believers to maturity instantly, bypassing the slow, awkward processes of human maturation. He could have ordained the church to multiply at dizzying, superhuman speeds. In our desire to see the unreached know him, we may wonder if God *should* have chosen to work in such ways!

But we risk paying a terrible price for imagining this. If God didn't require us to do excellent work—if it pleased him to move apart from our work, rather than *through* it—what would motivate missionaries to be trained in the Scriptures? What reason would they have to spend years of their lives mastering other languages or gaining expertise in other cultures? What would be the rationale for missionaries to spend years patiently teaching and discipling new believers?

Indeed, many have concluded that the slow, plodding path I've described is too cumbersome. Increasingly, young missionaries are told that the careful professionalism of past generations was mostly an exercise in self-reliance. They're encouraged to leave such paths behind and "get out of the way" so that God can work.[2] Those who point out that God has always chosen to communicate his message this way may find themselves dismissed as having "talking head syndrome."[3] They may be accused of "usurping God's role"[4] or of being "selfish and [trying] to keep control over God's Kingdom."[5]

2   Steve Addison, "David Watson Author of Contagious Disciple Making," *Movements with Steve Addison*, podcast audio, November 16, 2015, https://podcastaddict.com/episode /65667146.

3   David Watson, "What about Teaching and Preaching in Disciple-Making Movements?" Accessed March 10, 2017, https://www.davidlwatson.org/2013/08/27/what-about-teaching -and-preaching-in-disciple-making-movements/.

4   Jerry Trousdale, *Miraculous Movements: How Hundreds of Thousands of Muslims Are Falling in Love with Jesus* (Nashville: Thomas Nelson, 2012), 103–4.

5   Wilson Geisler, *Rapidly Advancing Disciples: A Practical Implementation of Current Best Practices* (2011), 89, accessed August 12, 2018, http://www.churchplanting

These accusations are nothing new. As we saw in chapter 1, a similar confusion about God's use of human agency led an older pastor to dismiss William Carey's missionary aspirations over two hundred years ago: "Young man, sit down! When God pleases to convert the heathen, he'll do it without your help or mine either."[6] We should reject such talk, as Carey did. If we imagine that our human efforts are too ordinary for God to use—if we forget that our efforts are the *means* by which God calls people to himself—then we'll have little motivation to give our best in missionary service. We'll be taking the first step down a road to quiet despair, a step toward failure in what God has given us to do.

Let's not take that step. God *does* work through our humble, human efforts. Within our limited capacities, we must devote ourselves to excellent, professional work. We may not see results immediately, but this shouldn't discourage us. Remember the proverb: "Everyone who is hasty comes only to poverty" (Prov. 21:5). Remember what Jesus tells us: it is not for us to know—or to hasten—the "times or seasons that the Father has fixed by his own authority" (Acts 1:7). He told us that his kingdom wouldn't come in ostentatious ways: "The kingdom of God is not coming in ways that can be observed, nor will they say, 'Look, here it is!' or 'There!' for behold, the kingdom of God is in the midst of you" (Luke 17:20–21).

Faithful and fruitful missionaries don't need a spectacular or eye-catching ministry. As Carey wrote, "I can plod. I can persevere to any definite pursuit. To this I owe everything."[7,8] So let us also plod ahead, relying on the Lord. Missionaries tend to pride themselves on being *doers* rather than *thinkers*, on making things happen. But it isn't only ac-

---

movements.com/images/stories/resources/Rapidly_Advancing_Disciples_(RAD)_Dec_2011.pdf.

6   Joseph Belcher, *William Carey: A Biography* (Philadelphia: American Baptist Society, 1853), 19.

7   William Carey, quoted in James Culross, *William Carey* (London: Hodder & Stoughton, 1881), 5.

8   See Donald Alban Jr., Robert H. Woods Jr., and Marsha Daigle-Williamson, "The Writings of William Carey: Journalism as Mission in a Modern Age," *Mission Studies* 22/1 (2005): 85–113.

tion that we need. We need steady action that's wisely directed: "A wise man scales the city of the mighty and brings down the stronghold in which they trust" (Prov. 21:22).

Indeed, wise missionaries may capture not only cities but the nations. Let those of us who have been given grace for the task approach it wisely and professionally, knowing what it may cost to succeed and—to that end—employing every human means within our grasp. Let's avoid shortcuts. As we plod year after year after year, may God answer our prayers and empower our efforts.

"Let us not grow weary of doing good, for in due season we will reap, if we do not give up" (Gal. 6:9).

Acknowledgments

JACK AND CLAIRE HELPED me refine these ideas over the past years, always ready to talk and to help me explore Scripture in greater depth than I could have on my own.

I'm grateful for the long hours Ron spent helping me refine this manuscript stylistically and missiologically. Chad Vegas looked over the manuscript for theological and scriptural soundness. This helped rescue parts of the manuscript when I had gotten too close to be able to see them clearly. Colleen Chao is an excellent editor and combed through the manuscript for content, style, and grammar—her insights and encouragement both helped immensely.

Brad Buser read through this manuscript before I had any real confidence in it and when it was simply a series of disjointed essays. Without his encouragement to refine it, I would never have imagined that it could reach publication. Brooks Buser also helped immensely in circulating it to people who had the influence and experience to bring it to publication—I don't know if it would have gone anywhere without his help.

Alex Duke patiently and carefully edited this manuscript to its final version, and I appreciate all I learned about writing in the process. As Mark Dever said in his foreword, we've never met, and I am extremely grateful for the generous foreword he wrote without even being asked.

My dad's careful reading produced edits which deepened this manuscript, adding theological wisdom, life experience, and pastoral perspective far beyond my own. My mother and brothers added per-spective and ideas through countless conversations, and never got tired of talking to me.

And my wonderful wife has always believed in this project. I am so grateful for her love and support.

General Index

2-3-4 method, 102

Abraham, 75, 97–98, 184
Addison, Steve, 48n6, 101, 103n128,
   105n132, 146n30, 253n2
Africa, missions to, 37, 80n50,
   101n117, 236n7, 243n21
   cultural differences in, 37, 89n85,
      135–36, 195, 197, 211
   language skills in, 37, 143, 147n38,
      167–68
ambassadors
   central task of, 117–23, 127–
      28, 136, 138, 143, 157–201,
      252
   go in the authority of Christ, 14,
      112–18, 175, 195
American Council on the Teaching
   of Foreign Languages (ACTFL),
   153, 177
Ananias, 94, 235n
angels, 88, 121, 124, 174, 235, 246–48,
   253
animism, 148, 169n15
Any-3 (missions method), 37–39, 51,
   67n1, 70, 147, 166n6
Apollos, 30, 86, 124, 126, 130
apostles
   boldness of, 172–73
   spiritual gifts of, 113–17, 121, 139,
      212–13, 235–36
   "super-apostles," 69, 112
Aquila and Priscilla, 124

audio Bibles, 61, 82, 179, 181–82
Ayub, Edward, 49, 57

Baal, 163, 240, 241n17
baptism, 51, 85, 178, 192
Barnabas, 128, 188, 225, 245n
Bethlehem College and Seminary,
   26n4
Bezalel, 31–32
Bhojpuri (people group), 48n8, 59–64,
   69, 146
Bible
   audio Bibles, 61, 82, 179, 181–82
   authority of, 57n37, 111, 206
   story of, 103, 116, 160, 163–65,
      181–83
   sufficiency of, 131, 182, 190
   translation of, 75, 104, 138–40, 147,
      150, 156–57, 179, 191n
Bible school, 137, 176
boldness
   by itself isn't enough, 27, 33
   in the New Testament, 122n, 128–31
   of missionaries, 14, 133, 172–74,
      178, 252
"breakthrough," in missions
   fasting and, 242–47
   language skills and, 60n47, 146, 243
   missions methods and, 60–61, 75,
      146n31
   prayer and, 37, 238
business as mission, 18, 117, 148, 155,
   176n, 177, 225

Camel Method, the, 18, 51, 70n19
Carey, William
  effectiveness of, 20, 30, 104–5, 120,
    251–54
  professionalism of, 20, 34–37,
    104–5, 139, 141, 174, 251–54
Chambers, Oswald, 238
"charter for Protestant missions," 34
children of missionaries, 141, 155,
  217–21
China Inland Mission, 141, 171, 214,
  233n, 242n
Christians
  identification as, 57n37, 58, 62
  missionaries are not superior
    Christians, 28–29, 218
  not all are ambassadors, 112–16,
    118, 218
churches
  definition of, 43n40, 190–91
  foundation of, 56, 74–75, 79, 90,
    102n123, 178, 187–88
  maturity of, 43, 90–91, 95–102,
    178–79, 187–95, 252
  sending role of, 144n25, 176, 198,
    203–4, 222
Church Planting Movements (CPM)
  influence on missions, 36–37, 54,
    69
  methods of. See CPM-style
    methods
  popularity of, 18, 36, 39, 49, 67,
    69–70, 196
CityTeam ministries, 70, 81n58–60
clarity
  fluency and, 138–57, 159, 173–74
  of Jesus, 124n
  of missionaries, 14, 35, 105, 133–58,
    177, 251–52
  in the New Testament, 123–25,
    130–31
contextualization, 169–72
Cornelius, 88, 94, 121, 124, 174, 235
counseling, 27, 29, 148, 211
CPM-style methods

aversion to teaching in, 40, 79–95,
  101–5, 117–18, 174, 185
"cultural contamination" in, 89–90,
  111, 174, 185
discipleship in, 57n37, 77, 95–101,
  135, 184
"DNA" for rapid growth in, 76–79,
  100, 105
emphasis on numbers in, 49–52,
  64–65
emphasis on rapid growth in,
  38–39, 51, 71–79, 84, 91–92,
  104–5, 157
false reports from, 47–50, 55–58,
  59n44, 103, 146, 199
goals of, 54, 72, 77–78, 104, 196
obedience-based discipleship
  (OBD), 57n37, 77, 95–101, 135,
  184
"person of peace," 91–95
positive traits of, 70–72, 82, 172
"silver-bullet" strategies in, 20,
  38–39, 48
"wrinkling time" in, 69n12, 104–5,
  104n129, 196n34
credibility, 14, 125–30, 133, 159–75,
  252
Cru (Campus Crusade for Christ), 43
cultural fluency
  importance of, 18, 26n4, 37, 89–90,
    105, 117, 134, 148, 159, 171
  lack of, 32, 37, 40n38, 62–63, 80,
    146
  minimized in new missions, 62–63,
    80, 87–89, 117
  slow process of, 104–5, 141, 156,
    174, 198, 252–53

Daniel, 244, 245n, 247–48
David, 74, 121, 242, 244
"day of small things" (Zech. 4:10),
  11, 75
decision-making, See guidance
Dent, Don, 188
Disciple Making Movements (DMM)

for missions, 44, 79, 93, 118, 179, 198, 205
of singleness, 215, 221–23
of teaching, 87–88, 179, 212–13
of tongues, 122n, 139, 141–42, 212, 233–34
spiritual warfare, 84, 126, 213, 238–39, 246–50
Stark, Rodney, 73–74
statistics, 18, 53, 62–65, 106
Stephen, 86, 126–29, 173
"storying," 180–85
Studd, C. T., 141, 233n
suffering
of Jesus, 123, 125
of missionaries, 27, 214–15, 219–21, 227–31
missionary response to, 119–21, 136–37
questions about, 40n38, 135, 150
supernatural events
deliverances, 233–34, 246n26
dreams, 47n4, 234, 253
healings, 94, 234–35, 241
miracles. See miracles
resurrections, 234
visions, 47n4, 94, 234, 248, 253
syncretism, 134–35, 148–49

targums, 138–39
Taylor, Hudson
example of, 36–37, 75, 171, 175, 242
language learning of, 141, 154, 214, 233n
professional skills of, 20, 36–37, 120, 139–40
"talking head syndrome," 105, 253
teaching
"able to teach," 86–88, 101–2, 172, 178, 187, 192
aversion to, 40, 79–95, 101–5, 117–18, 174, 185

central role of, 14, 43, 79, 87, 117–18, 130, 137, 174, 217
doesn't "usurp God's role," 80, 86–88, 105, 253
is a gift of the Spirit, 87–88, 179, 212–13
must be sound, 88–89, 101–2, 189
Timothy, 86–88, 101, 188–90, 198, 209
tongues, gift of, 122n, 139, 141–42, 212, 233–34
Training Leaders International, 26n4
Training for Trainers (T4T), 18, 39, 67n, 70–72, 145, 196
See also CPM-style methods
translators, 147–148
tribalism, 41, 148, 169n, 183, 195
Trinity, 149n40, 165–68
Trousdale, Jerry, 40, 53–54, 67n1, 69–70, 86, 97n112, 146, 253n4

Vegas, Chad, 96n110–11

Warren, Rick, 65–66
Watson, David and Paul, 60n53, 69–70
See also Disciple Making Movements (DMM)
Watson, Jan, 69
Willard, Dallas, 29–30, 184n22
Winter, Ralph, 43, 94n103
Wolf, Thomas, 91
worldview
communicating about, 159–165, 177–78
correcting, 84n69, 104, 148–49, 165–69, 174, 178–85
stories at the heart of, 162–164
word of God. See Bible
World Vision, 43
Wright, N. T., 162, 248n31

Zechariah, 11, 75, 121

Scripture Index

9Marks

Building Healthy Churches

9Marks exists to equip church leaders with a biblical vision and practical resources for displaying God's glory to the nations through healthy churches.

To that end, we want to see churches characterized by these nine marks of health:

1. Expositional Preaching
2. Gospel Doctrine
3. A Biblical Understanding of Conversion and Evangelism
4. Biblical Church Membership
5. Biblical Church Discipline
6. A Biblical Concern for Discipleship and Growth
7. Biblical Church Leadership
8. A Biblical Understanding of the Practice of Prayer
9. A Biblical Understanding and Practice of Missions

Find all our Crossway titles and other resources at 9Marks.org.

More Resources from 9Marks

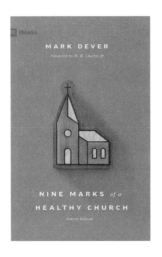

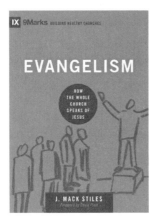

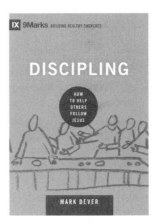

For more information, visit **crossway.org**.